GURU DEV

Paul Mason learned the practice of transcendental meditation in 1970 when he visited Maharishi's ashram at Rishikesh after having hitchhiked to India. This experience spurred him to dig deeper into the history of the teaching of meditation, which in turn led to his being commissioned by Element Books to write the biography of Maharishi Mahesh Yogi - published in 1994 as *'The Maharishi: the Biography of the Man Who Gave Transcendental Meditation to the World'*.

Maharishi's *guru,* referred to simply as Guru Dev, was Swami Brahmananda Saraswati, Shankaracharya of Jyotirmath (the most prominent religious position in Northern India). Paul Mason hopes that by offering Guru Dev's lifestory and teachings, readers will be able to obtain a clearer perspective on traditional Indian teachings.

Titles by Paul Mason:

Via Rishikesh: A Hitch-Hiker's Tale

The Maharishi: The Biography of the Man Who Gave Transcendental Meditation to the World
Element Books - First English edition 1994
Evolution Books - Revised English edition 2005
Maharishi Mahesh Yogi - Aquamarin - German edition 1995
O Maharishi - Nova Era - Portuguese edition 1997

Mala: A String of Unexpected Meetings

108 Discourses of Guru Dev:
The Life and Teachings of Swami Brahmananda Saraswati,
Shankaracharya of Jyotirmath (1941-53) - Volume I

The Biography of Guru Dev:
The Life and Teachings of Swami Brahmananda Saraswati,
Shankaracharya of Jyotirmath (1941-53) - Volume II

Guru Dev as Presented by Maharishi Mahesh Yogi:
The Life and Teachings of Swami Brahmananda Saraswati,
Shankaracharya of Jyotirmath (1941-53) - Volume III

Kathy's Story

The Knack of Meditation:
The No-Nonsense Guide to Successful Meditation

Dandi Swami: The Story of the Guru's Will, Maharishi Mahesh Yogi, the Shankaracharyas of Jyotir Math & Meetings with Dandi Swami Narayananand Saraswati

Roots of TM: The Transcendental Meditation of Guru Dev & Maharishi Mahesh Yogi

The Beatles, Drugs, Mysticism & India:
Maharishi Mahesh Yogi - Transcendental Meditation- Jai Guru Deva OM

* All titles are published by Premanand, other than *'The Maharishi'* biography

108 DISCOURSES
OF
GURU DEV

★

The Life and Teachings of
Swami Brahmananda Saraswati,
Shankaracharya of Jyotirmath (1941-53)

★

Volume I

★

by
Paul Mason

PREMANAND
www.paulmason.info
premanandpaul@yahoo.co.uk

First published by Premanand 2009

ISBN 978-0-9562228-0-0

Cover design by Premanand

Foreword

When in 1970 I travelled to the ashram of Maharishi Mahesh Yogi, across the river from the pilgrimage town of Rishikesh in Northern India, I was taught a system of meditation known as transcendental meditation. The teaching of transcendental meditation (TM) is preceded by a short ceremony, a *puja*, before a reproduction of a painting of Maharishi's master, 'Guru Dev', Swami Brahmananda Saraswati, Shankaracharya of Jyotirmath from 1941-53.

Despite crediting Guru Dev as being the inspiration behind the practice of TM, in the years of his mission to spread this teaching of meditation, curiously Maharishi seldom if ever quoted Guru Dev.

When I returned to India, in 1979, I made a pilgrimage to the monastery of Jyotirmath, high in the Himalayas, and was rewarded in obtaining two publications on the life and teachings of Guru Dev, in Hindi. There and then I made up my mind to learn Hindi in order to learn about his life and teaching.

'Shri Shankaracharya Upadesha'

One of the books was a collection of 108 '*upadesha*' or sermons of Guru Dev. It appears that these originally appeared in the ashram newletter *'Shri Shankaracharya Upadesha'* between 1949-1953 and were later reproduced as a paperback, by Rameshwar Tiwari.

My progress in Hindi was slow but eventually I made translations of both these books on Guru Dev. I also translated a third book, which I had discovered on a return visit to Jyotirmath. I uploaded my rough translations onto my website (www.paulmason.info) as I worked. But reading these quotations on a computer screen is far less pleasant than having them in a printed form, so I am happy to be able to present my translations in book form and make them available through the website.

So, here is the first volume of a series on Guru Dev, in which I have included Guru Dev's speeches in their original Hindi form. Titles have been revised to only include the words of Guru Dev. To render the Hindi (and the Sanskrit quotes with which he peppered his talks) I had first to re-type the text into ITRANS and convert this to a Devanagari font, which was achieved by using a computer program called Itranslator99. I am indebted to Omkarananda Ashram for developing and making this software freely available, and to Swami Satchidanand for working through some technical problems with me.

The whole process of translation was made so much easier with the help of Richard Mason, who is a whizz with computers and who suggested I start to create a database of Hindi words which would then be connected to MS Access with a little program he created called Handi Hindi Gizmo Innit. Thanks Richard, I don't know what I would have done without it.

Thanks go to Marek Reavis who helped by giving useful feedback and assisting in photo research. To Ajay Shankar for his support and assistance in obtaining images of Guru Dev (hand-tinted colour prints and hi-res black and white prints of many photos of Guru Dev can be had from Ajay at Delhi Photo Company). Thanks also go to L B Shrivers for sending me a photocopy of the text when my copy disappeared, and to Dr. Cynthia Humes (I look forward to seeing the publication of her translation of these teachings).

Premanand Paul Mason

Contents

20. Don't look at the defects of others, trace your own flaws up to the present and attempt to remove them.
21. For as long as you are breathing, pass the time praying to Bhagwan.
22. He who sings the prayers of Bhagwan, his conduct should be the best.
23. If you are ready in the first place, then there will be no suffering at the time of death.
24. By gaining the one Bhagwan everything is naturally obtained.
25. He who protected you inside the womb protects you right now too. Do not forget him.
26. However many days there is to stay, live in peace.
27. Develop one's own spiritual strengths.
28. Be collected in your own mind and don't get involved in any disputes about form and formless.
29. Don't disgrace the position of work that you occupy.
30. It is a dangerous thing to be greedy for wealth or for a woman or a son.
31. Make efforts so that a relationship of oneness with Paramatma occurs in this lifetime.
32. Worry is more powerful and dreadful than the funeral pyre; because the pyre is to burn the dead but worry burns the living.
33. He is seeing everything that everyone does. Nobody can escape his working being seen.
34. The senses and the body work only in accordance with man's mind. For this reason it is a necessity to take care of the mind.
35. Few people have a siddhi, but by their greediness for *siddhi* a good many people become cheated.
36. Showing the difference between the individual life and Paramatma (the Supreme Self) is like distinguishing between paddy and rice.
37. If you wish to experience happiness and peace then don't search for outer things, only seek inside yourself.
38. That which is ours cannot be another's.
39. If Bhagwan did not resolve to come in the shape of an *avataara* then how would publicity come for *bhakti yoga*?

40. Omnipotent Bhagwan is ready to take on the burden of all business management.
41. Certainly by singing *bhajan* of Bhagwan you will get *moksha*, and you will get wealth, food, reputation and respect too.
42. Only Paramatma is suitable to be with the mind, and anything else in worldly existence cannot satisfy the mind when it connects to it.
43. If someone has a thirst for a *seer* of water then how can that thirst be quenched with a sixteenth of a *seer* of water?
44. Apply the mind to business a little, and apply it a lot to *paramarth* (salvation).
45. How can the Omnipotent see his own devotees sorrowful?
46. All give help to him on whom the grace of Bhagwan comes..
47. Consider this that you are always thinking about insignificant things.
48. In darkness (nightime) you should sit with eye closed and do *japa* of the *mantra*.
49. 'Loss of the mind is defeat, mastery of the mind is success.'
50. Man acts according to the desire of the mind.
51. At whatever time there is attachment to worldly life then at the same moment bow in the direction of Paramatma.
52. People say:- 'So-and-so *mahatma* had fallen, so-and-so *maharshi* had fallen.'
53. That the mind is not inclined towards bad actions and that it flows toward good actions - this is really the man's primary effort.
54. When you can be in the diamond business then why are you blackening the hand in the brokerage of coal?
55. Now do such actions that do not become baggage for future suffering.
56. The are many *tyaagi* and there also are many who are generous; but make an effort to be attached and stingy!
57. In one's own life, most important is *paramarth*, understand that everyday business is secondary.
58. First do your own work, then help in the work of others.
59. Every moment of life is very precious.
60. To hope for happiness and peace by knowing *samsara* is desiring to search for light in darkness.

61. Don't suffer unrest by having pointless worries.
62. Why the insults and the red-coloured powder at Holi?
63. The *maharshi* people ate roots, tubers and fruits, and were drinking water, but had the power to command emperors.
64. If the value of one *shloka* of the *Gita* is understood or even one line of the *shloka* is understood, then there can be happiness.
65. There are various methods of remembering Bhagwan. You should understand one's own suitable methods from *gurus*.
66. That the food is not pure is the very reason that many thoughts occur.
67. The body of a human being is scarce, this is just what the *Shastra* says.
68. In truth worshipping any of the gods is really worship of Bhagwan.
69. 'Having taken one *guru*, another you should not' - this is all rubbish talk and is obstructive to the welfare.
70. Your own house is full of rubbish and you travel to sweep the house of another, this then is not intelligence at all.
71. Take a look and consider one time, who are you?
72. To drink Gangajal (water from the River Ganga) why will you drink from the gutter?
73. Some people set great measure by the magnificence of the *japa* of OM.
74. Kshatriya, vaishya, shudra and female sex are not for the purpose of position of *guru*.
75. The welfare of women is really only in the attachment to husband.
76. The *Shastra* is said to be the command of Bhagwan.
77. Bowing the head is to surrender one's *ahamkara* (ego)
78. What do we say is a *jagadguru*?
79. Meditating on insignificant things, the mind remaining in the cycle of *samsara*, he will continue to be giddy in the head.
80. One does not become a *mahatma* from clothes dyed in ochre or the mark of a *tilaka*.
81. Take more effort in purifying the mind than in collecting wealth.

82. By the fire of knowledge one's own mass of *karma* becomes ashes.
83. To withdraw from *samsara* and to apply oneself in the direction of Paramatma takes effort.
84. But when the wood is rubbed then it can be lit and can be used according to our wishes.
85. By searching in the vegetable bazaar you will not get a diamond no matter how much you want and try.
86. Chant worship of Bhagwan - whether the mind is attached or not attached.
87. Is it best to experience the *darshan* of Bhagwan by knowledge or with the sight?
88. Can anybody who is unwell become healthy from formless medicine?
89. If you will grow an acacia tree then you will really have a thorn in you, no mango will be grown.
90. Which people go to hell?
91. Don't get the mind excessively involved in *samsara*, apply it towards Bhagwan.
92. To reach towards Bhagwan, then take the assistance of his name.
93. Suffering exists only in appearance, it is not real.
94. The drunk happily accepts falling in the gutter and remains there.
95. The *nastika* (atheist) also has this wish that he is being happy and serene.
96. With worldly people only maintain good manners, they are not a basis for attachment.
97. Happiness will not be being born in any caste.
98. It is not proper to be wicked to the wicked, to go and be abusive to those who are abusive.
99. When *samsara* is separate from you, then what will you abandon?
100. All the pain and all of the unrest of *samsara* (worldly existence) is really caused by *aviveka* (absence of discrimination).
101. Self-interest is prevalent.
102. Materialism is not capable of giving happiness and peace.

103. 'If that is in our destiny, that is really certain that we will get it'
104. By self-restraint of the senses you will be happy in your self.
105. Live carefully - make proper use of existence.
106. Celestial vision is needed in order to see the heavenly form of Bhagwan.
107. Don't forget that everyday business is really the way of *paramarth* (salvation).
108. 'By performing *dharma*, sin becomes destroyed.'

॥ ॐ ॥

श्री शंकराचार्य उपदेशामृत

*

ब्रह्मलीन जगद्गुरु भगवान श्री शंकराचार्य

श्रीमद् स्वामी ब्रह्मानन्द सरस्वती जी महाराज

ज्योतिर्मठ, बदरिकाश्रम (हिमालय)

.. OM ..

Shri Shankaracharya Upadeshamrita

*

The Nectar Teachings of Shri Shankaracharya

*

Brahmaleen Jagadguru Bhagwan Shri Shankaracharya

Shrimad Swami Brahmananda Saraswati Ji Maharaja

Jyotirmath, Badarikashram (Himalaya)

1

जो सुखी है वही दूसरे को सुखी बना सकता है

*

परमात्मा के सम्पर्क में ही जीव वास्तविक सुखी हो सकता है क्योंकि उसी में सुख की पराकाष्ठा है

जिसके पास जो कुछ होता है। वही वह दूसरों को दे सकता है। किसी कंगाल से कोई धन की याचना करे तो मूर्खता ही तो है। जिस प्रकार धन की राशि से ही धन प्राप्त किया जा सकता है। विद्यानिधि यविद्वान्फ से ही विद्या की प्राप्ति हो सकती है। उसी प्रकार सुखराशि जो भगवान् हैं। उन्हीं से सुख की प्राप्ति हो सकती है।

संसार में भगवान् के कृपापात्र भक्तों को छोड़ कर कोई भी सुखी नहीं है। आध्यात्मनिष्ठ परमात्मा के भक्त ही यहाँ सुख का अनुभव करते हैं अन्यथा सभी को कुछ न कुछ दुःख घेरे ही रहता है। संसार में कोई सुखी नहीं देखा जाता। जिसके पास जो वस्तु नहीं होती वह दूसरे को उसके द्वारा सुखी मानता है। किन्तु जिसके पास वह है। उसको देखा जाय तो उससे वह अपने को सुखी नहीं मानता। जिसके पुत्र नहीं है वह पुत्रवालों को सुखी मानता है। पर पुत्र से कितना सुख है। यह किसी पुत्रवान से पूछो। मालूम होता है। वास्तव में किसी भी लौकिक-पदार्थ में सुख नहीं है। सुखस्वरूप तो सच्चिदानन्द-रूप परमात्मा ही है और उसी के सम्पर्क में आने से जीव भी सुखी हो सकता है और सुखी होने का दूसरा मार्ग नहीं है। परमात्मा ही ऐसा ल्जनरल मर्चेन्टह् है जिसके यहाँ सुख की किसी भी सामग्री का अभाव नहीं होता। किन्तु उसकी कृपा प्राप्त करने के लिये विधिवत् प्रयत्न करना पड़ेगा। केवल परमात्मा का माहात्म्य

पाठ करने से कुछ होगा नहीं। बीजक का पाठ करते रहो तो क्या धनी हो सकते हो?

संसारियों से सुख प्राप्ति को इच्छा करना भूल है। भला जो स्वयं दुखी है वह दूसरे को सुखी क्या बनायेगा संसार में जो सुख दिखता है वह सब सापेक्ष सुख है। किसी से कोई किसी अंश में सुखी है तो कोई अन्य किसी अंश में।

किसी से सुख की याचना करनी ही है तो ऐसी जगह के याचक बनो। जहाँ से सर्व सुख प्राप्त हो सके। स्मरण रखो कि जो परमात्मा की तरफ झुका है वही संसार में सुख-शान्ति प्राप्त कर सकता है। दूसरा नहीं। संसार में सुख ढूँढ़ना ऐसा है जैसा कि प्यास बुझाने के लिए ओस की बूँदों का संग्रह करना।

1

How Can You Become Wealthy By Studying A Catalogue?

Only by contact with Paramatma (God, the Supreme Self) can there be true happiness for the *jiva* (the individual soul), since in that is the highest happiness.

If one has something, the very same one can give to another. To demand any money from a pauper would really be a folly then. Wealth of that kind can only be gained by going to a mass of wealth. Only from a treasury of knowledge can knowledge be gained. That kind of treasure house of happiness, that form of happiness, is who Bhagwan (the Supreme Being) really is. Only from Them can happiness be gained.

In worldly existence devotees of Bhagwan are left to be vessels of grace and nobody else is happy. Only those devotees who desire spiritual contemplation of Paramatma have an experience of happiness - otherwise to all, little-by-little only suffering slowly is lived. In worldly existence nobody is found to be happy. If someone has a lack of something they regard someone who has that as the way to happiness. But the one who has, does not regard themselves as happy. He who has no son regards the one with sons as happy, but how much happiness is there from the son? Ask this of any with sons. It is already known, in truth in anything else earthly and material there is no happiness. The form of happiness then is the form of *sachchidananda* (Truth, Consciousness, Bliss), is really Paramatma and from coming in contact with that the *jiva* can become happy and there is no other way to be happy. Actually, Paramatma is like a *"general merchant"* in whose place there is no deficiency of any articles of happiness. But in order to gain his grace regular effort is required, not only some reading of the greatness of Paramatma. By studying a catalogue, how can you become wealthy?

To wish for happiness from worldly people is a mistake. Good. How can someone who is himself unhappy, make another happy? In worldly life those who are seen as happy, that is relative happiness. From any one thing someone is happy then someone is happy in another part.

If you are to ask for any happiness then beg from this place, from wherever all happiness can be gained. Remember this that whosoever bows in the direction of Paramatma the very same can obtain happiness and peace in worldly existence, otherwise not. To search for happiness in worldly existence is similar to quenching one's thirst by collecting drops of dew.

२

संसार में आये हो - ऐसी चातुरी से काम लो कि फिर लौट कर मल-मूत्र के भांड में न आना पड़े

भगवान् की कृपा से ही यह पल्लेदारी छूट सकती है।

जीवन जाने कितने जन्मों से पल्लेदारी करता चला आ रहा है - कभी हाथी का पचास मन का शरीर, कभी चींटी का आधीरत्ती का शरीर, कभी मनुष्य का शरीर, कभी किसी का शरीर - यह जो ढोना पड़ रहा है वह पल्लेदारी भगवान् की कृपा से ही छूट सकती है।

ऐसा करो कि इसी जीवन में भगवान् की कृपा प्राप्त हो जाय और मल-मूत्र के शरीर में फिर न आना पड़े। यह तभी होगा जब कि भगवान् की आज्ञाओं का पालन करोगे। वेद शास्त्र का आदेश ही भगवान् की आज्ञा है।

जिस वर्ण में हो और जिस आश्रम में हो, उसी के अनुसार स्वधर्म पालन करो और हर समय भगवान् का स्मरण करते रहो।

प्रतिदिन सायंकाल और प्रातःकाल नियमपूर्वक उपासना करो और अपनी व्यावहारिक व्यवस्था ऐसी रखो कि जहां तक हो सके अपने से दूसरों की भलाई ही हो और यदि किसी की भलाई ही हो और यदि किसी की भलाई न हो सके तो कम बुराई न होने पाये।

भगवान् को सर्वत्र उपस्थित देखना बहुत आवश्यक है। सर्वत्र

भगवान् को उपस्थित देखोगे तो कोई पाप नहीं होगा। पहले जो पाप हो गया वह तो नष्ट हो जायगा, पर जब से भगवान् के नाम को अपनाओ तब से पाप से बचो, नहीं तो उन पापों का छुटकारा कठिनाई से होगा। क्योंकि पहले के किये हुये पाप तो गंगास्नान से नष्ट हो जाते हैं; परन्तु गंगा में, तीर्थ में जो पाप करता है वह 'बज्र लेपो भविष्यति' अर्थात् वह पत्थर की लकीर के समान हो जाता है जो छुटाया नहीं छूटता। इसलिये भगवान् का स्मरण करते समय पाप करने से डरो।

स्वधर्म-पालन पूर्धक भगवान् का भजन करोगे तो पिछले सब जन्म-जन्मान्तरों के पाप कट जायेंगे और सुख-शान्ति का अनुभव करते हुए अन्त में भी सद्गति होगी।

2

It is very necessary to see Bhagwan present everywhere.

Only by the grace of Bhagwan can you gain freedom from portering. How many lifetimes have you existed working as a porter?

Sometimes in the body of an elephant weighing fifty *mana* (1 *mana* = 100 lb / 45.6 kg), sometimes with the body of an ant weighing *adhiratti* (half a *ratti*; *ratti* = the weight of half a seed of *abrus precatorius*), sometimes in the body of a man - only the grace of Bhagwan can give freedom to a porter who is carrying.

So do this in life so that the *kripa* (grace) of Bhagwan be gained and no more returning in a body of *mala-mutra* (excrement & urine). For this reason cherish the commands of Bhagwan. The instructions of the *Veda Shastra* are really the commands of Bhagwan.

Be one of that *varna* (caste), of that *ashram* (stage of life), do according to one's *dharma* and remember Bhagwan all the time. Every day regularly practice *upasana* (worship, meditation etc.) in the evening and early morning and perform one's customary fixed habits so that you can be of benefit to others and be good, and, if you can't be good then don't get a little bad.

It is very necessary to see Bhagwan present everywhere. If you will see Bhagwan present everywhere then nobody will be sinning. If sin has been committed before then that will be destroyed, but from when one appropriates the name of Bhagwan from then on refrain from sin. Don't sin then for those sins will be difficult to be liberated from. Since the sins committed earlier can be destroyed by bathing in the River Ganga, but that sin done in Ganga, in a sacred place, that is:-

"बज्र लेपो भविष्यति"

"bajra lepo bhavishyati"

- 'becomes cemented' - that is similar to a line on stone that is not erased.

[From an old Sanskrit saying:- *"anyakshetre kritam paapam, punyakshetre vinashyati, tirthakshetre kritam paapam, vajralepo bhavishyati."* - 'Sins committed at another place are destroyed at a holy place, but sins done at a holy place become cemented.']

Therefore fear committing sin whilst remembering Bhagwan.

Protect one's religion and worship Bhagwan then the sins of all one's previous lifetimes will be destroyed and experiencing happiness & peace there will be salvation at the end too.

'Two hill coolies yoked together under their load'
[*'Wonderful India'*, Statesman & Times of India Book Dept., 1936']

३

मनुष्य कर्म करने में स्वतंत्र है परन्तु फल भोगने में परतंत्र

*

इसलिये ऐसे ही कर्म करो जिसका फल उत्तम हो

चोरी करने में चोर स्वतंत्र है परन्तु फल तो न्यायालय के अधीन है, जितनी सजा दी जायगी उसको भोगना ही पड़ेगा - चाहे इच्छा हो या न हो। मनुष्य जैसा चाहे वेसा कर्म कर सकता है। पुष्य कर्मों को करके स्वर्गादि लोकों में जाकर दिव्य भोगों को भोग सकता है या पाप कर्म करके रौरव आदि महा भयंकर दुःखदायी नरक को प्राप्त हो सकत है।

मनुष्य-योनि कर्म-योनि मानी गई है। यहाँ मनुष्य कर्म करने में स्वतंत्र है अर्थात् वह जैसा कर्म करना चाहे कर सकता है। मनुष्य चाहे तो साक्षात् सर्वशक्तिमान सच्चिदानन्द परमात्मा से मिल सकता है।

मनुष्य जो कर्मं करता है उसका फल उसे अवश्य भोगना पड़ता है। कोई कर्मं मनुष्य कर ले और चाहे कि उसका फल न भोगना पड़े तो ऐसा नहीं हो सकता। हां, यह अवश्य है कि -

'धर्मेण पापमपनुदति'

धर्म करने से पाप नष्ट होता है। तो यदि किसी से कभी कोई पाप-कर्म हो गया हो तो उसे चाहिये कि उसको नष्ट करने के लिये पुण्य कार्य करे। पुण्य बढ जायगा तो पाप दब जायगा। इसीलिये कहा गया है -

'जपतो नास्तिपातकम्'

भगवन्नाम मंत्र का जप करने से पाप नष्ट होता है। इसलिए यदि किसी के द्वारा अभी तक अविहिताचरण और पाप-कर्म अधिक हुये हैं और वह उन समस्त पापों से छुटकारा पाना चाहता है तो पुण्य-कर्म (शुभ-कर्म) करने लग जाय और श्रद्धा-भक्ति पूर्वक अपने योग्य (उपयुक्त) भगवान् के नाम (मन्त्र) का जप करने लग जाय। ऐसा करने से धीरे-धीरे पिछले पाप नष्ट हो जायँगे और कुछ समय में वह गढ़ा पूरा होकर आगे के लिये शुभ फल संचित होने लगेगा और उसी के सहारे सद्गति हो जायगी।

अनिच्छा से भी यदि भगवान् का स्मरण किया जाय तो उससे पापों का नाश होता है। जैसे बिना इच्छा के भी यदि अग्नि छू जाय तो वह जला देती है। तात्पर्य यह कि जैसे अग्नि का स्वभाव है कि जो संपर्क में आये उसे जला दे, इसी प्रकार भगवान् का स्वभाव है कि जिसने उनका स्मरण किया उसके पापों को वे नष्ट कर देते हैं।

जन्म-जन्मान्तरों का बिगड़ा हुआ मन है, इसलिये भगवान् के प्रति प्रेम बनाने में तो कठिनाई है पर मलिन व दूषित मन से भी यदि भगवान् का चिन्तन किया जायगा तो भी भगवान् की कृपा प्राप्त होगी।

इसमें एक बात यह समझने की है कि मन पहले का चाहे जितना दूषित हो, पहले का चाहे जितना दुराचारी व पापाचारी हो, उसकी परवाह नहीं। परन्तु ऐसा नहीं है कि भगवान् के नाम की पापनाशनी शक्ति के बल पर पाप करते रहो।

3

Man certainly endures the fruits of his actions.

Really it is like this; do the *karma* (action) that has the best fruit.

A thief is free to steal, but the upshot is dependent on a court, really however much punishment will be given he is to suffer it, whether he desires it or not. Similarly man can do what he wants. He who does cherished works goes to Heaven etc. and can experience heavenly pleasure, or by doing *paapa* (sinful) *karma* you can obtain great ghastly distressing hell, *raurava* (a hell) etc.

Birth as a man means a birth of action. Here man is free to act, that is to say that he can do as he wishes. If man desires to he can meet with Paramatma the All-Powerful, *sachchidananda* (Truth, Consciousness, Bliss).

Man certainly endures the fruits of the *karma* he does. Any actions a man does but does not desire the fruit of, then such cannot be. Yes, it is certain that:-

"धर्मेण पापमपनुदति"

"dharmenna paapamapanudati"
[*Taittiriya Samhita (Mahanarayana Upanishad)*]

'*dharma* destroys sinful thoughts' - by performing *dharma, paapa* is destroyed. In case any sinful *karma* happens then you should do some holy work for destroying that. Merit will grow, then *paapa* (sin) will be controlled. Therefore it was said before –

"जपतो नास्तिपातकम्"

"japato naastipaatakam"

[From the sloka*: 'krishito naasti durbhiksham.japato naasti paatakam.mounena kalaho naasti naasti jaagarato bhayam.*' 'Ploughing eliminates famine, *japa* eliminates sin. Silence eliminates quarrels, eliminate fear by wakefulness.']

- 'by doing *japa* of the *mantra* of Bhagwan's name, *paapa* (sin) is destroyed.'

Therefore, if someone took a way that was prohibited and was more sinful and that they now desire to get rid of all sins, then do holy work, engage in doing good works and apply your own proper faith & devotion in doing the *japa* of the name of Bhagwan's name. After this manner, slowly, slowly past sin becomes destroyed and in a while is completely mended and additional good effects are collected which will assist with your salvation.

Even if one remembers Bhagwan unwillingly then from that action sins fade away. In the manner that also without desire the fire is blown and ignites. The significance of this is that it is the nature of fire to ignite on contact, this is the manner of the nature of Bhagwan that those who remember him, their sins are destroyed.

Over many lifetimes the mind has been spoiled, therefore it is difficult to create a love of Bhagwan with a filthy or corrupted mind, but if you will think of Bhagwan then you acquire Bhagwan's grace.

In this there is one thing to understand, that whatever the mind desired before, however much it was corrupted, however much you desired wicked or sinful living, it is of no concern. But the purifying strength of Bhagwan's name is not for doing sin.

४

उदर पोषण में ही सारी चातुरी समाप्त मत कर दो सब से चतुर वही है जो भगवान् की उपासना करता है

*

भजन करने से कोई बच नहीं सकता। भगवान को नहीं भजोगे तो राजा, रईस, सेठ, साहूकारों को भजना पड़ेगा

आजकल लोग अपने को बड़ा बुद्धिमान समझते हैं। पर उनकी सारी चातुरी पेट के आसपास ही रहती है। उदर में ही उनकी सारी चातुरी समाप्त हो जाती है। पेट के आगे बुद्धि ही नहीं जाती। वे उदर रूपी फोड़े की मलहम-पट्टी करने में ही सारा समय लगा देते हैं और इसी में सारा जीवन नष्ट कर देते हैं। वास्तव में, इससे अधिक घाटा मनुष्य जीवन में और दूसरा नहीं हो सकता।

भजन तो करना ही पड़ेगा। भजन करने से कोई बच नहीं सकता। 'सर्वज्ञ सर्वशक्तिमान कर्तुमकर्तुमन्यथाकर्तुसमर्थ' भगवान को नहीं भजोगे तो विषयी-पामर, राजा, रईस, सेठ साहूकारों को भजना पड़ेगा। किसी बड़े का सहारा नहीं लोगे तो छोटों का सहारा लेना पड़ेगा। इसलिए वृद्धिमानी इसी में है कि परमात्मा का सहारा लिया जाय जो लोक-परलोक दोनों जगह काम दे। मनुष्य चाहे जितना भी ऐश्वर्य सम्पन्न हो जाय पर फिर भी उसका ऐश्वर्य सीमित ही रहेगा और कभी भी प्रारब्ध बदलने पर, वह दीन हो सकता है। इसलिए जिसकी स्वयं की स्थिति निश्चित नहीं उसका सहारा लेकर घोखा ही तो उठाना होगा। सबसे चतुर वही है जो परमात्मा का भजन करता है, वह लोक-परलोक में सर्वत्र सुखी रहता है।

4

Nowadays people consider themselves to be very intelligent.

No one can avoid worshipping. If you do not worship Bhagwan then you will fall down worshipping the *raja*, the nobleman, the merchant and the moneylender.

Nowadays people understand themselves to be very intelligent. But all their cleverness continues to be about their stomach. All their cleverness is completely only in the belly. Really, beyond the belly the mind does not go. They are all the time applying ointment and bandages to the ulcer and in this all life is destroyed. In truth, there can be no greater loss in man's life.

Really then, fall down to do worship. No one can avoid worshipping.

"सर्वज्ञ सर्वशक्तिमान कर्तुमकर्तुमन्यथाकर्तुसमर्थ"

"sarvagya sarvashaktimaana kartumakartumanyathaakartusamarth"

'Omniscient, Omnipotent, active / inactive & capable of action in a different manner (miracles)'

Whoever will not worship Bhagwan is then a licentious & base person who will fall down and worship the *raja*, the nobleman, the merchant and the moneylender. If you will not get help from the greater then you will fall down and accept assistance from the lesser. Therefore it is the wise mind that goes for the support of Paramatma who gives what we desire in both this world and the next. However well off a man has become, afterwards his wealth will only remain limited and also sometimes shifts (worsens), that day can be. Therefore if you don't look for support from one whose condition is not settled then you will rise up. The most ingenious one of all is the one who worships Paramatma to always stay happy in this world and the other world.

५

वासनाओं को पूरा करने के पीछे मत पड़ो

*

शरीर यात्रा के लिये आवश्यक कर्मों को करते हुए मुख्य ध्यान परमात्मा की प्राप्ति में रखो

भगवान् विष्णु जिनके पुत्र रूप में आये और देवराज इन्द्र जिन्हें अपना अर्द्धासन देता था ऐसे समर्थ शक्तिशाली चक्रवर्ती नरेन्द्र दशारथ भी अपनी सारी वासनायें पूरी न कर सके - राम के राज्याभिषेक की वासना लिये हुए बैल के समान करण पीट-पीट कर उनकी मृत्यु हुई। जब इस प्रकार सामर्थ्यशाली पुरुषों की ही सब आशायें और वासनायें पूरी नहीं हुई, तब आप लोग अपनी सम्पूर्ण इच्छाओं की तृप्ति की आशा स्वप्न में भी मत रखो - जाग्रत अवस्था की तो बात ही क्या।

परमार्थ और व्यवहार दोनों साथ-साथ ही चलते हैं, क्योंकि स्वरूप से कर्मों का त्याग नही किया जा सकता। कर्मों के त्याग करने पर मनुश्य की शरीर-यात्रा भी सम्भव नहीं हो सकती। परन्तु इतना ध्यान अवश्य ही रखना चाहिये कि शरीर-यात्र के लिये आवश्यक कर्मों को छोड़कर शेष वासनाओम् को पूरा करने के पीछे न पड़ जाओ। संसार में बड़े से बड़े शक्तिशाली मनुष्य हुए परन्तु उनकी भी सम्पूर्ण वासनायें पूर्ण न हो सकीं। इसलिये शरीर यात्रा के लिये आवश्यक कर्मों को करते हुए मुख्य ध्यान परमात्मा की प्राप्ति में लगाओ।

विषयों को भोगकर इन्द्रियों को तृप्त करने की बात सोचना ऐसा ही है जैसे खुजलाकर खाज को अच्छा करने की आशा करना। संसार के व्यवहार उलझे हुए कच्चे सूत के समान हैं, जितना

सुलझाने की चेष्टा करोगे उतने ही ये उलझेगें। इसलिये बुद्धिमानी पूर्वक संसार का व्यवहार चलाते हुए मुख्य बुद्धि पर्मार्थ में ही रखना चाहिये।

5

Finding satisfaction in anything experienced by the senses is like imagining it is good to scratch an itch.

Vishnu.

[*'India and Its Inhabitants'*, Caleb Wright, Brainerd. 1856]

He whom Bhagwan Vishnu came to in the form of his son, and who Indra offered to share his throne, he was indeed one who possessed strength. He was king and emperor but King Dasharatha could not fulfil all his wishes - like a fool he died thrashing about because he had desired the coronation of Rama. Really, when these kind of capable people couldn't fulfil all their hopes and desires, then you people don't hope to satisfy all desires in dreams. What is the talk then of [satisfying all desires] in the waking state?

Really spiritual salvation and everyday affairs both go together, because by nature one cannot abandon actions. By abandoning actions it is not possible to maintain the body and get about. But really you should meditate on this that, certainly do those actions for the progress of the body whilst relinquishing the wish to fulfil remaining desires. In the mundane world there have been very strong people but they could not fulfil their desires. Therefore doing those actions for the progress of the body apply oneself in the primary consideration of gaining Paramatma.

Finding satisfaction in anything experienced by the senses is like imagining it is good to scratch an itch. The everyday affairs of the mundane world are similar to becoming entangled in raw threads, really however much you desire to become disentangled that much you become entangled. Therefore, performing the business of the mundane existence with prudence, you should set yourself in the topmost wisdom of *parmartha* (the ultimate good, salvation).

६

जो भाग्य में है वह आयेगा अवश्य और उसे भोगना ही पड़ेगा

*

इसलिये सम्पत्ति-विपत्ति जो जब आये धैर्य पूर्वक भोगते चलो

मनुष्य निष्क्रिय होकर कभी बैठ नहीं सकता। मन, बुद्धि, प्राण तथा इन्द्रियों के द्वारा कुछ न कुछ चेष्टा करते रहना मनुष्य का स्वभाव है। अपने अपने संस्कारानुसार प्रत्येक मनुष्य स्वभावतः ही कार्य में प्रवृत्त होता है। अतः क्रिया में प्रवृत्ति होना स्वभाविक है। यह सिद्धांत है कि जैसा कर्म होगा वैसा फल कर्म करने वाले को अवश्यमेव भुगतना पड़ेगा। अल्प समय में किये हुये कर्म का फल चिरकाल तक भोगना पड़ताँ है। अतः एक जन्म में किये हुये सम्पूर्ण कर्मों का फल दूसरे जन्म में भोगकर समाप्त नहीं किया जा सकता। बिना भोगे कर्मों की राशि सञ्चित् होती जाती है। जब तक

यह कर्मों की राशि समाप्त नही हो जाती तब तक जीव को पुनः पुनः गर्भ में आना ही पड़ेगा। अतः मनुष्य जीवन पाकर इस कर्म राशि को समाप्त करना चाहिये।

शास्त्रों ने कर्मों को तीन विभाग कर तीनों को समाप्त करने के उपाय बतलाये हैं। सञ्चित, प्रारब्ध और क्रियमाण - यह कर्म के तीन विभाग हैं। सञ्चित कर्म अनन्त हैं। वे भोग कर समाप्त नही किये जा सकते। उनको समाप्त करने का उपाय या तो ज्ञान की प्राप्ति है अथवा भगवान् के चरणों में अनन्य भक्ति। प्रारब्ध कर्म भोगने से ही नष्ट होंगे, अन्य कोई उपाय नहीं। अवश्यमेव भोक्तव्यं कृतं कर्मं शुभाशुभम्। क्रियमाण कर्म भगवान को अर्पण कर देने से बन्धन के हेतु नहीं होते। इस प्रकार सञ्चित कर्म ज्ञानाग्नि से दग्ध करके, प्रारब्ध कर्म भोग कर और क्रियमाण कर्म भगवान को समर्पण करके कर्म-बन्धन से मुक्त हो जाने को ही मोक्ष कहते हैं। यदि साधन हीन होने के कारण ज्ञान की प्राप्ति में देर है तो कम से कम क्रियमाण कर्म तो भगवान को अर्पण करते जाओ। ऐसा करने से इस जन्म के कर्म बन्धन के हेतु नहीं बनेंगे। साथ ही यह बिचार भीं पुष्ट करलो कि प्रारध्ध भोग तो भोगना हो पड़ेगा, ज्ञानी भी इससे बच नहीं सकता। अतः प्रारब्ध वश आये हुये दुःखों को वीरता पूर्वक सहन करो। आपत्तिकाल में भी धैय को न छोड़ो। इसी प्रकार सुख की प्राप्ति होने पर प्रमादी मत बनो। ऐसा करने से पुण्य का संचय होगा और लोक-परलोक दोनों बनेंगे।

6

The effects of the actions of a brief time are endured for a long time.

Therefore whether fortune & misfortune, they will come and should be endured together with courage.

Man can seldom sit and do no work, man, by means of the mind, breath and the senses little by little acts, this is man's nature. According to his own individuality every man is naturally inclined to some work. Therefore it is natural inclination of mind to be in action.

According to this theory people will necessarily suffer the effects of their actions. The effects of the actions of a brief time are endured for a long time. Consequently the actions of one lifetime cannot be finished and can result in suffering in another lifetime. Without experiencing them, a heap of actions will be gathered. Until such time as the heap of actions is finished then it will befall you to return again and again inside a womb in order to live again. Consequently having obtained this human life you should deal with this heap of *karma.*

The Shastas have divided actions into three types and explained the means to accomplish these tasks. These *karmas* are the three divisions - *sanchita* (collected *karma*), *prarabdha* (already commenced *karma*) and *kriyamana* (work now being done). *sanchita* (collected *karma*) is limitless. This [accumulated *karma*] cannot be dealt with by experience. The way to deal with [such *karma*] is by obtaining *gyaan* (knowledge) or by endless *bhakti* (devotion) to the feet of Bhagwan. One has to experience the *karma* that has already begun, there is no other way:-

"अवश्यमेव भोक्तव्यं कृतं कर्मं शुभाशुभम्"

"avashyameva bhoktavyam kritam karmam shubhashubham"

'One has to endure the consequences of one's *karma*, both virtuous and sinful'

By offering our *kriyamana karma* (current action) to Bhagwan there is no reason for it to be binding. In this way, by the method of burning the *sanchita karma* (accumulated action) in the fire of knowledge, experiencing *prarabdha karma* (action already begun) and dedicating *kriyamana karma* (current action) to Bhagwan - one will be liberated from being bound, and really find *moksha* (final liberation, beatitude, redemption, absolution, salvation, freedom).

If the reason that acquisition of knowledge is delayed because one's *sadhana* (spiritual practice) is neglected, then little-by-little offer your *kriyamana karma* to Bhagwan. Acting in the manner, there will be no reason for the *karma* of this life to be binding. Along with this thought be strong for the *prarabdha karma* which you will endure, which even the learned cannot escape. Therefore you should come with willingness to the suffering, with endurance and heroism. It is also necessary not to give up courage. Make no mistake, by this method is happiness gained. By doing this there will be an accumulation of *punya* (meritous) *karma*, and both this world and the next world will be prepared.

७

मनुष्य का शरीर मिला है, इसे व्यर्थ न जाने दो

*

अपने कल्याण का मार्ग समझो और उस पर चलो

पेट की चिंता में और शब्द, स्पर्श, रूप, रस, गंध आदि विषयों को भोगने की वासनाओं में ही पड़े रहकर जीवन का अमूल्य समय नष्ट न कर दो। यह तो पशु-पक्षी, कीट-पतंग आदि योनियों में भी करते आये हो। मनुष्य होकर भी यदि यही किया तो फिर उसी चौरासी लक्ष योनियों के चक्कर में पड़े रहोगे; छुटकारा मिलना कठिन है। मनुष्य शरीर की की कीमत करो। विचार से काम लो। अपने वास्तविक कल्याण का मार्ग समझो और ऐसा करो कि चार-चार

फिर गर्भ की काल-कोठरी में न आना पड़े।

अपने जीवन को धार्मिक बनाओ। धर्म का बन्धन स्वीकार करना कल्याणकारी है। स्वतंत्र हो गये हो तो ऐसा मत सोचो कि हम धर्म के तंत्र में भी नहीं रहेगे। धर्म के तंत्र में रहैओगे तो लोक में भी उन्नति करोगे और परलोक भी उज्ज्वल रहेगा।

धर्म-तन्त्र से अपने को मुक्त मानोगे तो उछृंखल अधर्म-तंत्र में फँस जाओगे और अपना सर्वनाश कर बैठोगे। स्वधर्म को अपनाओ। स्वथर्म-पालन ही एक ऐसा उपाय है जिससे मनुष्य-जीवन कृतार्थ हो सकता है।

अपने जीवन के व्यक्तिगत, सामाजिक, राजनैतिक, राष्ट्रीय एवं अन्तर्राष्ट्रीय सभी क्षेत्रों में स्वधर्म पालन की आवश्यकता है। सभी क्षेत्रों में देह, इन्द्रिय, मन और बुद्धि की हलचलों को धर्मानुकूल रखने से ही अधर्म से बचोगे।

धर्म की उपेक्षा करने का अर्थ है, अधर्म को अपनाना। जीवन के जिस क्षेत्र में धर्म की उपेक्षा करोगे उसी क्षेत्र में अधर्म का प्राधान्य हो जायगा और वह क्षेत्र तो कलुषित होगा ही, साथ ही उसके सारे अधर्म का फल व्यक्तिगत रूप से अकेले भोगना पड़ेगा। कर्त्ता ही कर्म का जिम्मेदार होता है। इसलिये जीवन दे व्यक्तिगत अथवा सामाजिक अथवा राजनैतिक किसी भी क्षेत्र में कोई भी काम करो तो विचार कर लो कि धर्म के विरुद्ध तो नहीं हो रहा है। जितना अंश धर्म के विरुद्ध हो उतना कार्यान्वित मत करो। धर्म-विरुद्ध कार्य किसी की रजोगुणी, तमोगुणी बुद्धि में भले ही लाभदायक जँचे, परन्तु परिणाम में वे बलहीन और अनर्थकारी ही होते हैं। तात्पर्य यह है कि धर्मावलम्बन सदा कल्याणकारी और अधर्मावलम्बन या परधर्मावलम्बन सदा अनर्थकारी होता है।

7

Value the human life. Act considerately.

Understand the path of your happiness and proceed upon it

In the thought of stomach and by sound, touch, form, taste and smell etc. one is falling into desires for experiences of the senses, don't destroy this priceless life. You have also been born [before] as beast & bird, worm & grasshopper etc. Even after becoming a human being then again you will fall into the circle of eighty-four hundred thousand births; it is difficult to gain release. Value the human life. Act considerately. Follow the real way to happiness and in this way one will not come four, four times (repeatedly) within the dark cell of wombs.

Make your life *dharmik* (virtuous, devout, religious, godly, upright, etc.). Happiness is acceptance of being bound by *dharma*. We have free will but don't consider that we can live without the system of *dharma*. Living in the system of *dharma*, then you will find advancement in this world and also stay bright in the next world.

Thinking that you are free from the system of *dharma* then you will be trapped in unrestrained *adharma* and will become habituated in destroying yourself. Do one's own *dharma*. Actually preserving one's *dharma* can be the single means of accomplishing man's life.

The life of the individual, society, the duties of the *raja*, national and international, in all fields it is necessary to preserve the *dharma*.

Really, by keeping all areas of the body from agitation, the senses, mind and intellect in keeping with *dharma* you will escape from *adharma* (unrighteousness).

Neglecting *dharma* means to appropriate *adharma*. By neglecting *dharma* in that field of life then in that area *adharma* will predominate and that area will be afflicted, and also you will fall to suffering alone for all the effects of the aspects of the *adharma*. The responsibility for the actions belongs to the doer. Therefore do the work in the given life, personal or in society or in politics, or in any other field. Be considerate then you will not bring any action contrary to *dharma*. Whatever part [of your activity] is contrary to *dharma* that you should not do.

Activity that is contrary to *dharma* is *rajoguni* (passion of love and pleasure), to the *tamoguni* (ignorant) mind this is really beneficial and good, but in effect they are altogether pointless and useless. The gist of this is that adhering to *dharma* always brings happiness and not adhering to *dharma* or doing the *dharma* of another is always without reward.

८

कर्म से भी मोक्ष सम्भव

*

निष्काम कर्मयोग का सहारा लेकर प्रत्येक मनुष्य भवसागर पार हो सकता है।

निष्काम कर्म का अर्थ यह नहीं है कि बिना कामना के कर्म करो, क्योंकि बिना कामना के तो कोई भी प्रवृत्ति नहीं हो सकती। प्रवृत्ति होने में दो हेतु हुआ करते हैं - एक इप्ट [इष्ट] साधन का ज्ञान अर्थात् इस बात का ज्ञान कि यह कार्य करने से हमें इष्टकी (सुख की) प्राप्ति होगी; और दूसरा कृत-साध्यता का ज्ञान अर्थात् यह ज्ञान कि इस कार्य को हम कर सकेंगे। यह दो बातें निश्चय हो जाने पर ही किसी कार्य में मनुष्य की प्रवृत्ति होती है। दो में एक भी बात में सन्देह हो जाय तो प्रवृत्ति नहीं होती। इसलिये कामना पूर्वक ही कर्म में प्रधृत्ति [प्रवृत्ति] होती है। अतः निष्काम कर्म का अर्थ यही निकलता है कि जो कर्म किया जाय भगवान को अर्पण करने के लिये ही किया जाय। भगवान के निमित्त किये हुए कर्म ही निष्काम कर्म कहलाते हैं। भगवान को जो कर्म अर्पण किये जाते हैं वह बन्धन के हेतु नहीं होते। तुम्हारा अधिकार केवल कर्म करने में ही है; फल की कामना कभी मत करो। क्योंकि जीव जन्म-जन्मान्तरों

से गरीबी भोगता चला आ रहा है; इसको माँगने का भी सहूर [सहार?] नहीं है, न जाने क्या माँग ले। जब कोई माँगता है तो अपनी हैसियत से माँगता है। जीव यदि कर्मों के फल को इच्छा करेगा तो अपनी हैसियत से छोटे फल की ही इच्छा करेगा और यदि भगवान पर ही सौंप दे तो भगवान जो सर्वज्ञ शक्तिमान हैं अपनी हैसियत से उसे ऊँचा से ऊँचा प्रदान करेंगे।

भगवदर्पण बुद्धिपूर्वक कर्म करने वाला मनुष्य भगवान के लोक को प्राप्त होकर निष्ठानुसार सालोक्य सामीप्यादि मुक्ति प्राप्त कर लेता है और जन्म-मरण के बन्धन से सदा के लिए छुट जाता है। कर्म करते हुए कर्मबन्धन से छुटकारा पाकर मोक्ष प्राप्त करने का यही उपाय है।

8

Your right is only in the action of *karma*; never desire the effects.

With the support of *"nishkama* (disinterested) *karma yoga"* every human being can come to the other side of the ocean of being

"nishkama karma" does not mean to do action without desire, because without desire then nobody can have the *pravritti* (tendency, inclination or perseverance) of mind [to perform action]. There are two causes of *pravritti* (tendency for activity), one is the knowledge of *"ishta sadhana"* that is information that by doing an action we shall gain fulfilment; and secondly the knowledge of *"krita sadhyata"*, knowledge that this work is feasible and possible for us to accomplish. Only by knowing these two pieces of information can there be a spur for any man to perform action. If there is any uncertainty about either of the two aspects then the spur to action will not occur. Therefore preceding a spur to action there must be the desire. Consequently the meaning of *"nishkama karma"* appears to be exactly this, that the *karma* suitable to be done is that which is fitting to offer to Bhagwan. *"nishkama karma"* is action done on Bhagwan's account. That *karma* that is to be offered to Bhagwan, and is not

on account of being attached. Your right is only in the action of *karma*; never desire the effects.

Because the soul's life has been suffering poverty from many lifetimes; it has no help with this call for assistance, not knowing what to ask for. When any demand is made then the demand is based on one's own merit. If the soul will wish for the effects of its *karmas*, then by one's merit there will be little effect desired, but if one surrenders to Bhagwan then Bhagwan who is All-Knowing, All-Powerful, from one's own merit offered to him on high he will give a high gift.

Intelligently, delivering to Bhagavat (God), doing action, man gains Bhagwan's world. According to devotion he receives salvation, freedom and deliverance and is always released from being bound to birth and death. Performing *karma* one gets freed from bondage of life and death, this is the means to acquire *moksha* (final liberation, beatitude, redemption, absolution, quietus, salvation, freedom, death).

९

जीना उन्ही का सार्थक है जो जीकर कुछ आगे के लियै बनायें

संसारी लोग जितनी चेष्टा धनवान, पुत्रवान, प्रतिष्ठवान बनने के लिये करते हैं उतना प्रयत्न भगवत् भक्त और ज्ञानवान बनने का नहीं करते। जो परम सुख का साधन है, उसकी उपेक्षा करके दुःख के साधनों का संग्रह करते हैं। किसी भी संसारी वस्तु से कोई कभी सुखी नहीं हो सकता है। संसारी वस्तुओं से सुख प्राप्ति की इच्छा उसी प्रकार है जैसे बन्ध्या के पुत्र के विवाह की तैयारी-वन्ध्या का पुत्र ही नहीं है तो उसका विवाह क्या होगा! धन, स्त्री, पुत्रादि संसारी वस्तुओं में सुख जब है ही नहीं, तो इनसे सुख मिलेगा कैसे! परन्तु अविवेक से अनिष्ट में इष्ट बुद्धि कर ली गई है।

जीना उन्हीं का सार्थक है जो जीकर कुछ आगे के लिये बनाना चाहते हैं। 'यदि झोली भरना और खाली करना इतना ही है', तो

मनुष्य जीवन निरर्थक ही जा रहा है, ऐसा मानो। 'उदर (पेट) की झोली सबेरे भरो और शाम को खाली करो' यदि इतना ही करते हुए जीना है तो जीना व्यर्थ ही है। जींने की इच्छा इसलिये रखो कि अभी भगवान् का दर्शन नहीं हुआ है उसी के लिये साधन करने के लिये जीना है।

बीज जब सेंक दिया जाता है तो फिर उसमें अंकुर नहीं निकलता। इसीं प्रकार मनुष्य का मन जब ज्ञान और भक्ति की गरमी से सेंक दिया जाता है तो फिर उसमें जन्म-मरण का अंकुर नहीं होता। इसलिये भक्तिमान् और ज्ञानवान् बनने का प्रयत्न करो। परन्तु ऐसे ज्ञानी न बनो कि धन, स्त्री, पुत्रादि से संसार में प्रेम तो बना रहे और 'शिवोहं शिवोहं, ॐ ॐ और अहं ब्रह्मास्मि' कहने लगे; लोग जब अपने को ब्रह्म कहने लगते हैं तो फिर धर्म-कर्म से भी दूर हट जाते हैं और उधर निष्ठा पुष्ट होती नहीं। इसलिये जब तक संसारी वस्तुओं से प्रेम नहीं हटा है तब तक ब्रह्म के फेर में न पड़कर भगवान की भक्ति करनी चाहिये। भक्ति करते-करते जब भगवान में अतिशय राग हो जायगा तो फिर जन्म-मरण के चक्कर से छूट जाओगे।

9

When a seed is roasted then no sprouting appears.

As much as *samsari* (worldly) people desire to obtain wealth, children and respect, that much effort is not made in worshipping Bhagavat (the Lord) and in becoming knowledgeable. That *sadhana* (means) of [obtaining] uttermost happiness is disregarded. *Sadhanas* of collecting and amassing suffering are done. From any worldly thing there can never be any happiness. From worldly things the pleasure gained is like the wish of a barren woman preparing for the son's marriage. If there is not a son who is fit to be reverenced then how will there be a marriage? At whatever time happiness is not really in worldly things such as wealth, woman, son etc., then how will happiness be got from these? But by absence of discrimination, the mind has gone in pursuit of *anishta* (mishchief, evil).

The purpose of life is to desire doing something for the future; 'If the bucket is to be filled, and is to be emptied, this is all there really is'. Then human being existence is going to be really useless. So consider; 'Fill the bucket of the stomach at dawn and empty it by the evening.' If this is really how life has been then to live is really useless. You desire life because just now you have not had *darshan* (vision) of Bhagwan. For this *darshan* one is alive, for doing *sadhana*.

When a seed is roasted then no sprouting appears. This is like the mind of a man when, from the heat of knowledge and devotion, it is roasted. Then afterwards birth and death does not sprout. Therefore, make an effort to become devout and knowledgeable. But similarly don't become a *gyaani* (a learned one) of wealth, woman, sons, in love with worldliness and at the same time chanting:-

"शिवोहं। शिवोहं"

"shivoham, shivoham"
'I am Shiva, I am Shiva'

[ref: *"chidananda rupah shivoham shivoham."* 'The Bliss Consciousness Form, I am Shiva, I am Shiva.' (*Atma Shatakam* or *Nirvana Shatakam* of Shankaracharya)]

"ॐ । ॐ"

"OM, OM"

and

"अहं ब्रह्मास्मि"

"aham brahmasmi"
[*Briharanyaka Upanishad* 1:4:10]

'I am Brahma'

When people call themselves Brahma then afterwards go far from *dharma* and *karma* too, in this way, that condition [of oneness with *Brahma*] is not nourished but is destroyed. Therefore, until you shrink from love of worldly things, then for as long as you are not returning to Brahma, you should do worship of Bhagwan. Keep doing *bhakti* and when you will very much desire Bhagwan, then afterwards you will be freed from *"janma-marana ke chakkara"* - the 'wheel of birth and death'.

१०

मृत्यु-काल की पीड़ा

जन्म लेने में जो कष्ट होता है उससे कई गुना अधिक कष्ट मरण काल में होता है। शास्त्रों मे कहा है कि सहस्त्रों बिच्छुओं के एक साथ दंश करने से जो पीड़ा हो सकती है उससे भी अधिक पीड़ा मरने में होती है। एक बिच्छू के दंश करने पर पीड़ा सहन करना कठिन होता है। यदि सहस्त्रों बिच्छू एक साथ दंश करें तो क्या दशा होगी! इसी से मृत्यु-काल की पीड़ा का अनुमान किया जा सकता है।

जन्म-मरण की पीड़ा के अतिरिक्त जीवन-काल की पीड़ाओं का

अंअन्त नहीं। बिना ईश्वर को प्राप्त किये इससे छुटकारा होना असम्भव है। संसार में जब तक मोह बना हुआ है तब तक पुनः संसार में ही आना पड़ेगा। अशुद्ध भावनाओं से अशुभ वासनाओं का वाध करना चाहिये और फिर केवल ईश्वर-प्राप्ति की ही एक वासना प्रबल करनी चाहिये। यह वासना इतनी पुष्ट हो जाय कि अन्य कोई वासना इसके सम्मुख उदय न हो सके।

10

Making the mistake of being worldly/transmigrated then you have to fall again and again.

In taking birth there is suffering; much more suffering there is at the time of dying. In the *Shastras* it is said that when you die the anguish can be greater than the stings of thousands of scorpions. If one scorpion stings it is torment to endure the pain. If thousands of scorpions sting then guess what may be the torment of the period of demise.

The pains of birth/death are additional to those of our lifetimes, which are without end. Without Ishwar (God) it is impossible to become released from this. Making the mistake of being worldly/transmigrated then you have to fall again and again. You should argue against desires that are impure and afterwards should have only one strong desire for getting God. You will not progress until this desire has become stronger than any other.

११

अन्त-काल न बिगड़ने पाये

प्रायः यह देखा जाता है कि जिस बात का जो अधिक चिन्तन करता है अथवा जिसका उसे अधिक अभ्यास होता है, अन्त समय में उसी का स्मरण आता है। यदि कोई वेद-पाठी पागल हो जाय तो अपने पागलपन में भी वह वेद की ऋचाओं को दोहरायेगा। मृत्यु-काल की पीड़ा में होश ठिकाने नहीं रहता है। उस समय उसी का स्मरण होने की सम्भावना अधिक है जिसका जीवन भर अभ्यास किया है। आदि की बिगड़ी बन जाती है परन्तु अन्त की बिगड़ी नहीं बनती। इसीलिये कहा है कि 'अन्त भला सो भला।' अपना अन्त-काल न बिगड़ने पाये, इसकी तैयारी अभी से करने लगो। यही बुद्धिमानी है।

11

'All's well that ends well.'

It is mostly seen that, that which is habitually thought about a lot, it is this that comes to be easily recollected at the time of death. If anyone who reads the *Veda* has gone crazy then in craziness too he will repeat the hymns of the *Veda*. At the time of death understanding does not remain. At that time it is most probable that the mind will recall that which has been the life's habit. If something has existed since a long time but at the end it is damaged then it cannot be repaired. Therefore the saying is that 'All's well that ends well'. One's own final time is not to be spoiled; do the work to prepare for this right now. This is prudence.

१२

जिसका वियोग निश्चित है, उसे सुख का साधन बनाना भारी भूल

संसार में प्रेम बढ़ाओगे तो जन्म-जन्मान्तर तक रोना पड़ेगा

सब का यहाँ नदी-नाव की तरह संयोग है। जहाँ हो, जिस परिस्थिति में हो, वहीं चातुरी से काम लो। सब का प्रोग्राम अपना अलग-अलग बना है। छान-बीन करोगे तो कोई किसी का साथी नहीं मिलेगा, केवल 'मैं और मेरा' ही दिख पड़ेगा। वास्तव में यहाँ संसार में किसी की अपनी स्थिति पुष्ट नहीं है तो दूसरे का कोई क्या होगा। सबका जीवन पत्ते के पानी की तरह है, चाहे जब ढल जाय। कर्माधीन जिसका जहां जन्म हों गया है, उसे वहीं अपना धर्म पालन करते हुए भगवान को स्मरण करते हुये समय को बिताना चाहिये। आवश्यक व्यावहारिक कार्यों को करो, परन्तु ऐसी बुद्धिमानी से करो कि वह कर्म आगे के परलोक-मार्ग में बाधक न हो। चातुरी वही है जो लोक-परलोक दोनों उज्वल बनाये। किसी को धोखा देकर उससे कुछ ठग लेना चातुरी नहीं, वह तो मूर्खता है। जिसको अपना भविष्य नहीं सूझ रहा है, क्या उसको चतुर कहा जा सकता है।

हमारा तो यही कहना है कि ठगो मत, चाहे ठगा जा। अपने धर्म-कर्म का भरोसा रखो। चालाकी और बेईमानी का भरोसा मत रखो। संसार में ऐसे रहो जैसे कि यहाँ का काम भी चलता जाय और परलोक का मार्ग भी उज्वल बनता जाय। यह तभी होगा जब अपने-अपने धर्म का पालन करते हुए भगवान का स्मरण करते चलोगे। ऐसा करोगे तभी जन्म-मरण के बंधन् से मुक्त होकर इस मलमूत्र के शरीर से छुटकारा मिलेगा। नहीं तो बार-बार इसी में लौट-लौट कर आना पड़ेगा।

संसार के सब पदार्थों का वियोग होता है। वियोगान्त वस्तु प्रेमास्पद (प्रेम करने योग्य) नहीं। जिसका वियोग निश्चित है उससे प्रेम करने की आवश्यकता नहीं। प्रेम करोगे तो रोना पड़ेगा और एक ही जन्म में नहीं रोना पड़ता, कई जन्म तक रोना पड़ता है। इस पर एक दृष्टांत है। एक बार महर्षि नारद किसी नगर से होकर जा रहे थे। एक वैश्य ने उनका आतिथ्य सत्कार किया। उसकी श्रद्धा-भक्ति देख कर उन्होंने उसका एक गिलास दुग्ध पी लिया। वेश्य ने पूछा -

महाराज, कहाँ से आ रहे हो?

नारद जी ने कहा - स्वर्ग से।

वैश्य ने पूछा - महाराज, अब यहाँ पधारोगे?

नारद जी ने कहा - थोड़ा मृत्युलोक में घूम कर फिर स्वर्ग लौट जायेंगे।

वैश्य ने प्रार्थना की - महाराज, लौटते समय हमें भी स्वर्ग लेते चलें तो बड़ी कृपा होगी।

नारद ने कहा - अच्छा ले, चलेंगे।

कुछ् दिनों के पश्चात् नारद जी घूम - फिर कर लौटे तो पूछा - सेठजी, स्वर्ग चलोगे?

सेठजी ने कहा - महाराज, चलना तो अवश्य है पर अभी ये लड़के बहुत छोटे नासमझ हैं। ये लोग गृहस्थी का काम संभाल नहीं सकेंगे। थोड़े दिन में ये काम-काज सँभालने योग्य हो जायँ तब चलेंगे।

नारद जी चले गये। थोड़े दिन में वे फिर लौटे। पूछा - सेठजी अब चलोगे?

सेठजी ने कहा - हाँ महाराज, अब तो लड़का बड़ा हो गया है, काम-काज भी कुछ देखने-सुनने लगा है, परन्तु यह अभी अपनी पूरी जिम्मेदारी नहीं समझता। अगले वर्ष इसका विवाह कर दें फिर निश्चिन्त हो जायँ तब चलेंगे। चार वर्ष बाद नारद जी। फिर लौटे तो दुकान पर लड़के से पूछा कि सेठ जी कहाँ हैं? लड़के ने कहा - महाराज, क्या बतायें। एक ही तो हमारे घर में पिता जी सब सँभाले हुए थे, उनका शरीर छूट गया, तब से हम तो बड़ी परेशानी में हैं।

नारद जी ने ध्यान लगा कर देखा तो मालूम हुआ कि सेठजी मर कर बैल हुए हैं। नारद जी बैल के पास गये और कहा कि सेठ जी अब तो मनुष्य शरीर भी छूट गया, अब स्वर्ग चलोगे न?

बैल ने कहा - महाराज! आपकी बड़ी कृपा है। मैं भी चलने को तैयार हूँ, पर सोचता हूँ कि घर के और बैल इतने सुस्त हैं कि आगे मैं न चलूँ तो कुछ काम ही न हो। कुछ नये बैल आने वाले हैं तब तक मैं इनका काम स ।भाल दूं, फिर आप कृपा करना मैं अवश्य चलूँगा।

नारद जी फिर दो-चार वर्ष बाद लौटे। उन्हें तो अपना वचन पूरा करना था और वैश्य का एक गिलास् दूध चुकाना था; इसीलिये बार-बार उसके पास आते थे। इस बार आये तो बैल नहीं दिखा। लड़कों से पूछा कि तुम्हारे यहाँ जो बूढ़ा बैल था वह कहाँ गया? लड़कों ने दुःखी होकर कहा कि महाराज! बड़ा मेहनती बैल था। सब से आगे चलता था। जब से मर गया है तब से वैसा दूसरा बैल नहीं मिला।

नारद जी ने ध्यान करके देखा तों मालूम हुआ कि इस बार सेठ जी कुत्ता होकर घर के आगे पहरा दे रहे हैं। कुत्तों से पास जाकर नारद जी ने कहा - कहो सेठ जी! क्या समाचार है? तीन जन्म तों हो गया, अब स्वर्ग चलने के सम्बन्ध में क्या विचार है?

कुत्तों ने कहा - महाराज! आप बड़े दयालु हैं। एक ओर मैं आपकी दयालुता देखता हूँ और दूसरी ओर लड़कों का आलस्य और बदइन्तजामी। महाराज! ये इतने आलसी हो गये हैं हि मैं दरवाजे पर न रहूँ तो दिन में ही लोग इन्हें लूट ले जाँय। इसलिये सोचता हुँ कि जब तक हूँ, तब तक इनकी रक्षा रहे तो अच्छा। थोड़े दिन में जरूर चलूँगा।

नारद जी फिर लौट गये। चार-छै वर्ष में फिर आये तो कुत्ता दर्वाजे पर नहीं दिखा। लड़कों से पूछा तो पता चला कि वह मर गया है। ध्यान लगाकर देखा तो मालूम हुआ कि इस बार सर्प होकर उसी घर के तलघर में कोष की रक्षा करते हुए बैठे हैं।

नारद जी वहाँ पहुँचे। कहा - कहिये सेठ जी! यहाँ आप कैसे बैठे हैं? स्वर्ग चलने का समय अभी आया कि नहीं?

सर्प ने कहा - महाराज! ये लड़के इतने फिजूलखर्ची हों गये हैं कि मैं न होता तो अब तक खजाना खाली कर देते। सोचता हूँ कि मेरी गाढ़ी कमाई का पैसा है, जितने दिन रक्षित रह जाय उतना ही अच्छा है। इसीलिये यहाँ मेरी आवश्यकता है, नहीं तो मैं तो चलने को तैयार ही हूँ।

नारद जी फिर निराश होकर लौटे। बाहर आकर उन्होंने बड़े लड़के को बुलाकर कहा कि तुम्हारे खजाने में एक भयंकर कालरूप सर्प बैठा हुआ है; ऐसा न हो कि कभी किसी को हानि पहुँचा दे। इसलिये उसे मारकर भगा दो। ऐसा मारना कि उसके सर में लाठी न लगे। सर में लाठी पड़ने से वह मर जायगा। मरने न पावे और कूट-पीट कर उसको खजाने से बाहर कर दो।

महात्मा का आदेश पाकर लड़कों ने वैसा ही किया। सारे शरीर में लाठियों की मार लगाकर उसको लस्त कर दिया और घर के बाहर फेंक आये।

वहाँ जाकर नारद जी उससे मिले और कहा - कहिये सेठ जी! लड़कों ने तो खूब पुटपुटी लगाई; अभी आपका मन भरा या नहीं? फिर वापिस जाकर घर की रक्षा करोगे या अब चलोगे स्वर्ग? सर्प ने कहा - हाँ महाराज! अब चलेंगे।

तात्पर्य यह है कि गृह में, पुत्र में, धन में, स्त्री आदि में प्रेम हो जाने पर कई जन्म तक वह प्रेम-बन्धन शिथिल नहीं होता और कई जन्मों तक उसी के कारण अनेक यातनायें सहनी पड़ती हैं। इसीलिये कहा जाता है कि संसार में प्रेम मत फँसाओ। यहाँ प्रेम करोगे तो कई जन्म तक रोना पड़ेगा।

12

Don't put your trust in craftiness and dishonesty.

All of us here are connected like boats and the river. Wherever you are, whatever the circumstances are, take care how you act here. All have made their own separate *"programme"*. If you examine then nobody will be found to be a friend, only *"main aur mera"* ('me and mine') are to be seen. In truth if our own situation here in worldly existence is not strong, then how will it be with someone else? All life is like water of a leaf, dropping as needed. Work wherever appropriate to one's life, preserving one's *dharma* here. One ought to pass the time in remembering Bhagwan. Do the necessary customary tasks but in such an intelligent manner that it will not trouble the future way to the next world. Cleverness is that which makes both this world and the other world bright. It is not clever to obtain anything by deception. That is ignorance then. One who has no perception of his own future, how can he be said to be wise?

Then we say exactly this; 'Don't cheat - let go of the desire to cheat. Put your trust in your own *dharma* and *karma*. Don't put your trust in craftiness and dishonesty. In worldly action behave in such a way that the road to the other world is made bright. This will be when one preserves one's own *dharma* and will remember Bhagwan. Thus for this reason you will become freed from the restriction of life and death, be released from this body of excrement and urine. If not then time and time again you will return to this.'

The whole meaning of the word *samsara* (worldly existence, mortal world, transmigration) is *viyoga* (separation, disunion, detachment etc.), *viyoganta* (at the end is separation) is not a thing suitable to be an object of love. There is no need to love that which we will definitely be separated from. Then you will weep and not only in one life you weep, but for many lives you will weep.

An example of this is:-

One time Maharishi Narada was going to a town. One *vaishya* (trader) greeted him respectfully and hospitably. Seeing his faith and service he (Narada) accepted a glass of milk to drink. The *vaishya* asked, 'Maharaja, from where are you coming?'

Narada ji answered, 'From Swarg (heaven)'

The *vaishya* asked, 'Maharaja, where will you be going now?'

Narada ji said, 'A little while in the world of mortality and then again I will return (to heaven).'

The *vaishya* prayed, 'Maharaja, when the time comes for you to return, I would like you to take me to heaven too, that would be a great kindness, you will be a benevolent teacher.'

Narada said, 'Okay, you should come.'

After wandering, some days Narada ji later returned and asked, 'Seth ji, we shall go to Swarg?'

Seth ji said, 'Maharaja, certainly we go but just now the children are very young and ignorant. These people cannot do the work of looking after the home, some day they will find suitable work then we will go.'

Narada ji went away. In a short time he returned to ask, 'Seth ji now you'll go?'

Seth ji said, 'Yes Maharaja, now that the children have grown up and are working, but now they see and hear little, at present they have not understood responsibility. Next year grant that they marry and after that then we shall go.

Four years later Narada Ji returned and asked the children at the shop, 'Where is Seth ji?'

The children said, 'Maharaja, what to say? Father looked after our house all by himself, he is now gone from his body, since when we are in big distress.'

Narada ji meditated and it became clear to him that after his death Seth ji had become an ox. Narada ji came near to the ox and said, 'Seth ji, now then, the man's body is gone, now shall we not go to heaven?'

The ox said, 'Maharaja! Your great kindness, graceful teacher. I am ready to proceed together with you, but am considering that the ox of the house is slow and in future, if I do not walk, then little work will be done. Some new ox is to come and until then I will keep watch over the work, then with your grace I will certainly proceed with you.

Narada ji returned two to four years later, to keep his word and repay the *vaishya* for the glass of milk. This time when he came, the ox was nowhere to be seen. To the children he asked, 'There was an old ox here, where has it gone?'

Hearing the words the children became sorrowful, 'Maharaja! It was a great hardworking ox. It walked ahead of them all. Since it died we have not been able to find another like it.'

Narada ji meditated and it became clear to him that this time Seth ji had become a dog and was keeping watch over the house.

Going near the dogs Narada ji said, 'Seth ji tell me what is the news? Three lifetimes have come, now do you consider you are ready to accompany me to Swarg?'

The dog said, 'Maharaja! You are very kind. On one side I see your kindness and on the other my children's idleness and bad judgement. Maharaja! They have become very idle and if I do not remain at the door then, in time, some people will come and rob them. Therefore consider that whilst I am here to protect them, it is good. In a short time certainly I will come.'

After six years Narada ji returned again, then there were no dogs to be seen at the door.

From the children he asked the whereabouts of the dog, which had died.

Meditating it became apparent that this time he had become a snake who was sitting in a space beneath the house, protecting the treasures hidden there.

Narada ji reached there and said, 'Seth ji you should say why are you sitting here? Right now, is it not the time to come to heaven?'

The serpent said, 'Maharaja! These children have become so lavish, if I were not here then the treasury would be empty. Considering this is my hard-earned cash, however many days guarding, that much is good. Therefore I must stay here, else I would be ready to go.'

Narada ji again left, disappointed. Outside he called the grownup children saying that, 'Seated on your treasure is a fearful black serpent; it could cause harm. Therefore, beat it so that it goes away. Do not hit it at the top (in the head), that would kill it. Not to kill it, give it a grinding and thrashing so that it goes away from the treasure.'

Getting the advice of the *mahatma*, the children did exactly what he said. The entire body got a beating, it became weary and was thrown outside the house.

Going there Narada ji met him and said, 'Seth ji, you ought to say the children have given you a good beating. Now is your heart full (you are happy) or not? Are you going to return to the house and protect it or will you go to heaven?'

The serpent said, 'Yes, Maharaja, Now we will go.'

The meaning of this is, if you find love for the house, for the son, for wealth, for a woman etc., then you will endure the torture of many lifetimes. Therefore it is said, 'Don't become ensnared by the love of worldly existence.' Here you will love, then for many lifetimes you will weep.

१३

शत्रु और मित्र में समभाव रखो
दोनों अपने ही दुष्कृत और सुकृत के फल हैं

*

न कोई किसी का शत्रु है, न मित्र। यदि कोई किसी का मित्र हो तो सदा उसे मित्र ही रहना चाहिये। पर ऐसा नहीं देखा जाता। जो मित्र रहता है वही कभी शत्रु हो जाता है। इसलिए स्वभावतः कोई किसी का शत्रु व मित्र नहीं है। अपने सुकृत का फल जिसके द्वारा आता है वह मित्रता का व्यवहार करता है और अपने दुष्कृत का फल जिसके द्वारा आता है वही शत्रुता का व्यवहार करता है। सुख और दुःख अपने ही कर्मों का फल है। न कोई किसी को सुख दे सकता है, न दुःख। शत्रु व मित्र केवल अपने सुकृत और दुष्कृत फल के वाहन हैं।

जिस समय हमारे सुकृत का फल उदय होता है उस समय सब लोग मित्र बनकर सुख पहुंचाते हैं और जब दुष्कृत का फल उदय होता है तो वही लोग शत्रु बनकर दुःख देते हैं। सुख-दुःख सर्वथा अपनी ही वस्तु है, उसका निमित्त चाहे जो बन जावे। यदि हमने किसी को मार डाला है तो हमें फांसी होगी। फांसी का दोष न जल्लाद को है और न उस जज को है जो फांसी का हुक्म सुनाता है। हमारी फांसी हमारे ही किये हुए कर्म का फल है। इसलिए जज से और जल्लाद से व्यक्तिगत शत्रुता मानने की क्या आवश्यकता है - जैसा कर्म जड़ है, वैसा कर्म का फल जड़ होता है जो किसी चेतन के सहारे कर्त्ता के पास आता है। जिसके द्वारा हमें सुख मिलता है वह हमारे शुभ-कर्मों के फल का वाहन है और जिसके द्वारा हमें कष्ट होता है वह हमारे पाप-कर्मों के फल का वाहन है।

सुख-दुःख तो सर्वथा अपनी ही वस्तु है। जिस पर आरूढ़ होकर

वह आता है वही हमारे सुख-दुःख का निमित्त बन जाता है। यह निश्चय करके राग-द्वेष से अलग रहना चाहिये। जब हमारी वस्तु हमारे निकट आ रही है तो उसमें दूसरे का क्या है? जिसको हमारे सुकृत के फल का निमित्त बनना है वह बने। हमें न किसी से प्रेम करना है, न द्वेष। निमित्त से क्या राग-द्वेष करना! जो मुख्य वस्तु सुख-दुःख है वह तो अपनी ही है; वह चाहे जिस वाहन पर चढ़कर आये। वाहन का क्या महत्व है?

इसलिये किसी से राग-द्वेष न करते हुए शान्ति पूर्वक धैर्य से अपने कर्मों का फल भोगना चाहिये, चाहे वह सुख रूप में आये या दुःख रूप में, दोनों अपनी ही वस्तु है। अपना संबधी चाहे अच्छा हो या बुरा, अपना ही है; समीप आने पर उसका स्वागत करना ही उचित है।

13

The enemy and the friend are only the conveyance of the effects of good and evil actions.

Nobody is an enemy or a friend. If anyone is friendly then they should always be a friend, but it appears not. The one who is a friend sometimes becomes an enemy. Therefore by nature someone is neither friend nor foe. The process of friendship is a way for the effects of good *karma* (action) to come, and the fruits of one's own sinful actions come through one's enemies. Happiness and sorrow are really the fruit of actions. Nobody can give happiness nor sorrow. The enemy and the friend are only the conveyance of the effects of good and evil actions.

That time when the fruit of our good actions arise, at that time all people are friends and are come to make us happy and when the effects of evil deeds arise then the same people become enemies and give sorrow. In every case happiness and sorrow are together the same thing, caused and made by one's own desires. If we were to kill someone then we would be executed. The executioner is not to blame for the noose, nor is the *"judge"* who makes the sentence. Our hanging is really the effect of our own action. Therefore what is the need to assume there is any personal enmity from the *"judge"* or the hangman? The action is devoid of feeling, so the fruit of action is without partiality, it comes to the living being who is the author. In this way we get happiness which are the effects of our good actions conveyed to us and by this way suffering is conveyed to bring the fruits of our evil deeds.

Happiness and sorrow then are always completely one's own stuff. On whosoever one becomes elevated, the very same we make to be the cause of happiness and sorrow. Certainly we should be separate from attachment and hatred. When our own things are coming close to us then why [think] of another? Whoever causes the fruits of our good actions [to appear], he makes. There is no love from us, no malice. For this reason why have attachment or enmity? The main thing is that the happiness and sorrow are our own; so why desire that by which the fruits have become conveyed on?

Therefore, without attachment or malice, peacefully and courageously, one should endure the effects of one's own actions, coming in the form of happiness or unhappiness. Both are one's own stuff. Be they good or bad they are related to you, really yours; when they come near, welcome them properly.

१४

दुष्कर्म हो जाय तो कह दो
और
सत्कर्म करो तो छिपाओ

*

यज्ञ का फल असत्य भाषण करने से नष्ट हो जाता है, तप का फल गर्व से नष्ट हो जाता है; ब्राह्मण की निन्दा करने से आयु क्षीण होती है, दान किया जाय और उसकी चारों तरफ कह दिया जाय तो उसका फल नष्ट हो जाता है। इसलिए जिसको नष्ट करना है उसको कह दो और जिसको संचय करना हो उसको छिपाओ। यदि कोई पाप हो जाय तो कह देने से पाप का फल बंट जाता है। इसी प्रकार यदि कोई पुण्य कर्म हो जाय और उसको लोगों से कह दिया जाय तो उसका फल भी बंट जाता है।

14

If any sin is done, then by telling the effects are distributed.

The rewards of *yagya* (religious sacrifice) become destroyed by telling a lie, the fruits of *tapa* (austerity) become destroyed by pride; by the scorn of a *brahmana* the duration of one's life is diminished, having given to charity and telling in all four directions then the advantage is destroyed. Therefore that which you want destroyed, talk about it, and that which we want to keep, about that be secretive.

If any sin is done, then by telling, the effects are distributed. In this way if any virtuous *karma* is done, and it is talked about with people, then the effects also will be distributed.

१५

ऐसा नहीं कि -
पाप करते जाओ, भगवान् को भजते जाओ

*

भगवान् की कृपा के बल पर पाप करने का विधान नहीं है। वास्तव में जो अनन्य भाव से भगवान् का भजन करेगा उससे कोई अविहिताचरण हो ही नहीं सकता।

अनन्यता का तो अर्थ है कि फिर भगवान् के सिवाय और कोई उसके लिये रह ही न जाय। जब इस प्रकार भक्त की निष्ठा हो जायगी तो फिर जो वह करेगा वह ऐसा ही होगा जिससे भगवान प्रसन्न हों। भगवान के नाम में पाप नाश करने की जितनी शक्ति है उतना पाप पापी कर ही नहीं सकता। बल्मीकि आदि महर्षियों के ऐसे ही उदाहरण हैं जो पहले बड़े पापी-दुराचारी थे, परन्तु अपनी बुराई छोड़कर जब से वे भगवान के भजन में दत्तचित्त हुए तब से बहुत अच्छे बन गये। पहले का चाहे जितना पापी हो, पर यदि वह भगवान के भजन में लग जाता है तो यह निश्चित् है कि उसकी सदगति होगी।

15

In the name of Bhagwan the strength of sin fades, so much so that wicked wrongdoings cannot be done.

The power of the grace of Bhagwan is not an arrangement to commit *paapa* (sin). In truth with the endless feeling from singing *bhajan* (hymns) to Bhagwan no forbidden behaviour can be practised.

Then there is infinite wealth, for without Bhagwan there is nothing. When this kind of condition of devotion will come, then only that which pleases Bhagwan will be done. In the name of

Bhagwan the strength of sin fades, so much so that wicked wrongdoings cannot be done. Valmiki is an example of *maharishis* (sages) who were very evil and wicked before but who let go of their own wickedness after being fully attentive to worshipping Bhagwan, from when they were made good. However sinful one is before, yet if he applies himself to worshipping Bhagwan, then *sadagati* (salvation, good conduct) will be certain.

१६

भगवान् की सेवा करना चाहते हो तो हनुमान जी का आदर्श पालन करो

हनुमान जी ने भगवान् की हर प्रकार से सेवा की, पर उसके बदले में कुछ नहीं चाहा। दास्य भाव को अपनाते हो तो हनुमान जी को उदाहरण में लो। निष्काम भक्ति का यही स्वरूप है। इष्ट के निमित्त कार्य करो और उसके फल रूप में अपने लिये किसी वस्तु की याचना न करो।

इष्ट प्रीत्यर्थ काम करना चाहिये। इष्ट की प्रसन्नता रहे, यही एक वासना हो। ऐसा नहीं कि शकरजी को एक लोटा जल चढ़ाया और प्रार्थना में कहने लगे कि लड़के की नौकरी लग जाय, स्त्री की तबियत् ठीक हो जाय या धन की कभी है अतः। रोजगार में वृद्धि हो जाय। इस प्रकार की संसारी वासनाओं को लेकर इष्टाराधन करते हो तो इष्ट भी घबराता है; क्योंकि याचक से सभी दूर भागते हैं। इसलिये इष्ट से कुछ याचना नहीं करनी चाहिये। बस, उसकी सेवा करते चलो। जब उसका ध्यान तुम्हारे प्रति आकृत्ष्ट हो और पूछे कि क्या चाहते हो, तब भी यही कहो कि 'आप की कृपा चाहते हैं, आपकी दृष्टि हम पर रहे, और कुछ नहीं चाहते।'

इष्ट की निष्काम सेवा का फल है अन्तःकरण की शुद्धि और

अन्तःकरण की शुद्धि का फल है यथार्थ बोध। इसलिये दास्य भाव का बड़ा माहात्म्य है। जिस प्रकार काष्ठ में अग्नि सर्वत्र उपस्थित है और रगड़ने से उत्पन्न होता है, उसी प्रकार परमात्मा चराचर में रमा हुआ है और उपासना से प्रकट होता है।

उपासना करो, परन्तु उपासना काल में याचना मत करो। भगवान् को ऋणी बनाकर छोड़ दो। जैसे हनुमानजी ने किया था। अन्त में भगवान् राम को कहना पड़ा कि हनुमान, तुमने जो मेरी सेवा की है, उसका बदला मैं कैसे चुकाऊँ? यह है भगवान् को ऋणी बनाना।

वास्तव में परमात्मा जितना दे सकता है उतना जीव मांग नहीं सकता। तुम याचना करोगे तो अपनी हैसियत से कोई छोटी चीज मांगोगे और परमात्मा देगा तो वह अपनी हैसियत से देगा। वह सर्वज्ञ है और सर्वशक्तिमान है; उसके लिये सब कुछ साध्य है। तुम अपना कार्य करो और पर्मात्मा को अपना कर्त्तव्य करने के लिये छोड़ दो, कभी टोटे में नहीं रहोगे।

16

In truth Paramatma can give so much that much one could not ask.

Hanuman ji did every kind of service of Bhagwan, but desired nothing in return. Having a temperament of service, then take Hanuman ji as the exemplification. Desirelessness, this is the true form of *bhakti* (service). Do work for the purpose of the *ishta* (deity) and do not ask for anything in return.

You should work for the sake of love of the *ishta*. The one desire is for pleasing the *ishta*. It is not that you cause to offer a pot of water onto Shankar ji (Shiva) and then ask the service of children, that a woman's temperament becomes good or to get promoted at work in order to get some money. Worshipping the *ishta* for these worldly kind of things then the *ishta* is confused as well; because everyone runs far away from a beggar. Therefore, from the *ishta* you should not ask for anything. It is enough to go and do their service. When through meditation [the *ishta*] becomes drawn to you and asks what you desire, then at that time say this; 'We want your blessing, you looking upon us, and nothing else is desired.'

The effect of desireless service to the *ishta* is purity of the inner self and the gain of purity of the inner self is to be aware of reality. Therefore the feeling of service has great value. In the same way that *agni* (fire) is always present in wood and becomes produced by rubbing, in that way Paramatma attracts and by prayer becomes manifest.

Do pray, but whilst in prayer do not make demands. Make Bhagwan free to be indebted, just as Hanuman ji did. In the end Bhagwan Rama fell to asking of Hanuman; 'You are the one who have done my service, how can I repay and recompense you?' This is to make Bhagwan indebted.

HANUMĀN, THE MONKEY GOD.
[*'Daily Life and Work in India'*, W J Wilkins, T Fisher Unwin, 1890]

In truth Paramatma can give so much that much one could not ask. If you will demand then you will demand something small and Paramatma is to give, then by one's own merit he will give. He is All-Knowing and is Almighty; so everything is possible. Do your own work and leave Paramatma free to do his work, you will not lose anything.

१७

शक्ति का अपव्यय और बुद्धि का दुरुपयोग न करो

जो कुछ करो उसे पहले भली प्रकार सोच-विचार लो; क्योंकि अच्छा या बुरा जो कुछ कर्म होगा उसका फल भुगतना पड़ेगा। पूर्व कर्मानुसार ही शक्ति और बुद्धि प्राप्त होती है। हमारा कर्त्तव्य है कि शक्ति का अपव्यय और बुद्धि का दुरुपयोग न करें।

सदाचार पूर्वक धर्माचरण करते हुए हम अपने लौकिक जीवन को भी सुखी बना सकते हैं और परलोक तो बनता ही है। कोई ईश्वर के अस्तित्व को नहीं मानता तो न माने, परन्तु यदि वह संसार में सुख-शांति का साम्राज्य देखना चाहता है तो अन्य जीवों को भी अपने समान समझना पड़ेगा। इस प्रकार भी धर्मिक सिद्धान्तों का पालन उसे करना ही चाहिये।

मनुष्य अधिकांश संगीत से ही सीखता है। अच्छि या बुरी जैसी संगति होगी वैसी ही बातें वह सीखेगा। विशेष बात तो यह है कि मनुष्य अपने साथ वालों को जैसा आचरण करते देखता है वैसा ही यत्किंचित् अंशों में जाने या अनजाने स्वयं भी करने लगता है। सिद्धान्त है कि संगति के अनुसार ही मनुष्य के आचार-विचार होते हैं। अतः यदि कोई कुसंग में पड़ गया तो वह आचार-विचारों से भ्रष्ट होकर न केवल अपने ही पतन का कारण होगा अपितु अपने संपर्क में आने वालों को भी ले डूबेगा। इसीलिये प्रयत्न करके सत्संग करना चाहिये।

17

The theory is that man's conduct and judgement are really according to association.

Before taking any action take good stock of the situation and consider; because that little action, good or bad, you will have to enjoy or endure the effects. According to previous actions, energy and intelligence are gained. Our duty is to not waste energy and not misapply intelligence.

Morality together with behaviour according to one's *dharma* can make earthly life more pleasant and then the other world is really prepared. For anyone who doesn't accept the existence of Ishwar (God) this has no meaning, but if he wishes to behold happiness and peace in worldly existence then he will understand that other lives similar to one's own will occur. This kind of principle, of *dharma*, he too should preserve.

For the most part humans learn by association. The goodness or badness will be similar to that of the acquaintance, that speech will be learned. Characteristic speech then is seen to be similar to a man's own companions, so we become connected and become a small part of those whom we know, and strangers too. The theory is that man's conduct and judgement are really according to association. From this, if anybody falls into evil company then his conduct and his judgement become fallen too - not only oneself falls but also, by contact, other people will also fall. Therefore you should make an effort to mix with good company.

१८

जैसा देव वैसी पूजा

*

जैसा रोग हो वैसी ही औषधि हो, तब लाभ होता है। क्षुद्र रोगों के लिये क्षुद्र औषधियाँ ही काम कर जाती हैं, परन्तु राजरोग के लिये विशेष औषधियों का प्रयोग करना पड़ता है। मनुष्य वासनाओं के चक्कर में पड़ा हुआ जन्म-जन्मान्तरों से भवरोग से पीड़ित है। इस महाव्याधि से मुक्त होने के लिए उतनी ही प्रभावशाली महौशधि चाहिए।

राजरोग और भवरोग में यह अन्तर है कि राजरोग मनुष्य के एक ही जन्म को बिगाड़ता है, परन्तु भवरोग जीव को अनेक योनियों में घुमाता हुआ जन्म-जन्मान्तरों तक जन्म-मरण के घोरातिघोर महा दुःखों में डाले रखता है। जन्म-मरण के महा दुःखों का एक मात्र कारण और भवरोग रूपी महा भयंकर वृक्ष का मूल (जड़) है वासना। वासना रूपी जड़ की अनेकानेक शाखायें फैलकर इस महा भयंकर भवरोग वृक्ष की पुष्टि करती रहती है।

जन्म-जन्मान्तर से इसकी जड़ पुष्टि होति चली आ रही है। इसे निर्मूल करने के लिए बहुत समय तक इसका छेदन करना पड़ेगा, तब यह कट सकेगी। इसलिए अनन्त जन्मों की वासनायें शान्त करने के लिए दीर्घकाल का अभ्यास आवश्यक है।

18

Possessed of birth-sickness, the root of that great terrible tree is desire.

According to the disease so indeed is the medicine, afterwards there is benefit. For the purpose of treating insignificant diseases, petty medicines are used, but for incurable illnesses, special drugs have to be used. Man who has fallen into the cycle of desires, is oppressed lifetime after lifetime by *bhavaroga* (birth-sickness). In order to be free from this great disorder you must have the influence of a very effective remedy.

The difference between an incurable illness and birth-sickness is that an incurable illness destroys only one life, however, life with birth-sickness is a giddiness in the head which occurs in many births, and life after life until one is having to live and die in great suffering. The great pains of life and death have just one little cause. Possessed of birth-sickness, the root of that great terrible tree is desire. Pointlessly rooted desire spreads its branches and this great fearful tree of birth-sickness stays nourished.

From lifetime after lifetime nourishment is pointlessly coming to this [rooted desire]. For the purpose of eradicating this [desire] a lot of time is to be spent until it is cut off, this can be cut then. Therefore, to calm the interminable lifetimes of desires a long time of meditation is necessary.

१९

झूठे आदमी को कभी शान्ति नहीं मिल सकती चाहे वह कुवेर के समान धनवान क्यों न हो

*

धर्महीन शिक्षा होने के कारण लोगों को कर्त्तव्याकर्त्तव्य का विवेक कम हो गया है। जैसा करने लगते हैं उसी को ठीक समझते हैं।

'पाप करेंगें तो नरक की यातनाएं भोगनी पड़ेंगी' - यह भावना प्रायः लोप सी हो गई है। यही कारण है कि आजकल समाज में असत्य का व्यवहार बढ़ गया है। प्रत्यक्ष में इन्द्रिय भोग-सामग्री का साधन अर्थ को ही लोग सब कुछ समझने लगे हैं। यही कारण है कि अर्थ संग्रह में विहताविहित का ध्यान नहीं रखते। किन्तु यह निश्चित है कि असत् व्यवहार से कभी भी शान्ति का अनुभव नहीं हो सकता।

सत्संग की कमी के कारण चरित्र-हीनता फैली है। आजकल् लोग यह विश्वास नहीं करते कि बिना बेइमानी किए उनका काम चल सकता है, न भाग्य पर भरोसा है और न विश्वम्भर पर ही विश्वास है। परमात्मा पर विश्वास रखो और कुछ समय सत्यता का व्यवहार करके देखो। इससे जीवन में सन्तोष का अनुभव होगा और संतोष ही सुख का स्वरूप माना गया है। यथा - 'सन्तोष परमं सुखम्'। झूठे आदमी को कभी भी शांति नहीं मिल सकती, चाहे वह कुबेर के समान धनवान क्यों न हो जाय। यह सदैव शंकित रहता है और उसका हृदय जलता रहता है। इस प्रकार वह इस लोक में भी सुखी नहीं रह पाता और परलोक तो उसका बिगड़ता ही है।

19

By lack of *satsang* (meetings with good men) is the reason that miserliness and poor conduct spreads.

The absence of instruction in *dharma* (duty) is the cause that people necessarily have been less intelligent. That which they are doing they understand to be reasonable. If you commit sin then you will suffer the torments of hell; this feeling has almost disappeared. This is the reason that untruth in everyday affairs has increased these days. Evidently, mainly people understand little about obtaining wealth for the means of sensory experience. Here is the very cause that there is no consideration given for how the wealth is collected. But this is certain, that by dishonest business there cannot be the experience of peace at any time.

By lack of *satsang* (meetings with good men) is the reason that miserliness and poor conduct spreads. Nowadays, people no longer trust that they can work without dishonesty, neither trusting in destiny nor trusting on the Almighty. Put the trust in Paramatma and see that for some time you do honest business. By living like this you will experience satisfaction and real contentment, the true measure of happiness comes. That is, *"santosha paramam sukham"* – 'supreme best happiness'. The dishonest man, wanting, cannot get *shaanti* (peace) anytime, even if he becomes as wealthy as Kubera (the god of wealth). He is always living in fear and he lives with a jealous heart. In this manner this world is not good and the other world is very spoiled too.

२०

दूसरे में नहीं -
अपने में दोष देखो

चरित्रवान मनुष्य की लोक-परलोक दोनों में शान्ति का अनुभव कर सकता है। जो चरित्र भ्रष्ट है उसे न इस लोक में शान्ति रहती है, और परलोक में उसके लिए शांति की बात ही क्या! दूसरों की बुराइयाँ मत देखो, अपने में ढुढ़ो कि कौन सी बुराई अभी तक है, उसे हटाने का प्रयत्न करो। अपने में दोष खोज-खोज कर निकाला तो कल्याण होगा।

कभी भी किसी के दोषों का चिन्तन मत करो। दूसरों में दोष ढूंढ़ने से अपना भी अन्तःकरण मलिन होता है। पाप कोई करे और उसका चिन्तन हम करें - यह तो कोई हमारे लाभ की बात नहीं। जब हम स्वयं पाप करने से डरते हैं तो दूसरे के पापों का चिन्तन

करके अपने मन को पापी क्यों बनायें?

दूसरे के दोषों का चिन्तन करोगे तो उसको तो कोई लाभ होगा नहीं, उल्टे दूसरे के दोष तुम्हारे मन में घुसेंगे। इसलिये ऐसा काम करो कि कम से कम अपनी रक्षा तो रहे। अपनी रक्षा का ध्यान न किया तो जैसे आंधी आयेगी उसी में उड़ जाओगे। अपने को ही देखने का अभ्यास करो। नित्य सायंकाल विचार करो कि आज हममें कितने गुण-दोष आये और कितने छूटे। अपने दोषों को देखने लगोगे तो फिर धीरे-धीरे दोष अपने आप छूटने लगेंगे। दोषों के सम्बन्ध में पहले अपनी चिन्ता रखो; दूसरे की बात सोचना अपने लिये घातक है। पहले अपनी रक्षा करो, बाद में दूसरे की चिन्ता।

20

Don't look at the defects of others, trace your own flaws up to the present and attempt to remove them.

A man of good moral character can experience *shaanti* (peace) in both this world and the other world. He whose conduct has not fallen remains in peace in this world, and so, what talk of peace in the other world? Don't look at the defects of others, trace your own flaws up to the present and attempt to remove them. In accomplishing searches for defects in yourself, then you will have happiness.

Don't ever think about the faults of others. By thinking about the faults of others one's own inner self becomes soiled. If anyone sins and we think about it, then there is no advantage talking about it. When we are frightened of doing sin ourselves then why will we be thinking about the sins of others?

Thinking about the sins of others will be of no advantage to anybody, the reverse will happen, the sins of others will enter into your mind. For this reason desire that little by little oneself is protected. Not having considered one's own protection then a tempest will come and in that you will fly away. Routinely look to yourself. Regularly, consider every evening, today how many sinful quality have come and how many set-off? You will look at your own defects, then afterwards, slowly, slowly one's own defects will be got rid of. In connection with defects first give consideration to one's own; talking about another's is ruinous to oneself. Firstly, protect oneself, afterwards thought for others.

२१

संसार प्रेम का पात्र नहीं –
इसमें मन को फँसाओगे तो धोखा खाओगे

यह लोक धर्मशाले का निवास है। यहाँ अपने मन को बहुत फँसाने लायक नहीं। साधारण रूप से काम करो और दृष्टि आगे की यात्रा पर रखो। इस धर्मशाले के प्रबन्ध में अपने को फँसा लेना मूर्खता ही है। जो जैसी चीज है उसके साथ वैसा ही बरतो। चार दिन के जीवन में बहुत हाव-हाव अच्छा नहीं। जब तक साँस चल रही हैं भगवान् का भजन् करते हुए समय को काटो। व्यवहार में शिष्टाचार करते चलो। मन को अधिक मत फँसाओ। मन में यदि व्यवहार घुस गया तो चार-चार लौटकर चौरासी लक्ष योनियों के चक्कर में घूमना पड़ेगा। इसलिये बड़ी सतर्कता से काम करो; तन और धन से तो व्यवहार चलाओ और मन से परमात्मा का चिंतन। ऐसा विभाग कर लोगे तभी ठीक से सुख-शान्ति का अनुभव कर सकोगे।

21

For as long as you are breathing, pass the time praying to Bhagwan.

This world is a *dharmashala* (a dwelling house for pilgrims). In this place it is not proper to involve the mind very much. The general way is to do the work and put your vision on the *yatra* (journey, pilgrimage). It is really a folly to ensnare oneself in the arrangement of this *dharmashala*. So, behave according to what a thing is. In four days of existence putting on a show of emotion is not good. For as long as you are breathing, pass the time praying to Bhagwan. In everyday affairs proceed with proper behaviour. In case everyday affairs have intruded into the mind, then again and again there is a return to the eighty-four hundred thousand births, fallen and rolling in the wheel. For this reason very carefully perform everyday affairs; by the body and wealth are everyday affairs done, and with the mind thinking of Paramatma. Apportioning in this way, on this account people can well experience happiness and peace.

२२

पुरस्कार के योग्य का पुरस्कार
और
तिरस्कार के योग्य का तिरस्कार करो

चरित्र-हीन लोगों से कथा-वार्ता सुनना व सत्संग करना वैसा ही है जैसा वेश्या के मुख से गीत-गोविन्द सूरसागर सुनना। गंगाजल पान करना है तो शुद्ध धारा से लो, नाबदान से गंगाजल बह कर आये तो उसको पीने का विधान नहीं है। यदि उपदेशक चरित्रवान है तब तो उसकी बात सुनो। चरित्र-हीन के शब्दों में केवल राग-रागिनी में मुग्ध हो जाना उसकी चरित्रहीनता को बढ़ाने में सहयोग

देता है।

जो भगवान् का भजन करता है उसका चरित्र उत्तम होना चाहिये। यदि चरित्र-हीन है तो उसे समझ लो कि भगवान् का भक्त नहीं है, लोगों को धोखा देने के लिये वह ऊपर से भक्ति का हाव-भाव दिखाता है। ऐसे धोखेबाज लोगों से स्वयं बचो और अपने सम्पर्क की भोली-भोली धार्मिक जनता को भी बचाओ।

मान-सम्मान उन्हीं का होना उचित है जो चरित्रवान् हैं। ऐसा ठीक नहीं कि घी का लड्डू टेढ़ा-मेढ़ा; जब घी का लड्डू है तो उसका स्वरूप भी ठीक रहना चाहिये, टेढ़ा क्यों हो। जब कोई भगवान् की भक्ति का उपदेश देता है, सत्संग करने का दावा करता है तो फिर उसको चरित्रवान् होना चाहिये। तभी तो जनता को विदित होगा कि भगवान् का भजन-पूजन करने से पुराने पाप कटते हैं और वर्तमान के दुर्गुण छूटते हैं।

यह सिद्धान्त बना लेना चाहिये कि तिरस्कार के योग्य जो हो उसका अवश्य ही तिरस्कार करो और पुरस्कार के योग्य का पुरस्कार करो। तिरस्कार के योग्य लोगों का पुरस्कार करने से उनकी संख्या बढ़ती है और समाज में गंदगी फैलती है।

22

He who sings the prayers of Bhagwan, his conduct should be the best.

To hear discourses from people whose conduct is worthless and to do *satsang* is really like hearing the *Gita* of Govinda and the Surasagara (the *Ramayana*) from the mouth of a *veshya* (whore).
Drinking the Gangajal (the sacred waters of the River Ganga), take from the clear current, Gangajal flows into the gutter but we don't make arrangements to drink from there. If the preacher is of

good character and conduct, then listen to his speech. In the sounds of someone of worthless conduct one only becomes ignorant of *raaga-raagini* (classical melodies), really that is only giving help in promoting his characterlessness.

He who sings the prayers of Bhagwan, his conduct should be the best. If the conduct is vile then understand that he is not devoted to Bhagwan, in order to deceive the people he displays the temperament of a devotee. Oneself should escape from people who cheat, and help those in the community who are but innocent folk.

Dignity and prestige is proper for those of good moral character and conduct. It is like the *laddu* made of *ghee* that is crooked and twisted; when making the *laddu* out of *ghee* the shape should be made properly. Why make them irregular? When someone is giving advise how to give devotion to Bhagwan, demand to meet with good men then he should have good character and conduct. For this reason then folk will be informed that by doing *puja* and worshipping with *bhajan,* old sins are cut away and existing faults are got rid of.

You should make this a principle, that; reproach only those who deserve to be reproached but respect those who deserve respect. By respecting those that deserve reproach then their numbers grow and dirtiness in society spreads.

२३

जो आया है वह अवश्य जायगा रहना यहाँ किसी को नहीं

*

हर समय बिस्तर बाँधे तैयार रहो। न जाने किस समय वारण्ट आ जाय। मृत्यु का वारन्ट गिरफ्तारी वारन्ट होता है, उसमें फिर अपील का गुंजाइश नहीं होती, तुरन्त सब छोड़ कर चलना पड़ेगा। जो जहां है वहीं पड़ा रह जायगा। पहले से तैयार रहोगे तो चलते

समय कष्ट नहीं होगा।

जो हर समय चलने के लिये तैयार रहेगा उससे कभी भी पाप नहीं होगा। परलोक को भूल जाने से ही दुराचार पापाचार होता है। यहि हर समय स्मरण रहे कि यह सब तो एक दिन छोड़कर ही चलना है तो फिर मनुष्य असत्य और अविहिताचरण को कभी न अपनाये।

विचार करो कि जब पिता, पितमह, परपितमह नहीं रहे तो ऐसा तो नहीं हो सकता कि हम रहें। जब चलना निश्चित है तो पहले से ही तैयारी कर लोगे तब यात्रा में आराम रहेगा; और पहले से तैयारी नहीं की तो फिर कष्ट ही होगा। सतर्क रहो कि – 'कोई काम ऐसा न हो जाय जिसके लिये चलते समय पछताना पड़े।'

यदि सतर्क नहीं रहोगे तो नीचे गिरने से बच नहीं सकते। संसार का प्रवाह ऐसा है कि नीचे की ओर ही ले जाता है। इन्द्रियों की प्रवृत्तियाँ मनुष्य को बहिर्मुखी बनाती हैं और बहिर्मुखता में वासनाओं के चक्कर में पड़कर फिर अधिक विचार करने की क्षमता नहीं रह जाती। इसलिये सदैव सतर्क रहने की आवश्यकता है।

मनुश्य अपने जीवन-काल में जो अच्छा-बुरा करता है वह मरणकाल में सब स्मरण आ जाता है। जो-जो पाप हुए रहते हैं उनके भयंकर फल का स्मरण करके जीव अन्तकाल में बहुत पछताता और बहुत दुखी होता है। इसलिये सतर्क रहना चाहिये कि ऐसा कोई पाप न हो जाय जिसके लिये अन्त समय में पछताना पड़े।

23

If you are ready in the first place, then there will be no suffering at the time of death.

Every day be ready, bedding packed. Nobody knows what time the *"warrant"* comes. Death *"warrant"* is the arrest *"warrant"* - for you there is no scope for *"appeal"*, all at once it occurs you are to leave. Wherever one is, at that very place you will be falling down. If you are ready in the first place, then there will be no suffering at the time of death.

He who remains ready to go, from him there will never be sin. Really it is by overlooking the other world that one becomes wicked and lives sinfully. If all this is remembered every day that one day one is going to let go, then henceforth a man will never lie or behave badly.

Consider this; that when father, grandfather, great grandfather is not living then it cannot be that we will remain. When it is settled that we will go, then really if we are ready beforehand, then the travelling will be a pleasure; but if one is not ready then afterwards you will be suffering. Be careful of doing any work that you regret afterwards, at the time of going.

If you are not careful then you cannot escape falling down. The stream of worldly existence takes a downward direction. The inclination of the senses is opposed to a man and in opposition one again falls into the wheel of desires, not considering the suitability. Therefore it is always necessary to be careful.

At the time of death that which was good and bad in a man's own lifetime all come to be remembered. That sin that has been done remains, the fearful effects are remembered at the time of death - much repenting and much sadness occurs. Therefore you should be careful that no sin occurs to be regretted at the time of death.

२४

भगवान् के भजन में लाभ ही लाभ है
जितना समय लगा अगे उसका मूल्य कई गुना ब्याज सहित मिलेगा

यह एक ऐसा रोजगार है जिसमें घाटे की शंका नहीं। भगवान् के भजन में लाभ ही लाभ है। पर बात यह है कि लाभ का रोजगार करने का भी भाग्य होना चाहिये। भाग्य-हीन मनुष्य तो उसी अव्यवसाय में लगेगा जहाँ घाटा हो। बड़े आश्चर्य की बात है कि धन और संसारी वस्तुओं की प्राप्ति के लिये लोग कितना अथक प्रयत्न करते हैं - दिन-रात एक कर देते हैं। परन्तु जिस भगवान् की प्राप्ति से सब कुछ सहज सुलभ हो जाता है उसके लिये उचित प्रयत्न नहीं करते। कितना बड़ा अविवेक है! इससे बड़ा आश्चर्य और हो ही क्या सकता है कि सुख-शान्ति के मूल कारण सर्वशक्तिमान् भगवान् की ओर ध्यान न देकर तुच्छ संसारी चीजों की प्राप्ति के लिये दिन-रात परेशान रहें। कहावत है -

'एकहि साधे सब सधे, सब साधे सब जाय ॥'

एक भगवान् की प्राप्ति हो जाने से सब कुछ सहज प्राप्त हो जाता है। भगवान को छोड़कर और सब वस्तुओं की प्राप्ति के लिये चेष्टा करते रहो तो कुछ भी प्राप्त नहीं होगा - जो प्राप्त भी होगा वह इतना न होगा कि सन्तोष हो जाय।

छाया को पकड़ना चाहते हो तो भी असली रूप को पकड़ो तो छाया तुरन्त पकड़ में आ जायगी। रूप को छोड़कर छाया के पीछे जितना भागोगे उतनी वह भी आगे भागती जायगी। इसलिये छायारूप संसारी ऐश्वर्य-यश आदि के पीछे भागना मूर्खता ही है। असली रूप पर्मात्मा को पकड़ो तो यह स्वयं तुम्हारे अधिकार में आ जायगा। स्मरण रखो कि भगवान् के भजन में लाभ ही लाभ है। जितना समय इसमें लगाओगे उसका कई गुना ब्याज सहित

अदा हो जायगा।

24

By gaining the One, Bhagwan, everything is naturally obtained.

This is one such occupation with no danger of loss. The advantage in worshipping Bhagwan is really such an advantage. But talk of this advantage of the occupation should be together with the destiny. The unfortunate man is connected in common with people where loss exists then. Greatly surprising is the talk that for gaining wealth and worldly things. How much tireless effort they make, day and night working for one thing? Yet they make no proper effort for gaining Bhagwan from whom all becomes natural and easy. What a great lack of discrimination this is. From this is a great surprise. How can this really be that the root of happiness and peace, the All-Powerful Bhagwan is not given meditation, yet night and day they will continue to be troubled for worthless worldly things? The proverb is; 'Aim for the one and everything is accomplished' - Aim for everything and all is in vain.

By gaining the One, Bhagwan, everything is naturally obtained. If Bhagwan is relinquished and one desires to gain all things then nothing will be gained and even those things that are acquired will not bring happiness.

If you try to take hold of a shadow then seize hold of the true form and the shadow will be captured. Relinquish the form then however much you run after the shadow that much it will run ahead. Therefore it is indeed folly to run after the shadow form of worldly wealth, reputation etc. Hold on to the true form of Paramatma, then this will automatically be your entitlement. Remember what an advantage worshipping Bhagwan really is. However much time you apply yourself in this there will be repayment together with many times the interest.

२५

परमात्मा विश्वम्भर है

*

वह तुम्हारा भरण-पोषण करेगा, उसको भुलकर तुम कृतघ्न मत बनो

जिसने तुमको उत्पन्न किया है वह सर्वशक्तिमान् है और उसका नाम विश्वम्भर है। विश्व का भरण-पोषण करने का भार उसने ऊपर लिया है। उस पर विश्वास करो - उसने पैदा किया है तो पालन भी करेगा। परन्तु यदि तुमने उसको भुला दिया तो कृतघ्नता का दोष तुमको लगेगा और तब उसकी उपेक्षा हो जाय तो कोई आश्चर्य नही।

"का चिंता मम जीवने यदि हरिर्विश्वम्भरो गीयते।
नोचेदर्भक जीवनाय जननी स्तन्यं कथं निस्सरेत्?"

यदि भगवान् का नाम विश्वम्भर (विश्व का भारण-पोषण करने वाला) है तो मुझे अपने जीवन में पेट के लिये चिन्ता करना व्यर्थ है। यदि परमात्मा की विश्वम्भरता पर किसी को विश्वास न हो तो हम पूछते हैं कि बालक के गर्भ में अन्दर रहते हुए ही उसके लिये दुग्ध भाता के स्तन में पहले से ही कैसे आ जाता है!

परमात्मा की विश्वम्भरता का इससे अधिक ज्वलन्त प्रमाण क्या हो सकता है कि भोक्ता के बाहर आने के पहले ही भोग्य तैयार है। इसलिए विश्वम्भर का विश्वास करो। जिसने गर्भ के अन्दर रक्षा की है वह अभी भी रक्षा करेगा। उसको भूलो मत।

25

He who protected you inside the womb protects you right now too. Do not forget him.

The one who has created you is Sarvashaktiman (Omnipotent, Almighty) and his name is Vishvambhara. He is there supporting the burden of everything in the universe. Trust on him, for that which he has created he will protect. But if you forget him then you commit the sin of ingratitude and then afterwards is it surprising if you become neglected?

"का चिंता मम जीवने यदि हरिर्विश्वम्भरो गीयते ।
नोचेदर्भक जीवनाय जननी स्तन्यं कथं निस्सरेत्?"

*"kaa chimtaa mama jiivane yadi harirvishvambharo giiyate.
nochedarbhaka jiivanaya jananii stanyam katham nissaret?"*
[*Chanakya Niti Shastra* 10:17]

'Why should I be concerned for my maintenance while absorbed in praising the glories of Lord Vishwambhara (Vishnu), the supporter of all?
Without the grace of Lord Hari, how could milk flow from a mother's breast for a child's nourishment?'

If the name of Bhagwan is Vishvambhara (Universal Support) then it is pointless to worry about the stomach in one's life. If you do not trust that Paramatma is Vishvambhara (the Supporter of the universe) then we ask how is it that whilst the baby is inside the womb the milk appears in the breast! What could be more convincing proof of Paramatma as Vishvambharata (supporter of all)? That which is fit to be enjoyed is there even before the one who is to enjoy it has come out! Therefore trust in Vishvambhara. He who protected you inside the womb protects you right now too. Do not forget him.

२६

जितने दिन जीना है शान्ति से जियो अधिक हाव-हाव करना व्यर्थ है

*

महाराजा दशारथ जैसे समर्थ चक्रवर्त्ती नरेन्द्र के भी सारे मनोरथ पूरे नहीं हुए। इसलिये अपने-अपने मनोराज्यों को पूरा करने में अहर्निश परेशान रहना भारी भूल है।

यह नहीं भूलना चाहिये कि एक दिन अवश्य ही यहाँ से चलना है। यहाँ का प्रोग्राम सब यहीं ऐसा ही रह जायगा। जो जहाँ है वह वहीं पड़ा रह जायगा। सब कुछ छोड़कर अकेले यात्रा करनी पड़ेगी। इसलिये जो छोड़कर जाना है उसके लिये व्यस्त मत रहो। जितने दिन रहना है शान्ति से रहो। जब यह निश्चय है कि कार्य कभा समाप्त नहीं होंगे, तो कार्यों के पीछे अधिक हाव-हाव करना व्यर्थ है। शान्ति पूर्वक स्वधर्मानुष्ठान करते हुए परमात्मा का स्मरण करते चलो।

जिसने पैदा किया है वह विश्वम्भर है। सबके भरण-पोषण का भार उस पर है, वह स्वयं प्रबन्ध करेगा। किन्तु यदि उस पर विश्वास न करके अपनी चातुरी-चालाकी, दगाबाजी-बेइमानी पर विश्वास करोगे तो जीवन भर अशान्ति रहेगी और आगे भी मार्ग में अँधेरा रहेगा। इसलिये ऐसा करो कि जीवन-काल में भी शान्ति रहे और आगे का मार्ग भी उज्ज्वल रहे।

26

However many days there is to stay, live in peace.

Even great kings such as the emperor Maharaja Dasharatha [the father of Lord Rama] did not fulfil all desires. Therefore it is a great mistake to be distressed day and night in fulfilling one's own fantasies.

This you should not forget, that one day you will have to go from here. The *"programme"* is only to be for this place. Wherever one is, right on that spot you will fall. It will befall you to relinquish everything and travel alone. Therefore don't worry for that which is to be relinquished. However many days there is to stay, live in peace. When this is a certainty that sometime work is not completed, then there is no purpose making a big fuss about jobs. Peacefully going about your everyday affairs, remember Paramatma.

He who created you, he is Vishvambhara. On him is the burden of cherishing and nourishing all, he makes his own arrangements. But if you do not trust in him, putting your trust in deceit and fraud, treacherousness and dishonesty then the complete life will be lived in dissatisfaction and the road forward will be in darkness. Therefore behave such that in your lifetime you stay peaceful and the road ahead is bright too.

२७

शक्ति प्राप्त करो

*

शक्तिहीन जीवन व्यर्थ है

शक्तिशाली होकर जीवन व्यतीत करो। मनुष्य का शरीर मिला है, पुरुषार्थ करके बलवान बनो। स्मरण रखो कि तुम उन्हीं महर्षियों की संतान हो जो संसार में सब कुछ कर सकने में समर्थ थे। अपने संकल्प से दूसरी सृष्टि रच देने का सामर्थ्य जिनमें था उन्हीं की तुम संतान होकर आज चारों तरफ से दुःख और अशान्ति से घिर रहे हो। अपने घर की निधि को भूल जाओगे तो फिर दरवाजे-दरवाजे ठोकर तो खानी ही पड़ेगी।

शेर यदि भेड़ियों के झुंड में जाकर भें-भें करने लगे और उसी में सुख मानने लग जाय तो यह उसके लिये कितने लज्जा की बात होगी। इसी प्रकार भारतीय यदि अपने पुराने आध्यात्मिक और आधिदैविक सम्पत्तियों को भूल जाय और ऊपरी शब्द, स्पर्श, रूप, रस, गंध आदि की भौतिक सामग्री को प्राप्त करके ही सुख-संतोष मान लें तो यह उनका कितना पड़ा पतन है।

शक्तिशाली बनने के लिये अपने पूर्वजों के अनुभूत नुसखों से काम लो। सर्वशक्तिमान् जगन्नियन्ता की शरण में आओ। अपनी आध्यात्मिक शक्तियों का विकास करो। जगन्नियामिका चेतन सत्ता पर अधिकार प्राप्त करो। तब वास्तव में शक्तिशाली बन सकते हो और वही स्थिर शक्ति सत्ता होगी। निश्चय रखो कि आज भी तुम त्रिकालदर्शी और तत्र-विजयी होकर समस्त ब्रह्माण्ड की शक्तियों को अपने अनुकूल कर सकते हो। भारत में तुम्हारा जन्म हुआ है। तुममें अनन्त शक्तियां निहित हैं। प्रयत्न करके उनका उद्घाटन करो

और शक्तिशाली होकर उन्नत मस्तक होकर रहो।

27

Develop one's own spiritual strengths.

Become one who possesses strength and get on with your life. Having obtained the body of a man, make vigorous effort to fulfill *purushartha* ("human wealth" = willpower), *kama* (love), *dharma* (duty) and *moksha* (liberation)). Remember that you are really the offspring of those *maharshiyon* (great saints) who were capable of doing anything in *samsara* (the mundane existence). You are the descendant of those that had the ability to create another world by their own willpower, yet today you are surrounded on all four sides by suffering and anxiety. You have forgotten the treasure in your own home, so it will befall you to go knocking door-to-door in order to eat.

If a tiger goes baa-ing and bleating amongst a herd of sheep and regards itself as content, then how much shame is this talk? In this way, if an Indian, whose own ancient spiritual and destined heritage, thinks that contentment and happiness lies in superficial words and feelings, forms, tastes and scents of material possessions, then how much have they fallen?

In order to make yourself strong take the tried prescription of one's own ancestors. Come into the protection of the Omnipotent Controller of the World. Develop one's own spiritual strengths. Gain entitlement to the power of the Almighty Being. Afterwards, in truth, you can become strong and you will have the very same powerful authority. Be sure that even today you can see the past, present and future, conquer the elements, and have the favour of the powers of the whole universe. Your birth has been in Bharat (India). In you are placed infinite powers. Attempt to release them and become strong, hold the head high.

२८

साकार-निराकार के झगड़े में न पड़ो

*

जो निराकार है वही साकार होता है। स्थिर प्रशान्त महासमुद्र ही तरंग के रूप में ऊपर उठकर दिखलाई पड़ता है। जैसे तरंग समुद्र की सीमा से बाहर चली गई मालूम पड़ती है और फिर लौटकर समुद्र में विलीन हुई प्रतीत होती है, उसी प्रकार निर्गुण निराकार व्यापक परमात्मा हो सगुण साकार रूप लेकर एक देश में आते हैं।

हम तो यह कहेंगे कि भगवान् के साकार रूप में प्रकट होने से ही निराकार परमात्म-सत्ता की प्रत्यक्ष सिद्धि होती है। काष्ठ में अग्नि सर्वत्र है, यह तभी प्रत्यक्ष रूप से सिद्ध होता है जब किसी स्थल को रगड़ने से वहाँ अग्नि प्रकट हो जाता है।

सिद्धान्त यही है कि निर्गुण निराकार ही सगुण साकार होता है और सगुण साकार से ही, निर्गुण निराकार की प्रत्यक्ष सिद्ध होती है। अतः निराकार-साकार के झगड़ों में न पड़कर कहीं भी अपने मन को जमाओ। निष्ठा जमाने से ही कल्याण होगा। निराकार और साकार के सम्बन्ध में झगड़ा मचाने से कोई लाभ नहीं।

तुम चाहे निराकार पर सील लगाओ या साकार पर, उससे निराकार या साकार का कुछ बने-बिगड़ेगा नहीं। अपने कल्याण के लिए कहीं भी निष्ठा जमाने का प्रयत्न करो। किसी सद्गुरु से अपने अधिकारानुसार उपयुक्त उपासना का प्रकार समझ कर उपासना कर चलो और विधान पूर्वक आत्मा या पर्मात्मा में निष्ठा जमाने का अभ्यास करो। साकार में भी निष्ठा पुष्ट हो जायगी तो भी जन्म-मरण का बंधन कट जायगा और लोक में भी सुख-शान्ति से जीवन बीतेगा।

28

Be collected in your own mind and don't get involved in any disputes about form and formless.

That which is formless is the very same as exists as form. The still calm ocean is seen to rise up in the form of a wave. The wave seems obvious at the point at which it appears above the sea and afterwards it seems to disappear, as it retreats into the ocean, just as pervasive, shapeless Paramatma, having no qualities, comes to take form in one place.

We say then that in manifesting as a form, Bhagwan (the Supreme god) the shapeless Paramatma is seen to successfully take form. *Agni* (the god of fire, fire) is always within wood, and then, by rubbing a spot, the fire takes form and can be seen visibly manifesting. The established truth is here, that which is formless and without qualities indeed becomes formed and possessed of qualities. By taking form the formless is perfectly visible. Be collected in your own mind and don't get involved in any disputes about form and formlessness. Really, you will happy if you consolidate your faith. There is nothing gained by making a controversy about the relationship of the formless and that with form.

If you wish to attach your *"seal"* on the formless or on the form, to formless or the form, nothing will be any different. Make an effort to consolidate your faith. Understand from any *sadguru* (genuine *guru*) the proper appropriate *upasana* (worship) and follow it. And by those means proceed to worship and practice, consolidating faith in the *atma* (soul) or Paramatma (Supreme Soul). When you will become strong in faith for the manifest [form of Paramatma] then the bond of life and death will also be cut, and happiness and peace will be lived in this world.

२९

जैसा काछो वैसा नाचो

*

जिस आसन पर बैठो उसे गन्दा न बनाओ जिस पद को स्वीकार करो उसको कलंकित मत करो या तो किसी चीज को अपनाओ मत, और यदि अपनाते हो तो उसको ठीक से निबाहो। जो पद अपनाओ उसकी रक्षा करो। जिस कार्य को हाथ में लेते हो, उसकों विधानपूर्वक पूरा करने के लिये प्रयत्नशील रहो।

जिस कार्य के करने की योग्यता हो और चाव हो उसी कार्य में हाथ लगाना चाहिये। केवल माहात्म्य देख कर कार्य आरम्भ कर देने से फिर आगे चलकर जब उसमें कठिनाइयाँ आती हैं तो अशान्ति होती है। इसलिये जगत् में ऐसे ही कार्य करो, जिसमें अशान्ति की शङ्का अधिक न हो। इस बात का सदा ध्यान रखो कि जिस पद को अपनाया है वह कलंकित न होने पाये। माता के साथ व पिता के साथ उत्तम व्यवहार रखो, जिसमें पुत्र का पद कलंकित न हो। बहिन-भाइयों से उत्तम प्रेमपुर्ण-व्यवहार रखो, जिससे भाई का पद कलंकित न हो। पत्नी से मर्यादापूर्ण उत्तम व्यवहार रखो, जिससे पति का पद कलंकित न हो। गुरु के साथ सदा विनम्र और पूज्यभाव रखो, जिससे तुम्हारा शिष्य का पद कलंकित न हो। यदि कहीं किसी सरकारी नौकरी में हो तो अपने पदानुकूल न्यायोचित व्यवहार करो और पद का दुरुपयोग करके उसे लोगों की दृष्टि में कलंकित मत करो। तात्पर्य यह है कि जहाँ जिस आसन पर बैठो उसे अपने द्वारा गन्दा मत बनाओ। ब्राह्मण, क्षत्रिय, वैश्य, शूद्र जिस भी कुल में जन्म हो गया है, उस कुल की मर्यादा को अपने द्वारा भ्रष्ट मत होने दो। ब्रह्मचर्य, गृहस्थ, वानप्रस्थ या सन्यास जिस आश्रम को अपनाओ उसके नियमों का पालन करते हुए उसे

गौरवपूर्ण ढङ्ग से निबाहो। कहीं ऐसा काम न कर बैठो कि तुम्हारा पद कलंकित हो जाय।

29

Don't disgrace the position of work that you occupy.

You should not make the seat on which you sit filthy, do not tarnish the post you accept, and do not misappropriate anything, and if you do appropriate anything make sure that all is well and proper. Own that position and protect it. Whatever the task you take in hand naturally make an effort to complete it properly.

Whatever work you have an aptitude and a keenness for, you should apply yourself to that work in hand. If you see only the glory of doing a job then later on when problems come then you will become dissatisfied. Therefore only do work in the world wherein there is not much anxiety and danger. Always heed this instruction and don't bring one's own occupation into disgrace. Keep an excellent relationship with mother and with father, do not disgrace the status of son. Behave with the greatest of love with sisters and brothers, do not besmirch that dignity of brother. Applying the highest standards of conduct with wife, do not defame the status of a husband. With the *guru* always be modest and respectful, thus not disgracing your position as *shishya* (pupil).

If you are somewhere in government service then perform only legitimate suitable everyday affairs and do not abuse your position and be disgraced in full view of the people. The meaning of this is that; whatever seat you occupy don't make it filthy oneself. Whatever group you are born in, *brahmana*, *kshatriya*, *vaishya*, *shudra*, don't break the rules of that group. Whether *brahmacharya* (student), *grihastha* (householder), *vanaprastha* (forest dweller), or *sanyasa* (renunciate), accept that *ashrama* (stage of life), take great pride and keep the rules. Don't disgrace the position of work that you occupy.

३०

प्रेम परमात्मा में और प्रेम की छाया संसार में

*

प्रेम का आन्तरिक मनोभाव सांसारिक वस्तुओं में न भी लगाया जाय, तब भी व्यवहार बन्द नहीं होगा, कार्य सब चलते रहेंगे। व्यवहार का संचालन तो प्रारब्ध-अदृष्ट करता है। जब तक शरीर है तब तक तो प्रारब्ध है ही। इसलिये इस बात की तनिक भी चिन्ता नहीं करनी चाहिये कि व्यवहार से प्रेम हट जायगा तो सारे कार्य ही समाप्त हो जायेंगे। पर यह भी बात है कि सर्वत्र एक सा प्रेम नहीं रहता। सांसारिक पदार्थों में और सम्बन्धियों आदि के साथ प्रेम् का तारतम्य (न्यूनाधिक्य) रहता ही है। इसलिये प्रेम का तारतम्य ऐसा जमाओ कि मुख्य प्रेम की 'सीट' में परमात्मा को बैठाओ और सामान्य प्रेम का स्थान सांसारिक व्यवहार को दो। व्यवहार संचालन के लिये अर्थात् प्रारब्ध को भोगने के लिये प्रेम की छाया से ही काम चल जाता है। जहां छाया से काम चल जाय वहाँ मुख्य वस्तु को लगाना उसका दुरुपयोग ही तो है।

व्यवहार संचालन के लिये सांसारिक पदार्थों को मुख्य राग का विषय बना लेना बड़े घाटे का व्यापार है। धन में या स्त्री-पुत्र में भीतर से ममत्व रखना ही खतरे की चीज है। इनमें यदि भीतर से प्रेम बड़ाया तो संसार में ही लटक कर रह जाओगे और आगे की यात्रा में अंधेरा ही रहेगा। इसलिये मुख्य प्रेम परमात्मा में और प्रेम की छाया व्यवहार में रखो, तो यहाँ का काम भी नहीं रुकेगा और आगे भी प्रकाश रहेगा।

30

It is a dangerous thing to be greedy for wealth or for a woman or a son.

Don't let your mentality be attached to an inner love of worldly things, for you there will be no end to work, staying all the time working. The running of the everyday affairs then is down to fortune and to *prarabdha* (current destiny). Whilst there is a body there is *prarabdha*. Therefore you shouldn't give even a little thought to it, putting any love of employment out of the way, then all work will be accomplished. The meaning of this is also not to love everything. In worldly things and with relatives etc. love should really be in proportion. Therefore save the main proportion of love for sitting in the *"seat"* of love towards Paramatma and give only general love in regard of worldly everyday affairs. For the management of running the everyday affairs, just suffer that *prarabdha* (current destiny) and go with just a shadow of love. Whenever the desire for the shadow is the most important thing, then that is really a big distortion of purpose. If the enjoyment of the everyday affairs of managing worldly matters is the main desire, then the work increases. It is a dangerous thing to be greedy for wealth or for a woman or a son. If you have an exaggerated love inside then you will stay bent in worldliness and you will remain in darkness on the journey in future. Therefore put the principal amount of love towards Paramatma and only the shadow of love in the everyday affairs, then your desires will not be hindered and the future will be bright too.

३१

देवत्व से मनुष्यत्व श्रेष्ठ है

*

उत्तम पुरुषार्थ करके मनुष्य जीवन सफल बनाओ

देवयोनि भी अन्य योनियों की तरह भोग-योनि मानी गई है। देवयोनि की प्राप्ति दिव्य भागों की लालसा रखने वाले, यज्ञानुष्ठान आदि दैवी कर्मों को करने वाले मनुष्यों को प्राप्त होती है। देवलोक में विषय-भोगों की प्रचुरता के कारण देवताओं की बुद्धि घूम-घूम कर उसी में रहती है, आगे उनसे पुरुषार्थ नहीं बन पड़ता। इसीलिये मनुष्य-योनि को श्रेष्ठ कहा गया है; क्योंकि यहाँ पर मनुष्य पुरुषार्थवान् होकर इतना पुरुषार्थ कर सकता है कि साक्षात् परब्रह्म हो सकता है।

मनुष्य स्वर्ण का पासा है और देवता तो बने हुए आभूषण के समान हैं। आभूषण तो जो बन गया सो बन गया; अब उसकी तरक्की समाप्त हो गई, आगे कुछ वह और अच्छा बन नहीं सकता। परन्तु जब तक स्वर्ण पासा के रूप में है, तब तक उसकी तरक्की की कोई सीमा नहीं, अच्छा से अच्छा काम उस पर किया जा सकता है, अच्छा से अच्छा उसका आभूषण बनाया जा सकता है। इसीलिये मनुष्य-योनि को सर्वश्रेष्ठ कर्मयोनि कहा गया है। इसमें आकर प्रमाद नहीं करना चाहिये। सावधानी के साथ उत्तम पुरूषार्थ करना चाहिये। स्वधर्मानुष्ठान करते हुए पर्मात्मा में निष्ठा बढ़ाना ही उत्तम पुरुषार्थ है। प्रयत्न करो कि इसी जीवनकाल में परमात्मा का अभेद सम्बन्ध हो जाय। वेदशास्त्र पर विश्वास करते हुए वेदशास्त्रीय सिद्धान्तों को मानने वाले संत-महात्माओं और विद्वानों से सत्संग करो तो मनुष्य-जीवन सफल रहेगा।

31

Make efforts so that a relationship of oneness with Paramatma occurs in this lifetime.

Divine birth and other kinds of birth are means to experience pleasure and pain. Divine birth is longed for by those wishing for a share of the Celestial, to be acquired by people who make specific religious sacrifices and works relating to the divine. In Devalok (heaven) the abundance of things to be experienced causes the minds of *devatas* (gods) to remain wandering endlessly, hence they do not make efforts to do *purushartha* ("human wealth" = willpower). Therefore birth as a human is said to be preferable; since here man can do *purushartha* and so can be in the presence of Parabrahma (the Supreme Soul)

Man has been made a lump of gold and a *devata* (god) then is similar to an ornament. The one who has been made as an ornament is thus an ornament; now his or her advancement has been achieved, so they cannot be made any better. However while in the form of a lump of gold, there is no limit to improvement if desired, the best ornament can be made. Therefore being born as a human being is said to be the best birth for action. You should not be confused about this form, vigilantly you should do the best *purushartha*. Undertake your own *dharma* - the greatest *purushartha* is really to enhance one's allegiance to Paramatma. Make efforts so that a relationship of oneness with Paramatma occurs in this lifetime. Trusting in *Veda Shastra* take *satsang* (good company) with those *"saint"*, *mahatmas* (great sages) and learned scholars who accept the principles of *Veda Shastra*. Then the human life will be fruitful.

३२

उसकी चिन्ता करो - जो सब चिन्ताओं से मुक्त कर सकता है

*

सुख-शान्ति का अनुभव तभी होगा जब मन से चिन्तायें निकल जायेंगी। यदि चिन्ताओं को समाप्त करना चाहते हो तो संसार के स्वरूप को समझ लो। संसार को जब जान लोगे तब संसार की वासनायें समाप्त हो जायेंगी। इसका स्वरूप ही ऐसा है कि एक बार ठीक से समझ लेने पर फिर इसमें भीतर से प्रेम नहीं रह सकता।

अनेक पदार्थोंण् में प्रेम रहने के कारण ही अनेक प्रकार की चिंतायें उठा करती हैं। चिन्ता ऐसी भयानक होती है कि सारी सम्पदा और मान-सम्मान रहने पर भी मनुष्य को व्याकुल बनाये रखती है। जैसे -

"चिता चिन्ता द्वयोमंध्ये चिन्त चैव गरीयसी।
चिता दहति निर्जीवं चिन्ता दहति सजीवकम्॥"

चिता से चिन्ता अधिक बलवती और भयानक मानी गई है; क्योंकि चिता तो मरे हुए को जलाती है परन्तु चिन्ता जीवित को हो जलाती रहती है। इसलिये चिंता-मुक्त होने का प्रयत्न करो। वही परमात्मा जो परम स्वतंत्र और परम निश्चिंत है तुम्हें सब चिन्ताओं से मुक्त कर सकता है। इसलिये उसके पाने की चिन्ता बढ़ाओ तो फिर सारी संसारी चिन्तायें सदा के लिये समाप्त हो जायेंगी।

संसार में व्यवहार तो करो। पर यह समझते रहो कि यह केवल व्यवहार ही की चीज है, प्रेम करने की चीज नहीं। मन यहाँ की किसी वस्तु में फँस जायगा तो फिर चिन्ताओं का पहाड़ लद जायगा और जीवन भी व्यर्थ हो जायगा। इसलिये मन को परमात्मा में लगाओ और संसार मे शिष्टाचार करते चलो।

32

Worry is more powerful and more dreadful than the funeral pyre; because the pyre is to burn the dead but worry burns the living.

You will be able to experience pleasure and peace when you will get rid of anxieties from the mind. If you want to finish with worries then you have to understand and have a correct impression of *samsara* (worldly existence). When worldly existence is understood then people's longing for *samsara* will be finished. Once you have gained a good understanding of the true appearance then there can no longer be any love inside for this.

The cause of there being so many sorts of loving is because there are so many sorts of worries. Worry becomes so dreadful that having all wealth, dignity and honour, man is still perplexed.

In the manner that;

"चिता चिंता द्वयोमंध्ये चिंत चैव गरीयसी ।
चिता दहति निर्जीवं चिंता दहति सजीवकम् ॥"

"chitaa chintaa dvayomamdhye chinta chaiva gariiyasi.
chitaa dahati nirjiivam chintaa dahati sajiivakam.."

The meaning of this is that *chita* (worry) is more powerful and dreadful than the *chinta* (the funeral pyre); because the funeral pyre is to burn the dead but worry burns the living.

[There is also an alternate version of this popular '*subhashita*' (well spoken or wise verse); *"chintaayaastu chitaayaastu bindu maatram visheshatah. chitaa dahati nirjiivam, chintaa dahati jiivitam.."* 'The difference between चिंता *'chi**n**ta'* (anxiety) and चिता *'chita'* (funeral pyre) is merely a dot ('the *'**n**'* dot, *anusvara,* the *bindu*). Whilst the funeral pyre burns the non-living, worry burns the living.']

Therefore make an effort to become free from worries. The very same Paramatma who is utterly independent and utterly free can liberate you from anxieties. Therefore grow in worry for obtaining That, then all worldly worries will always be accomplished.

Conduct everyday affairs in worldly life then. Understand this, that this is really only an everyday affair thing, not a thing of loving. If the mind will get trapped in anything here then it will become laden with a mountain of worries and life will have no purpose. Therefore attach the mind to Paramatma and behave properly in the worldly existence.

३३

जिसे भले-बुरे का न्याय करना है
बह तुम्हारे सब कार्यों की देख रहा हैं

*

परमात्मा अन्तर्यामी है। वह सबके हृदय में सदा विराजमान है। वह सबके सब कार्यों को देख रहा है। उसकी दृष्टि बचकर कोई कार्य नहीं किया जा सकता। किसी कार्य के लिये यह सोचना कि इसको कोई नहीं जानता, परमात्मा को अन्धा बनाना है। यह दूसरों को नहीं, अपने को धोखा देना है।

दुष्कर्म में संसारी मनुष्यों की दृष्टि बचा लेने से ऐसा मत सोचो कि कोई नहीं जानता। जिसे भले-बुरे का न्याय करना है वह तुम्हारे सब कार्यों को देख रहा है, उसकी दृष्टि नहीं बचाई जा सकती। जो कर्मों का फल देने वाला है उसकी दृष्टि नहीं बचाई जा सकती। जो कर्मों का फल देने वाला है उसकी दृष्टि तो बचा नहीं सकते और जो स्वयं बिगड़े हु हैं वे कुछ कर नहीं सकते। उनकी दृष्टि बचाने का प्रयत्न करते हो, यह कितना बड़ा अविवेक है। यदि किसी से डरना है तो सर्वज्ञ सर्वशक्तिमान से डरो। उसकी रुचि के विरुद्ध कोई कार्य मत करो। उसकी रुचि ही वेद-शास्त्र है। ऐसा कोई कार्य मत करो

जिसके लिए वेद-शास्त्र आज्ञा न देता हो।

परमात्मा को सर्वत्र उपस्थित मानोगे तो फिर तुमसे कोई पाप-कर्म नहीं होगा। इसलिये परमात्मा को व्यापक मानते हुये चरित्रवान् बनो, अपने आचरणों में पवित्रता लाओ, अपनी भावनाओं को शुद्ध बनाओ और स्वधर्मानुकूल व्यवहार करो। तभी तुमारा अन्तःकरण पवित्र होगा। अन्तःकरण की पवित्रता बढ़ने से तुम्हारे संकल्प में बल आयेगा, कार्य अधिक सुदृढ़ होंगे और परमात्मा में भी निष्ठा बढ़ेगी। परमात्मा में निष्ठा बढ़ने से हर प्रकार का मंगल होगा। इसलिए ऐसा ही मार्ग अपनाओ जिससे सब प्रकार का मंगल हो और लोक-परलोक दोनों बने।

33

He is seeing everything that everyone does. Nobody can escape his or her work being seen.

Paramatma pervades inside. He is shining in the heart of all. He is seeing everything that everyone does. Nobody can escape his or her work being seen. Anyone who considers that his or her work is not known about, is inventing Paramatma's blindness. This is deceiving oneself, not anyone else.

Having evaded earthly people seeing wrongdoing, don't suppose that nobody knows. By the rules of what is good and bad, he is looking at all your deeds, you cannot escape his seeing. You cannot escape him seeing, he who is the giver of the fruits of actions. You cannot escape him seeing, who is the giver of the fruits of actions, and those who have damaged themselves they can do nothing. What a great lack of discrimination it is to make attempts to escape others seeing. If there is fear of anything, that fear is the one who is Omnipotent All-Knowing. Don't do any work that is contrary to his liking. Really, his wish is the *Veda Shastra*. So don't do any work that the *Veda Shastra* does not give permission for.

If you will accept that Paramatma is present everywhere then no wicked action will be done by you. Therefore accept that Paramatma is pervasive, become of good moral character and conduct, introduce integrity into one's own behaviour, make one's own feelings pure, and do everyday affairs according to one's *dharma* (religion). On this account your inner conscience will be pure. From the growth of sanctity of the inner self will come strength in your resolve, work will be more powerful, and faith in Paramatma will also grow. From growth of faith in Paramatma there will be all kinds of prosperity. Therefore possess this very road from which all kinds of auspiciousness occur, preparing both this world and the other world.

३४

चार वृत्तियों में ही रहो
तभी लोक-परलोक दोनों बनेंगे

*

मनुष्य के जीवन में स्थूल शरीर की प्रधानता नहीं होती, सूक्ष्म शरीर की ही प्रधानता होती है। स्थूल शरीर तो ढाँचा मात्र है - उसका संचालक है सूक्ष्म शरीर, मन और बुद्धि। मनुष्य का जैसा मन होता है उसी के अनुसार ही उसकी इन्द्रियाँ और शरीर काम करता है। इसलिये मन को सम्भालने की आवश्यकता है।

मन को पवित्र बनाने के लिये योग-शास्त्र के प्रणेता महर्षि पातंजलि ने यह उपाय बताया है कि - "मन को मैत्री, करुणा, मुदिता और उपेक्षा इन्हीं चार वृत्तियों में रखा जाय।"

अपने बराबरी वालों में मित्रता की भावना, अपने से छोटों पर या अपने से दुखी लोगों पर करुणा (दया) का भाव, अपने से जो अधिक सुखी, अधिक विद्वान या किसी भी अंश में बड़े हो उनको देखकर प्रसन्नता का भाव बनाना और जो अपने से द्वेष-शत्रुता

आदि का भाव रखें उनके प्रति उपेक्षा की भावना रखना, यह नहीं कि उनके प्रति अपने मन में शत्रुता और द्वेष की भावना बनायें। इस प्रकार चार ही वृत्तियों में मन को रखने से ईर्ष्या, द्वेष, मत्सर आदि भाव कभी मन में उठने नहीं पाते और स्वाभाविक रूप से मन की पवित्रता बढ़ती जाती है। ऐसा करने से व्यवहार में कोई रुकावट नहीं पड़ती और मानसिक 'मल' की निवृत्ति होने से विषय-भोग की लालसा स्वाभाविक रूप से कम होती जाती है और तभी मन अन्तर्मुख होकर भगवान् के भजन में लगता है।

34

The senses and the body work only in accordance with man's mind. For this reason it is a necessity to take care of the mind.

In man's life the *sthula sharir* (gross body) is not the most important, the *sukshma sharir* (subtle body) is more important. The gross body is merely the frame, managing it is the subtle body, the mind and intelligence. The senses and the body work only in accordance with man's mind. For this reason it is a necessity to take care of the mind.

To make the mind pure, the author of the *Yoga-Shastra,* Maharishi Pajanjali, has instructed this method:-

'You should keep in mind these four conditions, *maitri* (friendship), *karuna* (compassion), *mudita* (delight) & *upeksha* (indifference).'
[*Yogadarshanam* 1:33]

A feeling of friendship amongst those people equal to oneself and a feeling of compassion for subordinates or those people that are sick. With those who are more happy, more wise or more learned, or surpass you to some degree, make sure you look at them with a feeling of happiness. And with those who have a feeling of malice and hostility with you, apply an attitude of indifference, so that you will not copy this feeling of enmity and hatred. In this manner, by keeping in mind these four *vrittiyon* (mental conditions, of friendship, compassion, delight & indifference), then envy, malice and jealousy etc. will not arise in the mind and the mind's innate spirituality grows. By so doing, no obstruction appears in everyday affairs and with the disappearance of mental filth the instinctive longing for sensual experiences becomes less and on this account the mind becomes opened inside, praising and worshipping Bhagwan.

३५

सिद्धियों के चक्कर में ठगाये मत जाओ

*

आजकल अधिकाण्श लोग सिद्धि ढूँढ़ते हैं, चाहते हैं कि किसी प्रकार से सिद्धि मिले। सिद्धि तो कम लोगों को होती है, परन्तु सिद्धि के लालच में ठगाये अधिक लोग जाते हैं। हमारा काम तो सचेत करने का है। जैसे ग्राम का पहरेदार आवाज देता रहता है कि जागते रहो, उसी प्रकार हम लोग भी जनता को सावधान करते रहते हैं कि धूर्तों से बचते रहो। चौकीदार आवाज लगाता है कि जागते रहो, वह अपनी 'डिपटी' करता है। फिर उस पर भी कोई बेसुध होकर सोता रहे तो उसका क्या दोष! जो सोता है वह लूटा जाता है। धर्माचार्य तो चौकीदार होते हैं। चौकीदारी करना हमारा काम है। स्वयं जागते हैं और दूसरों को जगातें हैं।

सिद्धियाँ पाँच प्रकार से आती हैं -

"जन्मौषधिमन्त्रतपः समाधिजाः सिद्धयः। - योगदर्शन् ४ ।१"

१ - - जन्म से ही कोई सिद्ध उत्पन्न होते हैं। पूर्व जन्म में उपासना की होगी, पर इतनी न कर सके होंगे कि भगवान् में मिल जायें तो ऐसे पूर्वोपास्ती लोगों में जन्म से ही सिद्धियों का चमत्कार रहता है, - - जैसे, जड़भरत जन्म से ही सिद्ध थे, उन्हें कहीं श्रवण मनन निदिध्यासन करने नहीं जाना पड़ा।

२ - - औषधियों के द्वारा अनेक प्रकार को सिद्धियां देखी जाती हैं। मैं जब जंगलों में रहता था तो ऐसे अनेक अवसर आये कि कोल-भिल्ल आ-आकर औषधियों के गुण बता जाते थे। एक बार एक भील एक ऐसी जड़ी लाकर दे गया कि जिसको दिखा देने से शेर दूर

से ही भाग जाता है। औषधियों के द्वारा कल्प करते हुए मनुष्य सैकड़ों वर्षों तक जीवित रह सकता है। इसी प्रकार की अनेक सिद्धियाँ औषधियों से होती हैं। ऐसी भी औषधियाँ होती हैं कि जिनको मुख में रख लेने से आकाश में उड़ने की शक्ति आ जाती है।

३ - - मंत्र से सिद्धियाँ आती हैं। मंत्र का देवता अनुकूल होने पर अपने सामर्थ्यानुकूल कार्य वह करता है। यही मंत्रों के अनुष्ठान से होने वाली सिद्धियों का स्वरूप है। साधारण लोग यक्षणी या कर्ण-पिशाची आदि भूत-प्रेत या छुद्र देवताओं की सिद्धि कर लेते हैं और लोगों की भूतकाल की और वर्तमान की कुछ बातें बताकर अथवा कुछ असाधारण चमत्कारसा दिखाकर जनता में सिद्ध योगी होने का ढोंग करते हैं। इसी में सीधे-सादे लोगों को धोखा हुआ करता है।

४ - - तप से सिद्धि होती है। ब्रह्मचर्य का पालन करना, उपवासादि रहना तथा भगवत्प्राप्ति के साधनों में कष्टादि का सहन करना सात्विक तप है, इससे शान्ति व सन्तोष बढ़ता है। किसी के लौकिक उत्कर्षापकर्ष या मारण, मोहन, स्तंभन आदि के लक्ष्य से तप करना राजसी-तामसी तप का स्वरूप है। इससे शान्ति व सन्तोष न होकर अशान्ति और उद्वेगादि की वृद्धि के साथ-साथ काम-क्रोध आदि आन्तरिक शत्रुओं की वृद्धि हो जाती है और साधक का पतन हो जात्ता है।

५ - - समाधि से सिद्धियाँ आती हैं। किन्तु ये सिद्धियां, साधक को सर्वोच्च स्थिति या जीवन्मुक्ति की अवस्था प्राप्त कराने में विघ्न रूप होती हैं। इन सिद्धियों से स्थिर कार्य होते हैं और यदि इनसे बहुत कार्य न लिया गया तो ये स्थायी हो जाती हैं।

तात्पर्य यह है कि किसी मनुष्य में कोई चमत्कार देखा जाय तो उसे सर्वथा योगी ही मान लेना ठीक नहीं। योगियों में जो चमत्कार

होते हैं वे गम्भीर होते हैं और उन चमत्कारों का लक्ष्य अपनी प्रसिद्धि या जनता से धनादि संग्रह करना नहीं होता। वे केवल लोक-कल्याण की भावना से किसी पर दया-दृष्टि होने से ही होता है। इन सिद्धान्तों को समझ कर जनता को भ्रम से बचाना चाहिये।

भगवान् का भजन करो। सिद्धियों के अधिकारी बन जाओगे तो सिद्धियाँ स्वयं तुम्हारे पीछे-पीछे फिरेंगी।

अधिकारी बनना क्या है। लोक-वासना का न होना। जब तक जगत में नाना प्रकार की, पुत्र की, धन की, स्त्री की, मान-प्रतिष्ठा की वासनायें रहेंगी तब तक बलहीन ही रहोगे। कहावत है कि मंगन से 'खुदा' भी डरता है। जगत की वासनायें हटाकर एक परमात्मा के मिलने की वासना बढ़ाओ तो सिद्धि-समूह तुम्हारे पीछे-पीछे फिरेगा, सिद्धि ढूँढ़ने की तुम्हें आवश्यकता नहीं पड़ेगी।

मार्ग वह अपनाना चाहिये कि जिसमें अपना गौरव नष्ट न हो। जहाँ तुम साक्षात् सर्वशक्तिमान परमात्मा से सीधा सम्बन्ध स्थापित कर सकते हो वहाँ तुम यदि छुद्र सिद्धियों के पीछे यहाँ-वहाँ ठोकर खाते फिरो तो तुम्हारा दुर्भाग्य है। निश्चय रखो कि यदि तुम सिद्धियों के पीछे भागोगे तो दूर से तुम्हें देखकर सिद्धियाँ दूर भागेंगी। यदि सिद्धियों की इच्छा न करके, सिद्धियों को अपनी आध्यात्मिक उन्नति मे बाधक मानते रहोगे तो हठात् तुम्हें घेर कर सिद्धियां तुम्हारे आसपास् रहेंगी। सिद्धियों को अपने वश में रखने का उपाय है कि निरन्तर भगवान् के तरफ झुके रहना और सिद्धियों से काम लेने की इच्छा न करना - यह है स्वाधीनता का मार्ग। यदि तुम्हीं सिद्धियों के पीछे-पीछे फिरने लगे तो होगा पराधीनता अपनाना। तब तो तुम सिद्धियों के स्वामी नहीं रह सकते, उनके दास ही कहे जाओगे। इसलिए सिद्धियों के दास नहीं, सिद्धियों के स्वामी बनने की चेष्टा करो। भगवान् के दास बनोगे तो सिद्धियों के स्वामी होकर रहोगे। भगवान् के सेवक बनकर रहोगे तो सब तुम्हारी सेवा करेंगे - यही

वास्तव में स्वतन्त्र और स्वावलंबी होने का मार्ग है।

35

Few people have a *siddhi*, but by their greediness for *siddhi* a good many people become cheated.

Nowadays most people seek the *siddhis*, desiring to meet with any kind of *siddhi*. Few people have a *siddhi*, but by their greediness for *siddhi* a good many people become cheated. Our wish then is [for them] to be wary. We are like the village guard who calls *"Jagtay raho!"* ('Be awake!'), in this way we people are remaining attentive. Be cautious folks, beware of cheats. The watchman's raises his voice, his *"deputy"* work is done. Later, how could he be blamed if anyone is senseless asleep! It is the one who is sleeping that gets looted. Our wish is to perform the everyday affairs of the watchman. We are awake and awakening others.

There are five kinds of *siddhis*:-

"जन्मौषधिमन्त्रतपः समाधिजाः सिद्धयः"

"janmaushadhimantratapah samaadhijaah siddhayah."
[*Yogadarshanam* 4:1]

'*Siddhis* are attained by birth, drug, *mantra*, *tapa* & *samadhi*.'

1.
Truly, it occurs that someone is born as a *siddha* (one who has supernatural powers). Must have worshipped in a former life, but not so much as to have merged with Bhagwan (God). So in this way, by previous worship, people actually have miraculous *siddhis* - in this manner Jada Bharata was a *siddha* from birth, who did not have to hear, learn and memorise in order to understand.

2.
Various kinds of *siddhis* are come to be seen by means of drugs. When I was staying in the jungles, on several occasions Kol and

Bhil (tribal peoples) came and informed me of the properties of drugs. One time a Bhil brought one such which would make a tiger senseless who saw only a little of it from afar. By means of drugs a human being can live several hundred years. By means of drugs many *siddhis* can come. So there are also drugs that give the strength to fly for the one who puts it in the mouth.

3.

From a *mantra* come *siddhis*. Once the deity of the *mantra* becomes favourable it will act according to its ability. The proper form of *siddhis* is of *mantras*. Common people receive *siddhi* from *yakshini, karna-pishachi* and *bhuta-preta* (demi-gods, demons and ghosts) or trifling deities. And dark spirits of people inform of the past and present or do amazing feats and [the medium] pretends to be a *siddha yogi*. This is how straightforward simple people are deceived.

4.

siddhi occurs by doing *tapa* (austerity). Maintaining *brahmacharya* (celibacy), fasting and enduring one's *sadhana* in order to gain God are performances of *tapa* which are *satvik* (pure). From this [*tapa*] peace and satisfaction grow. The *tapa* aimed at dishonouring, killing, bewitching, enchanting etc. are *rajasik* and *tamasik tapa.* By this there will be neither peace nor satisfaction, the intrinsic enemies of unrest and anxiety increase bringing about the downfall of the *sadhaka.*

5.

From *samadhi* come *siddhis*. But, these *siddhis* go to the *sadhaka* who has gained the supreme situation or *jivanmukti.* With these *siddhis* the duty is to be steady and if a good deal of work is not undertaken then the steadfastness is gone.

The significance of this is that if miracles are seen in any person this is not the true measure of a *yogi*. Seriously, there are *yogis* in whom miracles occur and they do not perform miracles for their wealth or reputation. They only want for happiness in the world, tenderness and compassion. Understand that folk should be saved from misunderstandings about these *siddhas.*

Do *bhajans* (hymns) to Bhagwan (God). You should become a ruler to the *siddhis* then *siddhis* will wander behind you.

How to be made a ruler? Not to belong to the world of the imagination. Until such time as your world is of a different kind, not longing for a son, for wealth, for a wife, for prestige and reputation, until then you will really be bereft of strength. The proverb is that 'God is scared of the beggar'.

Withdrawing from the fancies of the world, grow in desire of Paramatma (the Supreme Self, God) then a multitude of *siddhis* will wander behind you, but no *siddhi* will occur when you seek them. The way that one should possess is where one's own honour is not sacrificed. When you can be in the steady presence of the Almighty Paramatma, then it would be a calamity if you were to go stumbling behind, here and there, following trifling *siddhis*. Be sure of this, the *siddhis* behind you will run away when they see you. If you do not wish for *siddhis*, if you obstinately make a boundary with the *siddhis* that obstuct your spiritual progress, then *siddhis* will stay surrounding you.

The way to keep *siddhis* under control is by remaining bowed to Bhagwan (the Supreme Being) and don't wish for the *siddhis* - this is the way to freedom. If the *siddhis* wander behind you, then they will be subjected. At that time then, the *siddhis* cannot be the *swami* (master), say they will really be only slaves. Therefore don't be a slave to the *siddhis*, become a master of the *siddhis*. Becoming a slave to Bhagwan you will become a *swami* of the *siddhis*. Becoming a servant of Bhagwan then all your service will be performed - in this is true independence and a way to be self-reliant.

३६

जीव-ब्रह्म की एकता

*

निष्काम कर्म से जन्म-मरण की निवृत्ति। धर्माचरण से ही त्रण

अज्ञान का पर्दा हटाने पर जीव और ब्रह्म का अभेद स्पष्ट अनुभव में आता है। जीव और परमात्मा में जो भेद दिखाई देता है वह ऐसा है जैसा धान और चावल का भेद। जब तक भूसी है वह धान कहा जाता है और भूसी निकाल लेने से चावल तो वह है ही। इसी प्रकार जीव जब तक कर्म-बन्धन में पड़ा है तब तक पर्मात्म से भिन्न है। कर्म-बन्धन नष्ट होने पर वह पर्मात्मा ही है।

यद्यपि धान चावल ही है, परन्तु भूसी बिना निकाले कोई उसे उबाल कर नहीं खाता। इसी प्रकार कर्म-बन्धन को नष्ट किये बिना वेदान्त की पुस्तकें पढ़कर 'शुद्धोऽहं, विशुद्धोऽह' कहने लगने से कोई ब्रह्म नहीं हो जाता। कर्म-पाश से छुटकारा दिलाने का मार्ग बताने के लिये ही वेद और शास्त्र हैं। यदि हम क्रियमाण (आगामी) कर्मों को ही पर्मात्मा को अर्पण करते जाएं तो भी पुनर्जन्म के चक्र से छूट सकते हैं। यदि धान से समूची भूसी न हटे, केवल उसकी नोंक ही तोड़ दी जाय तो भी उसमें किसी प्रकार अंकुर नहीं निकल सकता। पुनः जन्म लेना ही कर्म का अंकुरित होना है। निर्मली में जल को साफ करने का गुण है, पर यदि उसे घिस कर पानी में न मिलाया जाय तो जल की गन्दगी नहीं हट सकती। उसी प्रकार सनातन वैदिक धर्म कितना ही अच्छा हो पर यदि उसे आचरण में नहीं लगाओगे तो तुम्हारा यह दुःख और दारिद्र्य दूर नहीं हो सकता।

36

Showing the difference between the individual life and Paramatma (the Supreme Self) is like distinguishing between paddy and rice.

By *nishkama karma* (action free from any wish) there is no more life and death. Really, virtuous conduct is a means of protection.

On removing the veil of ignorance, the oneness of the individual life and Brahma comes to be clearly experienced. Showing the difference between the individual life and Paramatma (the Supreme Self) is like distinguishing between paddy and rice. Whilst there is a husk it is said to be paddy but when the husk is removed it is then solely rice. In this very manner, when the individual befalls actions that bind, then he is separate from Paramatma. Yet on the destruction of the binding action, he is really Paramatma.

Although paddy and rice are really the same, however, without removing the husk the paddy cannot nor eaten even when boiled. Without destroying the binding actions you will study the books of *Vedanta*, but by some saying of *"shuddho aham, vishuddho aha"* ('I am perfect, I am pure') you do not become Brahma. The *Veda* and *Shastra* are there for the purpose of informing the way to get liberated from action that ties. If the actions we are now doing are offered to Paramatma then we can also be given freedom from the wheel of rebirth. If not all the husk is gotten rid of, but just the point of the chaff is broken then like this no sprout can appear. To take birth again is really the sprouting of *karma*.

Within *nirmali* [the seed *strychnos potatorum*) is the property of being able to purify water, but if you do not rub it into the water then you cannot get the impurities out. By the same token, however excellent *vaidika dharma* is, if you do not practice it, then your unhappiness and poverty cannot be far off.

३७

तृष्णा का त्याग और ईश्वराराधन से ही सुख संभव

*

जगत के पदार्थों से जब कोई निराशा आती है तभी परमात्मा को प्राप्त करने की इच्छा उत्पन्न होती है। राजा भर्तृहरि को अपनी स्त्री के दुश्चरित्र का पता लगने पर धक्का लगा। तुलसी और पिंगला के उदाहरण भी यही बात पुष्ट करते हैं कि जगत में सुख की आशा भंग होने पर लोग परमार्थ की ओर उन्मुख होते हैं। परन्तु फिर भी ऐसे कितने मूर्ख हैं जो बार-बार संसार की असारता का अनुभव करने के बाद भी पिशाचिनी आशा का त्याग नहीं करते।

निरन्तर सावधान होकर विचार करते रहने की आवश्यकता है। स्त्री, पुरुष, धन, परिवार, वैभव आदि इनके अभाव में यदि दुःख मानते हो तो जिनके पास यह सब हैं उनके जीवन को जाकर देखो। यदि उन्हें उनसे सुख मिलता हो तो तुम भी इन्हें प्राप्त करने का प्रयत्न करो। जिनके पास यह सब वस्तुयें हैं उन्हें और भी अधिक क्लेश है। इसलिये तृष्णा को त्यागो। सुख तो तृष्णा को त्याग कर ईश्वर की आराधना करने ही से मिलेगा। संसार में सुख की आशा से कभी भी किसी के सामने दीन मत बनो; क्योंकि सुख कभी किसी बाहरी वस्तु से प्राप्त नहीं होता। सुख का भंडार तो अपने अन्दर ही है। बाहर तों जो कुछ है सब दुःख का ही सामान है।

बाहर के सांसारिक पदार्थों में जो लोग सुखबुध्दि कर लेते हैं, उन्हें बाद में अनुभव होता है कि धोखा हो गया। मृग-मरीचिकी में जल की प्राप्ति तो हो नहीं सकती। यही है कि दूर से जल दिखेगा और उसकी प्राप्ति के लिये दौड़ते रहो। ठीक यही हाल उन लोगों का होता है, जो जगत् के पदार्थ धन, स्त्री, पुत्र आदि में सुख की

भावना करके इनके संग्रह के लिये परेशान रहते हैं। इसमें केवल परेशानी ही उनके हाथ लगती है।

यदि सुख और शान्ति का अनुभव करना चाहते हो तो उसे बाहर के पदार्थों में न धूँढ़ कर अपने अन्दर ही धूँढ़ो। सर्वान्तर्यामी परमात्मा ही सुखस्वरूप है और अपने हृदय में ही उसका नित्य निवास है। इसलिये अपने अन्दर ही उसे धूँढ़ो। अपने अन्दर ही उस धूँढ़ोगे तभी वह जल्दी मिलेगा।

37

If you wish to experience happiness and peace then don't search for outer things, only seek inside yourself.

At whatever time any despair comes from worldly matters, at the same moment a desire for Paramatma is born. Raja Bhartrihari (King Vikramaditya's brother) was shocked to discover the misconduct of his own wife. Tulasi (writer of the Hindi version of *Ramayana*) and Pingala (Bhartrihari's wife) are also strong examples of people whose hopes for happiness having been destroyed became eager for *paramarth* (salvation). But again how many are foolish, who after experiencing the worthlessness of mundane existence, again and again, do not abandon hope in a *pishachini* (she-devil)?

It is necessary to be constantly cautious, and to remain discerning. If you regard suffering as being the lack of woman, man, wealth, family etc. then go and look at the life of those who have all this. If you find happiness there then you too go and make an effort to acquire these. Those who have everything, also have considerable trouble. For this reason abandon this longing. Happiness will be found by abandoning longing and by worshipping Ishwar (the Lord). Don't make out as needy in front of others by the promise of happiness in the worldly existence; because happiness is not gained from outer things. The storehouse of happiness then is really inside oneself. So there is little outside, really possessions are all trouble.

Those who are happy thinking about outer material things later perceive that they have been deceived. The deer cannot find water in a mirage. From right here they can see water in the distance and they run to get it. This is the exact condition that those people exist in, who remain troubled, grasping to feel the happiness of worldly things, wealth, woman, son etc. In this their hands will hold only trouble.

If you wish to experience happiness and peace then don't search for outer things, only seek inside yourself. All-Pervasive Paramatma is the real form of happiness and constantly dwells in one's heart. Seek to him inside yourself. Seek inside yourself and quickly you will meet him.

३८

योजनायें बना-बना कर अपने जीवन को उलझन में न डालो

जगत् तो धर्मशाला है। चार दिन यहाँ रहना है, फिर आगे चलना है। धर्मशाला के निवास में कोई भी प्रबन्ध की उलझन में बहुत अधिक नहीं फँसता - - जैसे होता है काम निकाल लिया जाता है। किसी चीज की कमी भी होती है तो लोग अधिक परेशान नहीं होते-सोचते हैं 'कि धर्मशाले में दो दिन किसी तरह काट लो फिर तो इसे छोड़ ही देना है।' धर्मशाले में यदि कोई अपनी इच्छा के अनुसार प्रबन्ध करने लगे तो उसका सारा समय रहने का प्रबन्ध करते-करते ही बीत जाय और जिस कार्य के लिये वह उस नगर या ग्राम में आया है, वह कुछ न हो पाये।

जगत् को भी धर्मशाला ही मानना चाहिये। थोड़े दिन का जीवन है, यहाँ किसी को स्थायीरूप से रहना नहीं है। इसलिये जगत् के

प्रबन्ध में बहुत दिलचस्पी मत रखो। उतना ही भाग लो कि जिससे निर्वाह होता चले। यह सदा स्मरण रखो कि जितनी तुम योजनायें बनाओगे, वे सब कभी भी पूरी नहीं हो सकतीं। इसलिये व्यर्थ में 'स्कीमें' (योजनायें) बना - बना कर अपने को आशा के सूत्र में टाँगे रहना और उसी के सम्बन्ध में सोचते-विचारते रह कर रात-दिन अशान्त बने रहना, इसमें समय की बरबादी के सिवा और कोई लाभ नही है।

जगत् में कितना भी प्रबन्ध करो, फिर भी कोई कमी बनी ही रहेगा। इसलिये जो मद्द कभी पूरा होने वाला नहीं है उसमें हाथ लगाना ही व्यर्थ है। जीवन-यापन के लिये सामान्य रूप से शास्त्र विहित पुरुषार्थ करते चलो और मुख्य पुरुषार्थ उसमें करो जिससे स्थायी सुख व शान्ति की प्राप्ति होना है। भगवान् की प्राप्ति के लिये प्रधान रूप से पुरुषार्थ करते हुए लौकिक पदार्थों की प्राप्ति में यह दृढ़ विश्वास रखो कि 'यदस्मदीयं न हि तत्परेषाम्।' जो हमारा है वह दूसरे का नहीं हो सकता। जो अपने भाग्य (प्रारब्ध) में है वह अपने पास अवश्य हो आयेगा, उसे कोई रोक नहीं सकता। ऐसी धारणा बनाकर जगत् में लौकिक कार्यों के लिये अधिक व्यस्त न रहते हुए सामान्य लगाव से व्यवहार करते रहो। मुख्य लगाव परमात्मा में रखो। ऐसा करने से जीवन में शान्ति का अनुभव होगा और आगे का मार्ग भी उज्वल बनेगा।

38

That which is ours cannot be another's.

The world then is a *dharmashala* (a stopping house for pilgrims). Four days you remain here, then you proceed further. Don't get very involved in any of the difficulties in your abode at the *dharmashala*, accomplish the work needed in order to go. If there is anything lacking then people are not much troubled; considering that they are to stay in the *dharmashala* only two days then they will be permitted to leave. If arrangements at the *dharmashala* are to be in accord with one's own wishes then all the time passes in making arrangements, and the work for which he came from his town or village, that he will not obtain.

You should accept that the world is really a *dharmashala* too. Life is a few days, we are not to remain here permanently. For this reason don't put a lot of interest in arrangements of the world, do only that much to get that portion for one's maintenance. Always remember this, that however many plans you will make, they cannot all be fulfilled. For this reason, in making *"schemes"* one's hopes hang by a thread, restlessly thinking about them day and night, ruining this time and to no advantage.

However much you make arrangements in the world, afterwards there will still remain some lack. Therefore if there is an item you cannot own, there is really no purpose in trying to reach out for it. Exert yourself in the normal way passing your life according to the *Shastra* and importantly do *purushartha* from which you gain permanent happiness and peace. By performing *purushartha* principally for gaining Bhagwan, for gaining earthly things put your trust strictly in:-

"यदस्मदीयं न हि तत्परेषाम्"

" yadasmadiyam na hi tatparesham"
'That which is ours cannot be another's.'

That which is in one's destiny, that will certainly come into one's own possession, none can hinder it. So be resolute in the world. Don't become too busy on account of earthly tasks, perform everyday affairs as a matter of routine. Set the primary relationship in Paramatma. By so doing you will experience peace in life and the way ahead will also be made clear.

३९

भगवान् का अवतार किस लिये होता है?

गीता में भगवान् ने स्वयं अपने अवतार का हेतु यह बतलाया है कि "जब धर्म नष्ट होने लगता है तो उसका अभ्युत्थान करने के लिये, सज्जनों की रक्षा तथा दुष्टों का संहार एवं धर्म की संस्थापना करने के लिये, मैं युग-युग में अबतरित होता हूँ।"

प्रश्न हो सकता है कि भगवान् तो सर्वशक्तिमान् है, उनकी इच्छा मात्र से सारी सृष्टि का प्रलय हो सकता है, तब क्या बिना अवतार लिये ही वह धर्म की रक्षा और दुष्टों का संहार नहीं कर सकते? इसका उत्तर यह है कि अवतार धारण कर धर्म तथा धर्मिक जनों के उद्धार के लिये भगवान् जो लीलायें करते हैं, अपने जो यश का विस्तार करते हैं, उसका गान करते हुए भक्त जन मुक्त हो जाते हैं। ज्ञान-योग तो अत्यन्त कठिन है, सहस्रों में कोई विरला ही उसका अधिकारी है। परन्तु भक्ति-योग सुगम है और मनुष्य मात्र का उसमें अधिकार है। यदि भगवान् अवतार धारण कर साकार रूप में न आते तो भक्ति-योग का प्रचार ही कैसे होता।

भगवान् को साकार रूप में आ-आकर उन योनियों के सुख-दुःख भोगने की लीला नहीं करनी पड़ती, क्योंकि भगव अपनी योगमाया से शरीर धारण करते हैं - जैसे, नट नाना प्रकार के स्वरूप बनाकर उन्हीं के अनुरूप कार्य करने लगता है परन्तु उनके गुणों से अप्रभावित रहता है, वैसे ही भगवान् भी लीला मात्र ही करते हैं।

39

If Bhagwan did not resolve to come in the shape of an *avataar* then how would publicity come for *bhakti yoga*?

In the *Gita,* Bhagwan himself explained the reason that he incarnates:-

'When *dharma* becomes perished then for progress and protection of the gentle, the destruction of the wicked, and for establishing *dharma* (religion), I come down from age to age.'
[*Bhagavad Gita* 4:7 & 4:8]

The question can be asked that; as Bhagwan is Omnipotent and that by his mere wish can be annihilation, then why can't he protect *dharma* and destroy the wicked without becoming an *avataar* (descending in human form)? This is the answer to it; that it is the *leela* (play) of Bhagwan to revive *dharma* and protect those righteous people, as an *avataar*, spreading his own fame; having sung thereof his devotees become liberated. *Gyaan yoga* (*yoga* of the intellect) is very difficult then, it is rare that out of thousands anybody is a master. But *bhakti yoga* is easy and some few human beings are masters. If Bhagwan did not resolve to come in the shape of an *avataar* then how would publicity come for *bhakti yoga*?

In taking a form, Bhagwan comes and takes births; it is not to experience happiness and suffering because by his own *yogamaya* (inner power) his body is steady, in the manner which an actor plays various parts but remains unaffected by their qualities; for Bhagwan it is just a play.

४०

मन के थोड़े सहयोग से ही व्यवहार चल सकता है

*

प्रश्न यह उठ सकता है कि मन के सहयोग के बिना व्यावहारिक कार्य कैसे चलेंगे? इसका यही समाधान है कि जिस प्रकार कृपण (कंजूस) मनुष्य सब व्यावहारिक कार्य करते हुए भी अपने धन को मुख्य मानकर हमेशा मन से धन का चिन्तन करता है, धन का ध्यान हमेशा रखते हुए भी वह समस्त व्यावहारिक कार्यों को करता रहता है; इसी प्रकार मन से हमेशा भगवान् का चिन्तन करते रहने पर भी व्यावहारिक कार्य यथाविधि होते रह सकते हैं - - इसमें संदेह नहीं।

प्रधान व अप्रधान का भेद कर लेने से इस प्रश्न का उत्तर ठीक हो जाता है। एक बात और है - - मन जब परमात्मा में प्रधान् रूप से लग जाता है तब परमात्मा की कृपा प्राप्त होती है। परमात्मा सर्वशक्तिमान है। उसकी थोड़ी भी कृपा जीव का पूर्ण रूप से कल्याण कर सकतो है। ऐसे सर्वशक्तिमान भगवान् की प्रतिज्ञा है कि:-

अनन्याश्चिन्तयन्तोमां ये जनाः पर्युपासते।
तेषां नित्याभियुक्तानां योगक्षेमेंवहाभ्यहम्॥

अर्थात् - - जो मुझे अनन्य भाव से भजता है उसके लिये योग (अप्राप्त वस्तु की प्राप्ति) और क्षेम (प्राप्त वस्तु का रक्षण) का प्रबन्ध मैं ही करता हूँ। योग और क्षेम में ही मनुष्य का सारा व्यवहार आ जाता है। जब सर्वशक्तिमान भगवान् समस्त व्यवहार संचालन का भार अपने ऊपर लेने को तैयार हैं तब भी मनुष्य व्यवहार के पीछे परेशान रह कर मन को सदा व्यवहार में लगाये रहकर परमार्थ से

वंचित रहे इससे अधिक अज्ञानता और मूर्खता क्या हो सकती है!

भगवान् की जब यह प्रतिज्ञा है तब तो यह प्रश्न ही नहीं हो सकता कि मन को प्रधान रूप से भगवान् में लगा दें तो व्यवहार कैसे चलेगा। जब मन भगवान् में लग जायगा तो व्यवहार जो आवश्यक होगा, वह अधिक उत्तम रीति से चलेगा। यही उपनिषद् और गीता का सिद्धांत है और यही भगवान् के भक्तों का अनुभव भी है।

अभी थोड़े दिन की बात है - - ४० - ५० वर्ष हुए होंगे, अधिक समय नहीं हुआ कि चुनकाई दास नाम के एक कानिस्टबिल थे। उनका नियम था कि सबेरे उठकर स्नान करके रामायण का पाठ करके फिर कुछ काम करते थे। एक दिन रामायण-पाठ करते-करते उसी में तल्लीन हो गये, देर तक पाठ ही करते यह गये। डिवटी का समय आया और दो घण्टे की डिवटी का समय भी समाप्त हो गया तब उन्हें याद आई कि डिवटी पर जाना है।

पूजन से उठकर देख तो मालुम हुआ कि डिवटी का समय बीत गया। घबराये हुए दिवटी में गये और जो सिपाही पहरा से रहा था उससे बोले की बड़ी गलती हुई, आज इतनी देर हो गई कि डिवटी का पूरा समय बीत गया, आपको बड़ा कष्ट हुआ होगा।

डिवटी वाले सिपाही ने कहा कि चुनकाई दास तुमको क्या हो गया है। अभी तो तुम हमको अपनी डिवटी का चार्ज दे गये हो, और फिर लौट कर आ गर और ऐसा कह रहे हो, क्या तुम्हारा मस्तिष्क तो नहीं फिर गया है। चुनकाई दास ने कहा - "नहीं मित्र, मुझको आज पूजन में देर लग गई। मैं तो अभी भागा चला आ रहा हूँ।"

उस सिपाही ने बार-बार निश्चय कराया कि आप ने ही अभी डिवटी दी है और मेरे आने के पहले आप की ही डिवटी थी और

आप डिवटी पर बराबर थे। समय पूरा होने पर मुझको डिवटी देकर आप अभी गये हो। उसके बार-बार कहने पर चुनकाई दास को विश्वास हो गया कि मैं घर में भगवान् की आरधना में लीन था और यहाँ भगवान् ने स्वयं आकर मेरी डिवटी दी।

उसी समय चुनकाई दास ने नौकरी छोड़ दी। उसने कहा कि हमारे इष्ट को जब इतना कष्ट हमारी डिवटी के लिये करना पड़ा तो हम अब नौकरी नहीं करेंगे। नौकरी छोड़कर चुनकाई दास चित्रकूट चले गये और वहीं भगवान का भजन करने लगे।

ऐसे-ऐसे अनेक भक्तों को प्रत्यक्ष अनुभव हुए हैं जहाँ पर भगवान ने स्वयं उनके व्यावहारिक कार्यों को पूरा किया है। वेद-शास्त्र तो प्रमाणित करता ही है कि भगवान् की प्रतिज्ञा है कि जो अनन्य भाव से मेरा चिन्तन करता है उसका आवश्यक व्यवहार भी मैं संचालन करता हूँ, परन्तु भक्तों के अनुभव भी भगवान् की इस प्रतिज्ञा को प्रमाणित करते हैं। इतने पर भी कोई भगवान् के भजन-पूजन-चिन्तन में न लगे तो उसका दुर्भाग्य ही है और क्या कहा जा सकता है।

अन्त में हमारा यही कहना है कि मन को तो प्रधान रूप से भगवान् के स्मरण में लगाओ और तन-धन को शास्त्रानुसार व्यावहारिक कार्यों में लगाओ - लोक-परलोक दोनों उज्ज्वल रहेंगे।

40

Omnipotent Bhagwan is ready to take on the burden of all the management of everyday affairs.

This question can arise; 'How will everyday work proceed without the co-operation of the mind?'

This is the answer to it. In the way that a miserly person, whilst doing all everyday work, thinks foremostly about his own wealth, always thinking of wealth, always considering wealth while doing everyday tasks. But if he is always thinking about Bhagwan the everyday tasks can be accomplished properly - of this there is no doubt.

The answer to this question is achieved by differentiating between what is of principal importance, and that which is unessential. Furthermore, when the mind is primarily attached to Paramatma then it gains the *kripa* (grace) of Paramatma. Paramatma is Omnipotent. A little *kripa* (grace) can bless and make this life perfect. Thus the promise of Almighty Bhagwan is:-

"अनन्याश्चिन्तयन्तो मां ये जनाः पर्युपासते ।
तेषां नित्याभियुक्तानां योगक्षेमं वहाम्यहम् ॥"

*"ananyaashchintayanto maam ye janaah paryupaasate.
tesham nityaabhiyuktaanam yogakshemem vahaabhyaham.."*
[*Bhagavad Gita* 9:22]

That is; 'He who worships me with unbounded feeling, he obtains *yoga* (unity) - gains the thing unobtained and protection for arrangements - which I am doing.' In *yoga* and happiness all man's everyday affairs are done. Omnipotent Bhagwan is ready to take on the burden of all management of everyday affairs, but even then man is troubled because of everyday affairs. Always the mind is attached to everyday affairs, cheated from Paramatma, what can be more ignorant and stupid?

When Bhagwan has promised this then this question cannot really be, that; 'By attaching and putting the principal aspect of the mind to Bhagwan how can everyday affairs proceed then?' When mind will be connected to Bhagwan then everyday affairs will be consequential, it will proceed and be of the highest standard. This is the standpoint of the *Upanishads* and *Gita* and is also the experience of the devotees of Bhagwan.

Recently, some time ago, there was talk, that 40 - 50 years ago, no more time than that, Chunkayee Das was the name of the *"constable"*. It was his practise to rise early in the morning, have a bath, read the *Ramayana* and then do some work. One day he became deeply immersed in reading *Ramayana* and whilst reading he came to be delayed. The time came of his *"duty"* and when there was only two hours left of his duty he remembered. Rising from his worship he saw how much time of his duty had elapsed.

Embarrassed, he explained the big mistake about the duty to the Sepoy guard that; 'Today I have been delayed for the time of the duty and this will have been a big hardship for you.'

The Sepoy on duty said; 'Chunkayee, what has become of you? Just now then you passed your charge of duty to me, and you have come back and are talking like this, have your senses since gone?'

Chunkayee Das said; 'No. Friend, today I have been delayed in *pujana* (worship). I have just now come running here.'

That Sepoy again and again confirmed that; 'Before I came you had just now been on duty before and it was the entire duty. On fulfilling the time just now you handed the duty to me.'

Having been explained this again and again, Chunkayee Das believed; 'When I was was at home absorbed in worship of Bhagwan, Bhagwan was here doing my duty.'

At that time Chunkayee left his job. He said that; 'When our *ishta* (god) takes this much hardship doing our duty then now we no more do service.' Renouncing his work, Chunkayee went to Chitrakoot and at that very place sang *bhajan* (prayers) to Bhagwan.

Similarly, many devotees have experienced that Bhagwan has completed their everyday tasks himself. The *Veda Shastra* then is proven, that, the promise of Bhagwan; that whoever is in the unbounded experience of thinking about me, I take care of the management of all their everyday business. The experience of devotees authentically proves this promise of Bhagwan. But otherwise, if anybody is not thinking of and worshipping Bhagwan, then it is really a calamity and what can be said?

In the end we say this; 'Principally apply the mind in remembering Bhagwan, and in accordance with the *Shastra* apply yourself in suitable work for the body and wealth. This world and the other world will both be bright.'

४१

लोक-परलोक में सर्वत्र सुख-शान्ति चाहते हो तो सर्वशक्तिमान परमात्मा की शरण लो

मोक्ष तो मिलेगा ही, धन-धान्य व मान-प्रतिष्ठा भी मिलेगी।

यह न समझो कि परमात्मा के भजन से केवल मोक्ष ही मिलेगा - निश्चय रखो कि भगवान् के भजन से मोक्ष भी मिलेगा और धन-धान्य, मान-प्रतिष्ठा भी मिलेगी।

इसका कारण यह है कि भक्त भगवान् की उपासना करता है और भक्ति की पहली सीढ़ी ''श्रवण' दूसरी सीढ़ी 'कीर्तन' और तीसरी सीढ़ी 'स्मरण' को पार करके जब चौथी सीढ़ी में पहुँच कर 'पाद सेवन' अर्थात् मन से निरन्तर भगवच्चरणों का ध्यान करता है तो अहर्निष भगवत्पाद-सेविनी लक्ष्मी को भय हो जाता है कि कहीं भगवान का प्रेम अपने इस भक्त पर अधिक न हो जाय।

स्त्री यह कभी नहीं चाहती कि उसका पति किसी दूसरे से प्रेम करे। इसलिये उस भक्त को भगवच्चिन्तन से हटाने से लिये विघ्न रूप में लक्ष्मी उसे धन, यश, मान, प्रतिष्ठा देना प्रारम्भ करतो है जिससे

वह इसी लौकिक जाल में पड़ जाय और भगवान् को छोड़ दे। इस प्रकार भगवान के भक्तों के पास लक्ष्मी विघ्न रूप में आती है।

आज आप जिसका इष्ट बुद्धि से चिन्तन करते हुए रात दिन परेशान हों और मारे-मारे भटकते हों वही रुपया-पैसा, मान-प्रतिष्ठा जबरदस्ती बिना आवाहन के आप के पास आयेगा, आप भगवान् की तरफ तो झुको।

गति-मुक्ति के लिये तो भगवान का भजन है ही, किन्तु लौकिक ऐश्वर्य चाहते हो तो भी भगवान् की शरण में आओ। साधक जब तप करता है तो देवराज इन्द्र का आसन डोल जाता है और वह तप में विघ्न करने के लिये नाना प्रकार के प्रलोभन सामने उपस्थित करता है इसी प्रकार भगवान का स्मरण छुटाने के लिये लक्ष्मी लौकिक ऐश्वर्य सामने लाती है। जिस प्रकार जब कोई कुत्ता काटने को दौड़े तो रोटी का दुकड़ा फेंक दो, वह उसी में उलझ कर रह जाता है; ठीक उसी प्रकार लक्ष्मी भी सोने का टुकड़ा फेंकती है कि जिससे वे भक्त मेरे पति भगवान् के निकट न आवें तो अच्छा है!

भगवान के स्मरण से गति-मुक्ति भी होगी और लक्ष्मी भी धक्का खाएगी। व्यापार ऐसा करो जिसमें अधिक लाभ हो।

तात्पर्य कहने का यह है कि भगवान के भजन से सब कुछ हो जाता है। जब तुम सर्वशक्तिमान का ध्यान अपनी तरफ खींच लोगे तो तुम्हारे लिये क्या अप्राप्त रह सकता है। आजकल अपना घर छोड़ कर भी लोग सेठों के यहाँ धक्का खाते-फिरते हैं। उन्हें धनवान का विश्वास है; परन्तु सर्वशक्तिमान का विश्वास नहीं है। तभी दरवाजे-दरवाजे वे ठोकर खाते हैं।

जिन्हें भगवान का विश्वास है उनके पीछे संसार आज भी धक्का खा रहा है। इसलिये जब किसी का स्तोत्र करना ही ह तो भगवान का ही स्तोत्र करो जिससे लोक-परलोक दोनों बने।

लौकिक वासना कम करो और परमात्मा में राग बढ़ाओ। मनुष्य शरीर का यही उपयोग है कि विचार करके उस रास्ते पर चलो जहाँ सब प्रकार की सुविधा मिले।

41

Certainly by singing *bhajan* of Bhagwan you will get *moksha*, and you will get wealth, food, reputation and respect too.

Don't think that by chanting bhajans of Paratmatma you will get only *moksha*. Certainly by singing *bhajan* of Bhagwan you will get *moksha*, but you will get wealth, food, reputation and respect too.

The reason for this is; devoted worshipping of Bhagwan. Devotion is the first step - *'shravana'* (devotion), the second step is *'kirtana'* (singing praise of God) and the third step is *'smarana'* (remembrance). Then you have arrived at the fourth step, *'pada sevana'* - that is unceasing meditation on the feet of Bhagwan, then Lakshmi (Bhagwan's consort) becomes alarmed that somewhere there is night and day worship of Bhagwan's feet, worried that Bhagwan's love for the *bhakta* (devotee) will not be excessive.

The wife never wants the husband to love another. Therefore in order to stop the devotee thinking of Bhagwan, Lakshmi begins to give obstacles such as wealth, fame, reputation and honour, so these ensnare him and Bhagwan is spared. In this way Lakshmi comes to devotees of Bhagwan in the form of obstacles.

Today that which you are desiring, thinking about and worrying about night and day, and on account of which you are deceived, the very same *rupees* and *paisa*, honour and reputation, will be yours without asking, if you bow in the direction of Bhagwan.

For salvation and absolution then chant *bhajan* to Bhagwan, but really if you desire earthly wealth then also come take refuge in Bhagwan. When the *sadhaka* (one devoted to spiritual accomplishment) does *tapa* (devotion, penance) then Devaraj Indra (Indra, King of the gods) moves from his seat and places all kinds of temptations in order to obstruct *tapa*. In this way Lakshmi brings earthly wealth in order that Bhagwan be forgotten. This is similar to the way that if a dog is running to bite you, then you would throw a piece of *roti* (bread) so he might get distracted; in this exact way Laksmi throws a piece of gold. The *bhakta* will not come close to my husband, then that is good!

By remembering Bhagwan you will attain salvation and absolution and you will also give a shock to Lakshmi. Do such everyday affairs as will be the greatest advantage. The meaning of what is said is this; by singing *bhajan* of Bhagwan everything is gained. When working to pull oneself towards meditation on the Almighty, then what cannot be obtained by you? Nowadays people leave their homes only to be pushed about in the place of wealthy people. Their faith is in the wealthy; but no trust is in the Almighty. For this reason they suffer stumbling from door to door.

In the absence of trust in Bhagwan, today they stumble suffering *samsara* (the worldly existence). Therefore, when *stotra* (hymn of praise) is performed, then perform the *stotra* of Bhagwan by whom both this world and the other world are made.

Lessen your worldly desires and let your love grow for Paramatma. Man's body is for the use of contemplation, get on that path where all kinds of benefits are obtained.

४२

मन को संसार में कोई नहीं चाहता तन और धन से व्यवहार करो मन परमात्मा में लगाओ

*

इष्ट मित्र कुटुम्बो आदि सब अपनी आवश्यकताओं की पूर्ति चाहते हैं। आप के मन को कोई नहीं चाहता! अपने पुत्र को लिखने-पढ़ने की सामग्री का प्रबन्ध मत करो और पास बैठा कर कहो कि बेटा हम मन से तुमको प्यार करते हैं, तो क्या वह संतुष्ट रहेगा? अपनी स्त्री की आवश्यकताओं की पूर्ति मत करो और उससे कहो कि हम हमेशा तुम्हारा स्मरण करते रहते हैं, मन से कभी तुमको नहीं भूलते, तो क्या वह संतुष्ट रहेगी?

इष्ट मित्र जो तुमसे व्यवहार में सहायता या सहयोग चाहते हैं उनको कुछ सहयोग न दो और कहो कि मन से हम आपको बहुत मानते हैं। वे यही कहेंगे कि अपना मन अपने पास रखिये, बन सके तो हमारा अमुक-अमुक कार्य कर दीजिये।

तात्पर्य यह कि संसार में कोई भी आप का मन नहीं चाहता। यहाँ सभी तुम्हारे तन और धन के ग्राहक हैं। मन तो तुम जबरदस्ती दूसरों के गले लगाते हो।

स्मरण रखो कि जिस मन को संसार में कोई नहीं चाहता वही मन परमात्मा के निकट पहुँचने में काम आता है। इसलिये संसार के बाजार में तन और धन से व्यापार करो और परमात्मा के मार्ग में मन को लगाओ, तो संसार का व्यवहार भी नहीं बिगड़ेगा और परमार्थ का मार्ग भी साफ होता चलेगा।

जिसकी जहाँ जरूरत है उसको वहीं लगाना बुद्धिमानी है। मन को संसारी कार्यों में मत फँसाओ। मन का बहुत थोड़ा सहयोग देने से व्यवहार चलता जायगा। अधिक मन भीतर-भीतर परमात्मा में लगाओ।

जो संसार यहीं छूट जाने वाला है उसमें यहीं छूट जाने वाले तन और धन को लगाओ। जिस परमात्मा का कभी वियोग नहीं होना है उसमें सदा अपने साथ जाने वाले मन को लगाओ।

जैसा सौदा हो वैसा दाम चुकाओ। क्षणभंगुर सांसारिक व्यवहार में क्षणभंगुर तन और धन को ही लगाओ। मन तो सदा साथ रहने वाली स्थायी चीज है, परलोक में भी साथ ही रहेगा। इसलिये इसके साथ स्थायी वस्तु का सम्बन्ध जोड़ो। परम स्थायी चराचर में रमा हुआ सर्व व्यापक सदा सर्वत्र विराजमान जो परमात्मा हैं उसके साथ मन का सम्बन्ध जोड़ो। परमात्मा ही मन के साथ सम्बन्ध कराने योग्य है। और कोई वस्तु संसार में ऐसी नहीं है जिसके साथ मन का सम्बन्ध जोड़कर मन को संतुष्ट किया जा सके।

आप लोगों को स्वयं अनुभव है कि मन को आप धन में, स्त्री में, पुत्र में या इष्ट मित्र में लगाते हैं। पर क्या कहीं पर मन स्थिर रहता है? एक स्थान में अधिक समय तक नहीं ठहरता। यदि मन को धन से संतोष हो जाय या पुत्र से संतोष हो जाय तो वह फिर दूसरी जगह क्यों जायगा। किन्तु मन कभी भी एक पदार्थ में नहीं टिकता; यही इस बात का प्रमाण है कि मन को कोई भी सांसारिक पदार्थ अच्छे नहीं लगते। किसी पदार्थ को अच्छा मानकर उसके निकट जाता है; परन्तु थोड़ी देर में उससे हट जाता है। इससे मालूम होता है कि कोई भी सांसारिक पदार्थ मन को संतुष्ट नहीं कर सकता।

इसलिये सिद्धान्त यही निकलता है कि संसार में मन को कोई नहीं चाहता और मन भी किसी संसारी वस्तु से संसुष्ट नहीं होता -

तात्पर्य यह कि न मन संसार के योग्य है और न संसार मन के योग्य है।

मन जब परमात्मा को पा जाता है तो वहीं स्थिर हो जाता है, फिर कहीं किसी दूसरी वस्तु की इच्छा नहीं करता। इसलिये यही निश्चय होता है कि मन के योग्य परमात्मा ही है। अतः जो वस्तु जिसके योग्य हो उसको वहीं लगाओ।

42

Only Paramatma is suitable to be with the mind, and anything else in worldly existence cannot satisfy the mind when it connects to it.

Beloved friends and family etc. all desire to fulfil their own needs. Nobody wants your mind! If you don't give your own son the means to read and write but sit beside him and say 'I love you with all our mind', then how will he be content? Not fulfilling the needs of one's wife but saying 'I am always thinking about you with all my mind, I never forget you', then how will she be satisfied? The beloved friend who desires some assistance from you, to them you give no help but you say 'With the mind I have a high regard for you.' They will say 'Can you keep your mind to yourself, you ought to do such-and-such work.'

The meaning of this is that in the worldly existence nobody wants your mind. In this place all are customers for your body and means. Embracing with the mind, you oppress others. Recognise this that the mind that nobody wants in *samsara*, that same mind does the work of arriving close to Paramatma. In the bazaar of worldly existence do your work with body and means, and in the search for Paramatma apply the mind, and then worldly business will not be spoiled and the way to *paramarth* (salvation) will become clear.

Wherever there is a need, apply the intelligence to it. Don't get the mind involved in worldly tasks. With very little assistance of the mind the everyday business will proceed. Apply greater amount of mind within on Paramatma.

If you want to get release from mundane existence, right here have freedom, apply your body and means. Never become separated from Paramatma, always apply oneself with one's mind. According to the bargain, so repay the cost. In passing transitory worldly transactions only apply the body and means. The mind is always with you, it is a lasting thing, it remains with you in the other world. Therefore affix it in a relationship with something that lasts. The utmost and lasting thing which plays in the world is complete, many-sided, always everywhere, shining, that is Paramatma, connect the mind thereof. Only Paramatma is suitable to be with the mind, and anything else in worldly existence cannot satisfy the mind when it connects to it.

You people, it is your experience that your mind is attached to wealth, wife and son, or to a beloved friend. But does the mind stay steady on anything? It does not stay in any one place for much time. If the mind becomes satisfied by wealth or becomes satisfied by a son, then why does it again go elsewhere? But the mind seldom stays with one thing; This is truly said that it is not a good thing to get attached to anything in *samsara* (worldly existence). It goes well to appreciate something nearby; but after a short time it shifts away. It becomes obvious that anything worldly cannot satisfy the mind.

Therefore, the established truth really appears to be that the mind is not satisfied with anything worldly it desires - the moral being that the mind is not suited to the world and the world is not suited to the mind.

When the mind gets to Paramatma then it becomes still, afterwards it does not desire anything else. Therefore it is certain that Paramatma is suitable for the mind. Therefore, attach it to that thing it is suited to.

४३

पतन से बचना चाहते हो तो पाप से बचो और पुन्य को बढ़ाओ

*

जो शास्त्रानुकूल पुरुषार्थ है वही पुण्य है और वही अभ्युदय, लौकिक उन्नति और मोक्ष का देने वाला है।

जो काम जितने पुरुषार्थ से होने वाला है उतने ही पुरुषार्थ से होता है। जितने पुण्य से भवसागर से पार होते हैं उतने पुण्य के बिना पार होना संभव नहीं। किसी को एक सेर जल की प्यास लगी हो तो वह एक छटांक जल से कैसे बुझ सकती है!

धार्मिक ग्रंथों के पढ़ने से पुण्य अवश्य होता है। गीता, रामायण आदि का पाठ पुण्य-प्रद होता है। परन्तु केवल पाठ से इतना पुण्य संग्रह नहीं होता जो भवसागर से पार कर दे।

धार्मिक ग्रंथों के पाठ का खंडन यहाँ नहीं कर रहे हैं। - पाठ तो करना चाहिये; परन्तु पाठ करके ही अपना कर्त्तव्य समाप्त नहीं मान

लेना चाहिये। जो उसमें लिखा है उसको कार्य रूप में लाने का प्रयत्न करना चाहिये, तभी उसका पूरा पूरा उपयोग माना जा सकता है और तभी विशेषरूप से पुण्य का संचय होगा। यदि पतन से बचना चाहते हो तो पाप से बचो, शास्त्र-विरुद्ध पुरुषार्थ मत करो; पाप से बचो और पुण्य करो, यही उन्नति का प्रकार है।

43

If someone has a thirst for a *seer* of water then how can that thirst be quenched with a sixteenth of a *seer* of water?

The effort that is made according to the *Shastra,* that is *punya* (meritous action) which gives rise to earthly advancement and *moksha* (salvation).

However much *purushartha* (willpower) is needed for a task, that much effort is to be made. However much *punya* (meritous action) is needed in order to cross *bhavasagar* (sea of experience), without that *punya* it is not possible to get to the other side. If someone has a thirst for a *sera* of water then how can their thirst be quenched with a *chatanka* (a sixteenth *sera*) of water?

Certainly, by reading holy books you can become holy. Studying the *Gita*, the *Ramayana* etc. gives *punya* (merit). But by reading, the amount of *punya* acquired is not enough to cross *bhavasagar* (the ocean of experience).

I am not negating the value of reading holy books - you should read; but by studying alone one's duty is not finished, you should obtain its value. You should make an effort to apply what is written, in the form of work. Only then can it be completely useful, and then abundant *punya* will be accumulated. If you wish to be saved from downfall then escape from sin, don't make any effort to do anything contrary to the *Shastra*; escape from sin and do meritous action - this the way to progress.

४४

मन को संसार में लगाओ पर इतना ही कि परमार्थ न बिगड़े

*

हमारा तात्पर्य यह नहीं है कि आप लोग सब विरक्त बन कर व्यवहार छोड़ दो और भगवान् के भजन में लग जाओ। व्यवहार करो, परन्तु उसी प्रकार से करो कि जिससे व्यवहार भी भद्दा न हो और परमार्थ भी न बिगड़े। मन को संसार में लगाया और कहीं अधिक लगा दिया तो फिर रोजगार घाटे का हो जायगा।

जैसा लिफाफा हो वैसा ही गोंद लगाना चाहिये। किसी छोटे लिफाफे में ज्यादा गोंद लगा दी जाय तो गोंद से लिफाफा भी गन्दा हो जायगा और गोंद तो व्यर्थ जायगा ही।

मन तो गोंद के समान है, जहाँ लगाओ वहीं चिपक जाता है। व्यवहार में मन को विचार पूर्वक ही लगाना चाहिये। किस स्थान में मन को कितना लगाया जाय, यह अवश्य ही विचार कर लेना चाहिये। मूल बात यही है कि व्यवहार में मन को कम लगाओ और परमार्थ में अधिक लगाओ।

व्यवहार में यह ध्यान रहे कि जहाँ तक हो सके शास्त्रानुकूल ही व्यवहार किया जाय और मन का बहुत थोड़ा अंश उसमें लगाया जाय। मन से भीतर-भीतर परमात्मा का चिन्तन करते लगोगे तो व्यवहार भी सुन्दर रहेगा और परमार्थ भी उज्ज्वल बनेगा।

44

Apply the mind to everyday affairs a little, and apply it a lot to *paramarth* (salvation).

Apply the mind to *samsara* (worldly existence) only so much that *paramarth* (salvation) is not spoiled. Our drift is not that all you people should become detached (from the world) and go and apply yourself to chanting *bhajan*. Do everyday affairs, but not the kind of everyday affairs that is unseemly and which spoils the chance of salvation. The mind was applied to worldly business but somewhere the mind was applied too much then again everyday affairs will suffer.

Just as you want an envelope to be "gummed". If you apply too much gum then the envelope will become filthy and the gum will have gone to no purpose.

Mind is similar to gum, it sticks wherever it is placed. In everyday affairs one's mind should be applied together with discernment. How much to apply the mind? In which place? You should take notice of this for certain. Essentially the meaning is really this; apply the mind to everyday affairs a little, and apply it a lot to *paramarth* (salvation).

In everyday affairs heed this, that wherever you can, do everyday affairs according to *Shastra* and do not apply a very large part of your mind. With the mind inside applied to thinking of Paramatma then everyday affairs will be beautiful too and you will also make clear *paramarth* (salvation).

४५

भगवान का भक्त दुखी नहीं रह सकता

*

हमने घोर जङ्गलों में वर्षों रहकर भगवान् की सर्वज्ञता और सर्वशक्तिमत्ता का अनुभव किया है। जहां कोई भी लौकिक प्रबन्ध नहीं होता, वहाँ भगवान् के भक्तों के लिये समय पर सब आवश्यक प्रबन्ध हो जाते हैं।

राज्कुमार भी अपने राज्य में किसी वस्तु का अभाव अनुभव कर सकता है? सर्व समर्थ भगवान् का भक्त त्रैलोक्य में कहीं भी रहेगा आनन्द से रहेगा। भला जो सर्वशक्तिमान् है वह अपने भक्त को दुःखी देख सकेगा!

अपनी श्रद्धा-भक्ति और विश्वास के द्वारा भगवान् के प्रति अनन्य होकर एक बार भगवान् की कृपा प्राप्त कर लेने की आवश्यकता है। फिर तो भगवान् स्वयं सब देख-भाल रखते हैं, उनसे प्रार्थना करने की आवश्यकता नहीं पड़ती।

जब पुत्र बीमार होता है तो वह पिता से प्रार्थना करे, तभी पिता उसकी चिकित्सा कराये - ऐसी बात नहीं है। पिता स्वयं ही अपने पुत्र को रोगी नहीं देख सकता, बिना कहे ही वह रोग को हटाने का प्रयत्न करता है। इसी प्रकार जो भगवान् को अपनाकर उनके हो जाते हैं, जो एक बार भगवान की कृपा खींच लेते है, उनके लिये भगवान् बिना प्रार्थना किये ही सब कुछ करते रहते हैं। यह अनुभूत सत्य है कि भगवान् का भक्त कभी दुःखी नहीं रह सकता।

45

How can the Omnipotent see his own devotees sorrowful?

The years when we lived in the inaccessible jungles we experienced the Omniscience and Omnipotence of Bhagwan. Wherever there were no arrangements for worldly needs, there necessary arrangement was made on time for devotees of Bhagwan.

A prince cannot experience lack of anything in his own kingdom. The devotees in the three worlds of the All-Capable Bhagwan (heaven, earth and lower region) will live with *ananda* (bliss). Well, how can the Omnipotent see his own devotees sorrowful?

One's own endless reverence, devotion and faith are the way to return to Bhagwan. It is necessary to gain the grace of Bhagwan once then afterwards Bhagwan sees and investigates all himself, it is not necessary to make a request of them.

When the son is unwell then it is not necessary for him to pray to his father for a remedy. The father cannot see his own son unwell. Without being asked he makes an effort to remove the disease. In this way, the one who comes to Bhagwan, who one time has taken pity, does everything for them without being asked. Honestly, this is experienced, that detovees of Bhagwan can never be unhappy.

४६

कुटुम्बियों की अश्रद्धा होने के पहले ही भगवान् की ओर झुक जाओ

*

निश्चय है कि वृद्धा-अवस्था में जब शरीर शिथिल हो जाता है और धन कमाने की शक्ति नहीं रह जाती तब कुटुम्बीजन और इष्ट मित्र भी उपेक्षा करने लगते हैं। भगवान् का सहारा लोगे तो फिर और किसी के सहारे की आवश्यकता नहीं पड़ेगी। फिर चाहे सारा संसार विमुख हो जाय तो भी कुछ बिगाड़ नहीं सकेगा।

और बात जो कुछ ऐसी है कि

"जापर कृपा राम की कोई।
तापर कृपा करें सब कोई॥"

जिस पर भगवान की कृपा हो जाती है उसको सभी के द्वारा सहयोग मिलने लगता है; क्योंकि भगवान तो सर्वशक्तिमान हैं। एक साधारण राजा जिस पर कृपा करने लगता है उसे राज्य भर के लोगों का सहयोग प्राप्त होने लगता है। इसी प्रकार जगन्नियन्ता सर्वशक्तिमान परमात्मा की ओर जो झुकता है, उसके अनुकूल जगत् की सारी शक्तियाँ बर्तने लगती हैं।

46

All give help to him on whom the grace of Bhagwan comes.

It is certain that when you are old your body will become weak and you will not have the strength to earn money, then householders and also beloved friends neglect you. People, if you get the support of Bhagwan then any other support will not be necessary. Afterwards if the whole of the worldly existence is indifferent to your needs, even then nothing can be spoiled. It is said something like this:-

"जापर कृपा राम की कोई।
तापर कृपा करें सब कोई॥"

*"japara kripa raama ki koi.
tapara kripa karen sab koi.."*
[*Shri Gayatri Chalisa* v26]

'All give help to him on whom the grace of Bhagwan comes.'

Because Bhagwan then is Almighty.

If one ordinary *raja* gives his favour, help will be gained from everyone in the kingdom. It is really in this manner of bowing in the direction of the controller of the world, Omnipotent Paramatma, that all favourable energies of the world are applied and put to use.

४७

भगवान् की प्रतिज्ञा अपने भक्तों के लिये - "मैं सब कुछ करने को तैयार हूँ"

अनन्याश्चिन्तयन्तो मां ये जनाः पर्युपासते।
तेषां नित्याभियुक्तानां योगक्षेमं वहाम्यहम्।

अनन्य भाव से मेरा चिन्तन करते हुए जो मनुष्य मेरी उपासना करते हैं उनके लिये योग और क्षेम का प्रबन्ध मैं स्वयं करता हूँ अर्थात् उन्हें जो अप्राप्त रहता है उसकी प्राप्ति कराता हूँ (योग), और जो उन्हें प्राप्त है उसका रक्षण (क्षेम) मैं ही करता हूँ - यह सर्वशक्तिमान भगवान की प्रतिज्ञा है। इस पर विश्वास करके भगवान के भजन में लगाओ।

आजकल लोग साधारण मनुष्यों का तो विश्वास कर लेते हैं, परन्तु भगवान के शब्दों पर विश्वास नहीं करते। जो सब कुछ कर सकने में समर्थ परमात्मा है उसकी प्रतिज्ञा पर विश्वास करो तो लोक-परलोक दोनों उज्ज्वल बनेगा।

विचार करो कि तुम तो सदा तुच्छातितुच्छ वस्तुओं का चिन्तन करते रहते हो, खेती के लिये मल-मूत्र मय खाद का चिन्तन करते हो, बन्दरों से वस्तु को बचाने के लिये कंटक को भजते हो तो जो मन कंटक और मल-मूत्र तक का चिन्तन करता है, वह यदि थोड़ी देर भगवान का भजन कर लेता है तो कोई बड़ी बात नहीं है, बड़ी बात तो यह है कि जो पूर्ण काम सर्वशक्तिमान भगवान हैं वह अपने भक्तों का चिन्तन करने के लिये तैयार हैं।

इस पर भी यदि मनुष्य भगवान की तरफ न झुके तो सिवाय दुर्भाग्य के और क्या कहा जा सकता है।

47

Consider this, that you are always thinking about insignificant things.

The promise of Bhagwan for his own devotees is 'I am ready to do everything.'

"अनन्याश्चिन्तयन्तो मां ये जनाः पर्युपासते ।
तेषां नित्याभियुक्तानां योगक्षेमें वहाभ्यहम् ॥"

*"ananyashchintayanto mam ye janah paryupasate.
tesham nityabhiyuktanam yogakshemem vahabhyaham."*
[*Bhagavad Gita* 9:22]

'That person who thinks about me with endless feeling, who does my worship, for him I myself make arrangements for his *yoga* and *kshema* (prosperity).' That is to say;

'I am obtaining that which he doesn't have, and I am protecting that prosperity he already has.'

- this is the promise of Omnipotent Bhagwan. On this have trust, apply yourself in chanting *bhajan* of Bhagwan.

Nowadays folk have trust in human beings, but they do not have trust in the words of Bhagwan. He who can do anything is Paramatma, trust on his promise then this world and the other will be made bright. Consider this that you are always thinking about insignificant things. For farming you are thinking about manure full of excrement and urine, with monkeys the thing you are serving for the purposes of defence is the thorn, then the mind is thinking of thorn, excrement and urine. If a little time is to be taken chanting *bhajan* of Bhagwan then it isn't any great news. The great news then is that Omnipotent Bhagwan, who is capable of doing all work, that he is ready to think of his own devotees.

Contrariwise, if a man does not bow to Bhagwan then it is more than bad luck! What can be said?

४८

रात्रि में सोने से पहले कुछ जप और ध्यान अवश्य करें

*

प्रातःकाल और दिन में जो पूजन, जप, ध्यान, आदि करते हो सो तो ठीक ही है, किन्तु रात्रि में सोने से पहले १०-१५ मिनट अपने इष्ट मंत्र का जप और इष्ट मूर्ति का ध्यान अवश्य करना चाहिये। इससे उपासना में जल्दी उन्नति होती है।

अँधेरे में आँख बन्द करके बैठ जाना चाहिये और मंत्र का जप तथा नेत्र बंदकर मन से अपने इष्ट का ध्यान करना चाहिये। उनके सम्पूर्ण शरीर पर नहीं, चरण में या मस्तक पर (मुख-मंडल पर) देखना चाहिये कि हमारे इष्टदेव हमारी और करुणा भरी, दयाभरी दृष्टि से देख रहे हैं। इष्ट की दृष्टि ही अपने काम की होती है। अपने इष्ट को आंख बन्द किए हुए नहीं देखना चाहिये। इस प्रकार अपनी ओर दयाभरी दृष्टि से देखते हुए इष्ट का हृदय में ध्यान करते हुए इष्ट मंत्र का जप करते रहना चाहिये। इससे इष्ट के प्रति दृढ़ता बढ़ेगी और यदि मन ने दृढ़ता के साथ इष्ट को पकड़ लिया तो अन्त में यही निष्ठाकाम आयेगी। इसी के बल पर संसार-सागर से पार हो जाओगे।

48

In darkness (nighttime) **you should sit with eye closed and do *japa* of the *mantra***

At daybreak and in the day do that *puja* (ritual worship), *japa* and *dhyaana* (meditation) etc. which is appropriate, but at night you should certainly do 10-15 minutes of *japa* (repetition) of the *ishta mantra* and *dhyaana* of the *ishta murti* (desired form) before sleeping. Rapid advancement occurs by this *upasana* (sitting near / devout meditation).

In darkness (nighttime) you should sit with eyes closed and do *japa* of the *mantra*, and in the same way with eyes closed you should do *dhyaana* of the *ishta* with the mind. Not on their whole body, you should look on the foot or on the mouth area of the head, seeing our favourite *ishta* full of compassion, looking infused with tenderness. The vision of the *ishta* becomes one's own desire. You should not envisage the eye of the *ishta* to be closed. This manner of having seen the vision of the infusion of tenderness, doing *dhyaana* of the *ishta* in the heart, you should remain doing *japa* of the *ishta mantra*. From this, the image of the *ishta* will grow and provided that the mind gets strengthened and held with the *ishta* then in the end it will stay in this condition. You will be going across the ocean of *samsara* (worldliness) on the strength of this.

४९

इन्द्रियों के भोग-विलास में जो निमग्न रहता है वह किसी काम का नहीं रह जाता

*

जितना सत्संग करो, उससे अधिक कुसंग को त्यागो

जिस भूमि से जल हमेशा बहता रहता है वह किसी काम की नहीं रह जाती। बहते हुए जल को रोक कर, बाँधकर, उस भूमि को बहुत उपजाऊ बना लेते हैं, उसी प्रकार जिसकी इन्द्रियों में सदा विषयों का प्रवाह जारी रहता है वह बिल्कुल बेकाम हो जाता है, किसी काम का नहीं रहता - न वह अपना ही कुछ उत्थान कर सकता है और न दूसरों का ही उससे कुछ उपकार हो सकता है।

विषयोपभोग से विषय-चिन्तन अधिक हानिकर है। शास्त्रानुकूल मर्यादानुसार विषय-भोग किया जाय तो उससे उतनी हानि की शका नहीं होती। किन्तु यदि भाग-वासना से प्रेरित होकर मन को सदा विषय-चिन्तन में लगाये रहोगे तो अन्तःकरण दुर्बल पड़ जायगा और मानसिक शक्ति क्षीण होती जायगी, जीवन भार हो जायगा और लोक-परलोक कहीं के न रहोगे। इसलिये विषयों से बचो, परन्तु उससे अधिक मन को विषयों से बचाना आवश्यक है।

"मन के हारे हार है, मन के जीते जीत।"

मन यदि पराजित हो गया, मन पर यदि विषयों का कब्ज़ा हो गया, तो जीवन ही विषयाधीन हो जायगा। विपयाधीन जीवन, परवश जीवन, दुःखद ही रहता है। यदि विषय मन के अधीन रहेगा तो विषयों को जीतने वाला मन, विजेता की भांति सदा आनन्द में रहता है। इसलिये विजेता बनकर रहो, स्वतन्त्र रहो, स्वतन्त्रता में ही जीवन की सार्थकता है।

अतः जितना साक्षात् विषयों से बचो, उससे अधिक विषयों के चिन्तन से मन को बचाओ।

49

'Loss of the mind is defeat, mastery of the mind is success.'

With the land always flowing with water, there can be no working it. By restraining the flow of the water, a dam, that land is made to be very productive. In this way if the senses are always remaining in the running stream of worldly pleasures then all become idle, no work is done - he cannot make any progress himself nor can be of any benefit to others. Thinking about things enjoyed by the senses is more detrimental. If anything is enjoyed within the limits applied by the *Shastra* then there is no risk of that much loss. But if a portion of the mind is directed to longing, you will remained attached to constantly thinking of worldly pleasure, then the inner self becomes spiritless and the strength of the mind will become feeble - life will become a burden and you will not have this world or the other world. Therefore refrain from things to be perceived by the senses, but more than that, it is necessary to save the mind from things perceived by the senses.

"मन के हारे हार है मन के जीते जीत।"

"mana ke hare hara hai. mana ke jite jita."
'Loss of the mind is defeat, mastery of the mind is success.'

If the mind becomes overcome, if the mind becomomes grasped by worldly pleasures, then really the life will become dependent on things perceived by the senses. Life dependent on anything perceived by the senses, a subservient life, indeed is giving trouble. If worldly pleasure will remain subordinate to the mind, then worldly pleasures are conquered. In that way the mind is a conqueror, always remaining in *ananda* (bliss). Therefore become victorious, be independent, really in independence living has a meaning.

Therefore escape from the presence as much worldly pleasures, and more, defend yourself from thinking of worldly pleasures.

५०

मन की प्रवृत्ति जिधर होती है, वह स्वयं रास्ता निकाल लेता है

*

मन कों सदा पवित्र रखना आवश्यक है

सारी बात मन के ऊपर ही निर्भर है। मन जैसा चाहता है वैसा ही मनुष्य कार्य करता है। प्रवृत्त-निवृत्ति सब कुछ मन पर ही निर्भर है। विहित-अविहित कोई भी कैसा कार्य हो, यदि मन ने करने का निश्चय कर लिया तो वह उसका रास्ता निकाल ही लेता है। मन जितना पवित्र होगा, प्रवृत्ति उतनी ही पवित्र होगी और कार्य उतने ही बलशाली और स्थायी होंगे। मन जितना मलिन और अपवित्र होगा, प्रवृत्ति भी उतनी ही दूषित होगी और कार्य भी उतने स्वल्प प्रभावशाली तथा उतने ही अस्थायी महत्व के होंगे।

इसीलिये लौकिक और पारलौकिक सब प्रकार की उन्नति के लिये मन को पवित्र रखना और उसकी पवित्रता रखना और उसकी पवित्रता बढ़ाते रहना आवश्यक है। इसी के लिये सत्संग करना और कुसंग से बचना, नित्य स्वाध्याय करना, आहार शुद्धि का ध्यान रखना, भगवान् का भजन-पूजन व जप ध्यान करना, सत्य व अहिंसा आदि का पालन करना, सदाचार का पालन करना और अपने को सदा मर्यादा के अन्दर ही रखना आवश्यक है।

50

Man acts according to the desire of the mind.

Wherever the mind is inclined to, it is drawn on that path by itself. It is necessary that the mind is always kept pure, all speech is dependent of the mind. Man acts according to the desire on the mind. Whether engaged in work or repose, everything is dependent on the mind. Any action, whether approved of or forbidden, if the mind is resolved then on that path it will be drawn. As pure as the mind will be, the inclination will be to purity and that work will be powerful and steady. However much the mind is filthy and impure, the inclination will be that corrupted too and that work will have very little influence and will be of temporary importance.

Therefore for all kinds of progress in this world and the next world keep the mind pure and to keep spiritual too, it is necessary to maximise spirituality. For this do *satsang* (keep the company of good men) and avoid *kusang* (the company of evil men)), regularly study the *Vedas*, pay attention to eating pure food, chant *bhajan* of Bhagwan, do *puja* and do *japa* meditation, preserve truth and *ahimsa* (non-violence, inoffensiveness, benevolence) etc., cherish virtue and it is necessary to always keep within one's own code of conduct.

५१

राग ही सर्वनर्थ का मूल है

*

ज्ञानी में राग नहीं रहता, अज्ञानी में राग रहता है। ज्ञानी का व्यवहार राग रहित होकर प्रारब्धानुसार चलता है और अज्ञानी का भी व्यवहार प्रारब्धानुसार ही चलता है; पर उसका उसमें राग रहता है क्योंकि अज्ञानी का चिन्ह राग माना गया है। राग ही जन्म-

मरण की शृंखला में जीव को बाँधे रहता है। राग न रहने से जीव मुक्त हो जाता है। तथा -

'वीतरागजन्मादर्शनात्'

यह रोग शास्त्र का सूत्र है - अर्थात् राग नष्ट हो जाने से फिर जन्म नहीं होता। इसलिये महाबन्धनकारी सर्वानर्थ के मूल 'राग' को हटाने का प्रयत्न करो। संसार से राग तभी हटेगा जब परमात्मा की ओर झुकगे।

51

At whatever time there is attachment to worldly life then at the same moment bow in the direction of Paramatma.

In the *gyaani* (one possessing religious wisdom) no *raaga* (attachment) remains. In ignorance attachment remains. The everyday affairs of the *gyaani* commences and proceeds without *raaga* (attachment) and the everyday affairs of the ignorant one also commences; but is attached to it because that has been the mark of the ignorant. Really *raaga* (attachment) remains the fetter that fastens a soul to birth and death. When the attachment does not remain the soul becomes liberated. In the same way as:-

"वीतरागजनादर्शनात्"

"vitaraagajanaadarshanaat"

This is a *sutra* of the *Rog Shastra* (*roga* = disease) - that is to say;

'After *raaga* (attachment) becomes destroyed then there is no birth.'

Therefore being greatly attached is the root of destruction - make an effort to remove *"raga"* (attachment). At whatever time there is attachment to worldly life then at the same moment bow in the direction of Paramatma.

५२

विघ्नों के भय से मार्ग नहीं छोड़ना चाहिये
गिरने का कोई भय नहीं, भगवान् रक्षा करेंगे

भगवान को जान लेने के बाद, फिर कोई वस्तु जानने योग्य नहीं रह जाती। एक बार भगवत्तत्व का रसास्वादन हो गया कि फिर वृत्ति अन्यत्र कहीं विषयों में फँस नहीं सकती। कोई राजा कैसे दो गाँव की जमींदारी की इच्छा कर सकता है। जो आनन्द समुद्र में अवगाहन कर रहा है वह क्षणिका - नन्द-विषयानन्द - के लिये कैसे इच्छा करेगा? लोग कहते हैं - 'अमुक महात्मा गिर गये, अमुक बड़े महर्षि गिर गये'। परन्तु छोटे-बड़े की पहचान क्या है? महात्मा कभी नहीं गिरे और न गिर ही सकते हैं, गिरते हैं साधक लोग, जिन्हें अभी वस्तु की प्राप्ति नहीं हुई है। किन्तु जिन्हें भगवान् का साक्षात्कार हो गया है, उनकी वृत्ति कभी विषयानन्द के लिये लालायित नहीं हो सकती। महात्मापन और बड़ापन वृत्ति में होता है। किसी की निष्ठा को अन्य कोई नहीं जान सकता - तह स्वसंवेद्य विषय है।

भगवान् ने कहा है कि मेरी त्रिगुणात्मिका माया दुरत्यय है अर्थात पार करने के लिये कठिन है। परन्तु जो मेरी शरण आते है वे मेरी इस दुरत्यय माया को भी पार कर जाते है -

"दैवी ह्येषा गुणमयी मम माया दुरत्यया।
मामेव ये प्रपद्यन्ते मायामेतां तरन्ति ते॥"

अतः विघ्नों के भय से मार्ग नहीम् छोड़ना चाहिये। भगवान सब प्रकार से रक्षा करते हुए अपने समीप बुला लेते हैं। गिरने-गिराने का डर नहीं है, मार्ग पर चलते जाओ।

52

People say:- 'So-and-so *mahatma* had fallen, so-and-so *maharshi* had fallen.'

After taking knowledge of Bhagwan, then nothing remains which is fit to be known. Once the Bhagavat *tatva* (essence of the divine) has been tasted then you cannot be trapped in things elsewhere. How can any *raja* (king) desire to be a landlord of a couple of villages? He who is immersed in the ocean of *ananda* (bliss), how can he desire the happiness of transitory pleasures of things? People say:- 'So-and-so *mahatma* (great soul) had fallen, so-and-so *maharshi* (great *rishi*) had fallen.' But how is small or great recognised? A *mahatma* never fell and really cannot fall. Those *sadhaka* people (ones engaged in spiritual achievement) are to fall, those who right now have not been getting something. But those who have been perceiving Bhagwan, they are never in the condition of wishing eagerly for the joy of anything perceived by the senses. Being a *mahatma* and being great is to be in that condition. Nobody else can know the certainty of this, it is intelligible only to oneself.

Bhagwan has said that; 'It is difficult to cross over the *maya* (delusion) of the three *guna* (qualities) of myself', that is to say that; 'It is difficult to get to the other side. But whoever comes to my shelter they will get over this *maya duratyaya* (the delusion that is difficult to cross).'

"दैवी ह्येषाँ गुणमयी मम माया दुरत्यया ।
मामेव ये प्रपद्यन्ते मायामेतां तरन्ति ते ॥"

*" daivii dyeshaan gunamayii mama maaya duratyayaa.
maameva ye prapadyante maayaametaam taranti te. "*
[*Bhagavad Gita* 7:14]

'Verily, this *maya* of mine,
made of *gunas,* is difficult to cross over,
they who take refuge in me will cross over.'

Therefore you should not forsake the path out of fears. Bhagwan protects from all manner of things and invites you near to him.

Without fear of falling, go proceed on the way.

५३

प्रवृत्ति को अशुभ से रोक कर शुभ में लगाना - यही मुख्य पुरुषार्थ है

अशुभ कर्मों में प्रवृत्ति न हो और शुभ कर्मों में ही प्रवृत्ति रहे, यही मुख्य पुरुषर्थ है। अशुभ वासनायें उठें तो मन को जप, कीर्तन या स्वाध्याय तोत्र या भगवच्चरित पाठ आदि में लगा देना चाहिये। यहीं उपनिषद् का सिद्धन्त है -

शुभाशुभाभ्यां मार्गाभ्यां वहन्ति वासना सरित।
पौरुषेण प्रयत्नेन योजनीया शुभो पथि ॥

मुक्तिकोपनिषत्।

वासना रूपी नदी शुभ और अशुभ दो मार्गों से बहती है। अपने पुरुषार्थ के द्वारा प्रयत्न करके उसे शुभ मार्ग में ही बहाना चाहिये। पुरुषार्थ का स्वरूप यही है कि जब कोई अशुभ वासना उठे तो मन को दुसरे तरफ लगाओ या फिर उस कार्य को टालने का प्रयत्न करो। अभी थोड़ी देर में कर लेंगे, फिर कर लेंगे, कल कर लेंगे - इस प्रकार मन को समझाते हुए कुछ समय बिता दो तो वह वासना अवश्य ही शिथिल पड़ जायगी। यदि कोई शुभ वासना मन में उठे तो जल्दी से जल्दी उसमें प्रवृक्त होने का यत्न करो। हो सके तो कुछ न कुछ उसी समय कार्यारम्भ कर दो।

अशुभ वासनायें मन में उठे तो उन्हें रोकना और किसी तरह उसमें प्रवृत्त न होना और शुभवासना उठें तो यथाशीघ्र प्रवृत्त होने का प्रयत्न करना, यही पुरुषार्थ है।

53

That the mind is not inclined towards bad actions and that it flows toward good actions - this is really the man's primary effort.

That the mind is not inclined towards bad actions and that it flows toward good actions - this is really the man's primary effort. If bad desires will arise then you should apply the mind to *japa* (silent repetition of a *mantra*), *kirtana* (singing in loud tone in praise of God) or *swadhyaya*, study of *stotra* or accounts of Bhagwan. This is the doctrine of the *Upanishad*:-

"शुभाशुभाभ्यां मार्गाभ्यां वहन्ति वासना सरित ।
पौरुषेण प्रयत्नेन योजनीया शुभो पथि ॥"

*"shubhaashubhaabhyam maargaabhyaam vahanti vaasanaa sarita.
paurushena prayatnena yojaniiya shubho pathi."*
[*Muktika Upanishad* 2:5]

Good and bad impressions take the form of a river flowing with two ways. By way of exerting one's own effort you should really cause to flow in the way of happiness. The real form of *purushartha* (willpower) is really this, that when any bad desires arise then apply the mind in the other direction or again put aside any effort to do that action. 'I will take this after a little while', 'Afterwards I will take', 'Tomorrow I will take' - Having been thinking in this manner, give a little time, then this desire very certainly will become weak. If any good thought arises in the mind then quickly, quickly make an effort to engage in the undertaking. You can then start the work in very little time.

If bad desires arise in the mind then stop them and by any means avoid doing that action, and if good desires arise then quickly, in whatever manner, make an effort to engage in the action, this is *purshartha* (exertion, the object of a man's creation and existence).

५४

परमात्मा से विमुख हो रहे हों - इसी से नाना प्रकार की विपत्तियाँ आ रही हैं

जिसके राज्य में रहो उसका नियम पालन करने से ही सुख-शान्ति पूर्वक रह सकते हो। राजा की आज्ञा का उल्लंधन करोगे तो दण्ड अवश्य मिलेगा। समस्त ब्रह्माण्ड का स्वामी ब्रह्माण्डनायक परमात्मा ही है। उसकी इच्छा के विरुद्ध आचरण करोगे तो दण्ड के भागी बनोगे। आजकल लोग परमात्मा से विमुख हो रहे हैं इसी से अशान्ति, असंतोष और दुःख दिनोंदिन बड़ते ही जा रहे हैं।

ईश्वरीय नियम सब के लिये समान रूप से कल्याणकारी है। जो जितनी उत्तमता से उनका पालन करता है उसको उतनी ही अधिक सुख-शान्ति का अनुभव होता है। वेदशास्त्र ही सर्व कल्याणकारी पर्मात्मा का विधान है। उसी का पालन करने से सर्वविधि उन्नति सम्भव है। वेदशास्त्रों में ऐसे ही नियमों का उल्लेख है जिनके पालन से मनुष्य अपनी शक्ति, सामर्थ्य, ज्ञान और आनन्द की इतनी वृद्धि कर सकता है कि जिसका कोई अन्त नहीं।

जब तुम हीरे का व्यापार कर सकते हो तो कोयले की दलाली करके क्यों हाथ काला करते हो? जब तुम परमात्मा की विधिवत् आराधना करके अनन्त आनन्द की प्राप्ति कर सकते हो तो इस क्षणभंगुर इन्द्रिय सुखों के साधन संग्रह करने में क्योम् अहर्निश परेशान हो? थोड़ा विचार-शक्ति से काम लो; काल के प्रवाह में आँख बन्द करके मत वह चलो। दिन-रात तो अपने समय पर बीतते जायेंगे, परन्तु तुम्हें एक-एक क्षण का दुरुपयोग करके अपनी उन्नति करनी है। अतः परमात्मपरायण रह कर स्वधर्मानुकूल आचरण करो - यही सर्वोन्नति का मार्ग है।

54

When you can be in the diamond business then why are you blackening the hand in the brokerage of coal?

From being indifferently disposed towards Paramatma many kinds of difficulties are coming. Only by keeping the rules of he whose kingdom you live in can you be happy and peaceful. If you will contravene the commands of the *raja* (king) then certainly you will meet with the stick (you will be punished). The master of the whole universe is really Paramatma. If you will behave contrary to his wishes then you will be prepared to flee the stick (punishment). Nowadays people are being indifferent with Paramatma, only from this are anxiety, dissatisfaction and pain going to increase day after day.

The *ishvariya niyama* (divine regulation) is for the equal happiness of all. However much you preserve Them to the best, that much happiness and peace your will experience. Really the *Veda Shastra* is the regulation of Paramatma for all happiness. By protecting Them all manner of progress is possible. By protecting all the regulations in the *Veda Shastras* man's own strength, ability, knowledge and pleasure can be increased so much, almost without end.

When you can be in the diamond business then why are you blackening the hand in the brokerage of coal? When you regularly worship Paramatma you can gain unlimited *ananda* (bliss), so why are you troubled day and night devoted to collecting these sensory sense pleasures? Take the task with a little power of discernment; don't proceed in the current of time with eyes closed. Day and night then, one's own time will pass; but if you misapply even a moment it is your own evolution. Consequently, conduct yourself devotedly to Paramatma, behaving according to one's own *dharma* (religion, duty) - this is really the way to all progress.

५५

प्रारब्ध से पुरुषार्थ बलवान् है

पिछला किया हुआ पुरुषार्थ ही आज तुम्हारे सामने प्रारब्ध बनकर आ रहा है। बासी पुरुषार्थ ही ताजा प्रारब्ध है। यदि आज कुछ बनाकर रख लोगे तभी तो कल के लिये वह बासी होगा। जो चीज आज बनाओगे वही कल तुम्हारे सामने आयेगी; जो पहले बनाया है वही आज सामने आ रहा है और जो आज बनाओगे वही भविष्य में सामने आयेगा। आज जो सुख-दुख सामने आ रहा है वह पूर्व के शुभाशुभ कर्मों का ही फल है। अब ऐसा करो कि भविष्य के लिये दुःख की सामग्री न तैयार हो। यह निश्चय है कि जो कर्म करोगे उसका फल भोगना ही पड़ेगा। विहित कर्मों, शुभ कर्म करोगे तो उसका फल सुख होगा और अविहिताचरण करोगे तो परिणाम में दुःख सामने आयेगा।

यदि चाहते हो कि आगे प्रारब्ध अच्छा बने तो इस समय अपने पुरुषार्थ को संभालो, उत्तम कार्य करो। किसके लिये क्या उत्तम है, यह शास्त्र-दृष्टि से निश्चय करो। अपने अधिकारानुसार शुभ कर्मों में प्रवृत्त रहोगे तो वर्तमान में शान्ति-सन्तोष की वृद्धि होगी और भविष्य के लिये उत्तम प्रारब्ध का निर्माण होगा।

इस समय जो शुभाशुभ तुम्हारे सामने आ रहा है वह निश्चय ही तुम्हारा प्रारब्ध है जो भोग रूप में उपस्थित है। परन्तु ऐसा नहीं कि जो आये सब भोगते जाओ। प्रारब्ध को भी विचार पूर्वक ही भोगना उचित है। यदि मद्य-मांस सामने आये तो उसे किसी पुराने पाप-कर्म का फल समझ कर विवेक के द्वारा उसे हटाओ, उसे मत स्वीकार करो और उस पाप-फल को जप-तप के द्वारा नष्ट करो।

सिद्धान्त है कि 'जपतो नास्ति पातकम्'।

जप करने से पाप नष्ट हो जाते हैं। इसलिये विहित प्रारब्ध को भोगो और अविहित को जप-तप से नष्ट करो। इस प्रकार विवेक से व्यवहार करोगे तो तरक्की करते जाओगे और यदि व्यवहार में सतर्क न रहे तो कूकर-शूकर की तरह कीचड़ में नीचे गिर जाओगे।

55

Now do such actions that do not become baggage for future suffering.

The human effort that is begun is strong. That effort that you made in the past is today coming in front of you. Stale *purushartha* (willpower) is begun afresh. People, for this reason if today you make anything then this will be stale tomorrow. Whatever thing you will make today, that very same thing will come in front of you tomorrow; that which was made before, that is what is coming in front of you; and that which you are making today will come in front of you in the future. Today that happiness and/or pain is coming in front of you - this is really the fruits of those previous good and evil actions. Now do such actions that do not become baggage for future suffering. This is certain you will undergo the fruits of the actions that you will do. Permitted actions - you will do good action - then the fruit will be happiness and if you will do actions forbidden by law then in consequence suffering will come before you.

If you desire that good is prepared for the future then at this time make an effort to help yourself. Do the best works. What is for the best? From looking at the *Shastras* - do that! If you will be inclined to good works according to your own occupation then you will have happiness and satisfaction in the present and be creating the best destiny for the future. That pleasantness and/or unpleasantness that is coming in front of you, that is certainly your destiny in the present form of experience. But it is not that you experience whatever comes. Consider before what is reasonable to endure. If wine and meat are put in front of you then understand this to be the fruit of any old evil *karma*. By this way of reasoning push it away, do not accept that, and destroy that fruit of sin by way of *japa* (silent repetition of a *mantra*) and *tapa* (penance). The principle is that;

"जपतो नास्ति पातकम्"

"japato naasti paatakam"
'Sins become destroyed by doing *japa*.'

Therefore, experience the arranged good destiny and that destiny which was caused by breaking the law, destroy it by *japa* and *tapa*. If by this kind of reasoning you will do your everyday affairs then you will advance but if you are not careful then you will sink down in the mud like a dog or a wild hog.

५६

त्यागी और उदार तो बहुत हैं किन्तु रागी और कृपण बनने का प्रयत्न करो

सबसे बड़ा त्यागी वही माना जा सकता है जिसने सबसे बड़ी वस्तु का त्याग किया हो। संसार में सबसे बड़ी वस्तु परमात्मा है। परमात्मा को जो त्यागे बैठे हैं, भगवान् से जो विमुख हैं, वे ही सबसे बड़े त्यागी हैं। उदार उसको कहा जाता है जो दूसरे के लिये कार्य करता है और कृपण वह है जो अपने लिये ही करता है। जो कमाई कर करके सब अपने नाम से बैंकों में इकठ्ठा करता जाता है वही कृपण कहलाता है।

सच्चा रागी वह है जिसकी वृत्ति रागास्पद पदार्थ से हटती नहीं है। मन जहाँ लगा है वहाँ से उठे नहीं, यही राग का लक्षण है। ऐसा राग तो परम रागास्पद पदार्थ परमात्मा में ही होता है। जिसका मन भगवान में लग गया हो और फिर वहाँ से उसका वृत्यन्तर न होता हो-वही सच्चा रागी है, ऐसे रागी बनो। संसार के

त्याग की आवश्यकता नहीं है, परमात्मा के प्रति राग बड़ाओ और सच्चे रागी बनो।

जो लोग हमेशा संसारी कार्यों में ही लगे रहते हैं वे ही वास्तव में उदार हैं, क्योंकि उन्होंने जो किया वह सब दूसरों के काम आयेगा, उन्के साथ कुछ नहीं जायगा। और जो लोग दान, धर्म, जप, तप, आदि करके पुण्य संग्रह करते हैं वे ही 'वास्तव में कृपण' कहे जा सकते हैं। क्योंकि यहाँ जो कुछ वे कर रहे हैं उसका सब फल वे अपने नाम 'पार्सल किये दे रहे हैं। आगे उन्हें ही वह प्राप्त होगा - और दूसरे को नहीं। इस प्रकार पुण्यात्मा लोगों को ही वास्तव में कृपण कहा जा सकता है। ऐसे कृपण बनो तो लोक में भी यश होगा और परलोक में भी उत्तम गति प्राप्त होगी, यही वेद शास्त्र का सिद्धान्त है।

56

There are many *tyaagi* and there are also many that are generous; but make an effort to be attached and stingy!

There are many *tyaagi* (unattached renunciates) and there are also many who are generous; but make an effort to be attached and stingy! The best *tyaagi* of all is he who can become unattached to the best thing of all. In *samsara* (worldly existence) the best thing of all is Paramatma. The one who sits abandoning Paramatma, who is indifferent to Bhagwan, they are the greatest *tyaagi* of all! It is said that he is generous who does work for others and a skinflint is one who only works for himself. He who works to accumulate in the banks under his own name is said to be stingy.

True attachment is that state where there is no getting out of the way of that to which one is attached. The mind, wherever it is attached, from there it is not arising, this is really the characteristic of attachment. Such attachment, then to the best place of attachment, is really in Paramatma. He whose mind has become attached to Bhagwan and no occurrence can take from there - that is really attachment, so be a *raagi* (attached). Abandoning *samsara* (worldly existence) is not necessary. Increase attachment to the likeness of Paramatma and become a true *raagi*.

Those people who are always attached to worldly works, in truth they are generous, since the work they do will come for all others, none will go to them. Besides, those people who are giving, doing the *dharma* (duty), practising *japa* (repetition of *mantra*), doing *tapa* (penance) etc., are collecting *punya* (meritous action). In truth they can really be called stingy because all fruits of anything they are doing here are made into a *"parcel"* in their own name, in the future only they will obtain it - nobody else. In this manner those people who are said to be *punyatma* (pious) in truth can be said to be stingy. Thus become a skinflint, then you will be celebrated in this world and will get the Supreme state in the other world, this is really the principle of *Veda Shastra*.

५७

एक भगवान् को मजबूती से पकड़ो तो अनेक की खुशामद नहीं करनी पड़ेगी

अपना प्रधान-इष्ट सर्व-समर्थ सुख-स्वरूप भगवान् को बनाओ और उनके प्रति अनन्यता का भाव रखो तो कभी भी किसी वस्तु की कमी नहीं रहेगी। एक को मजबूती से पकड़ लो तो अनेक की खुशामद करने से बच जाओगे, नहीं तो लावारसी कुत्ते की तरह दरवाजे-दरवाजे पूंछ हिलाते फिरोगे और अपना अमूल्य जीवन भोजन-वस्त्र में ही समाप्त कर दोगे। लावारिस कुत्ता रोटी तो कहीं-कहीं पाता भी है, पर डंडे सब जगह खाता है। जिसने अपना कोई इष्ट नहीं बनाया वह हर समय अनाथ सा ही रहता है, उसे चाहे धन-दौलत कितनी भी मिल जाय।

इष्ट के प्रति अनन्य होने का तात्पर्य यह है कि इष्ट की आराधना के समय में यदि कोई व्यावहारिक कार्य आ जाय तो उसकी उपेक्षा कर दो, पर आराधना से उठो मत। अपने जीवन में परमार्थ को मुख्य और व्यवहार को गौड़ समझो। भगवान् की प्रतिज्ञा पर विश्वास करो तो संसार और परलोक दोनों में ही सिर ऊँचा रहेगा।

"नन्याश्चिन्तयन्तो मां ये जनाः पर्युपासते।
तेषां नित्याभियुक्तानां योगक्षेमं वहाम्यहम्॥"

अर्थात् जो अनन्य भाव से मेरा चिन्तन करते हैं उनके लिये योग (अप्राप्त की प्राप्ति) और क्षेम (प्राप्त वस्तु का रक्षण) मैं करता हूँ - यह भगवान् की प्रतिज्ञा है। इस पर विश्वास करके सदा के लिये सुखी हो जाओ।

57

In one's own life, most important is *paramarth*, understand that everyday business is secondary.

Make the All-Capable Blissful form of Bhagwan one's chief *ishta* (desired god) and place unbounded feeling on their image, then there will never be a miserly deficiency of anything. With firmness seize the One then you will escape from flattery of the many. If not then you will turn from door-to-door like a stray dog and one's own priceless life will be given over only to getting food and clothing. At some places the stray dog obtains *roti* (flat bread), but at all places it endures the *dande* (stick). He who has not made any *ishta* (chosen god), all that time he is an ownerless orphan, [no matter] however much wealth he wishes, however much he gets.

The significance of endless [attention] to the *ishta* is this, that at the time of worship of the *ishta*, if any everyday issue arises then disregard it. Do not get up from the worship. In one's own life, most important is *paramarth* ('best wealth', salvation), understand that everyday business is secondary. Trust on Bhagwan's promise then you will hold the head up high in both the worldly existence and the other world:-

"नन्याश्चिन्तयन्तो मां ये जनाः पर्युपासते ।
तेषां नित्याभियुक्तानां योगक्षेमं वहाम्यहम् ॥"

"nanyaashchintayanto maam ye janaah paryupaasate.
teshaam nityaabhiyuktaanaam yogakshemam vahaamyaham."
[*Bhagavad Gita* 9:22]

That is to say;

'He who with unbounded feeling thinks of me, he obtains *yoga* (unity) - gains the thing unobtained and protection for arrangements - which I am doing.'

This is the promise of Bhagwan. Having trust in this, go and be happy always!

५८

संसार जैसा है वैसा ही पड़ा रहेगा
जब तक यहाँ हो अपना काम बना लो

बड़े-बड़े प्रतापी और पुरुषार्थशील महारथी हुये, पर सब काल-कवल हो गये, आज किसी का पता नहीं। पर यह संसार ज्यों का त्यों प्रवाह रूप से चला जा रहा है। बुद्धिमानी इसी में है कि जब तक यहाँ हो तब तक अपना काम बना लो। अपने जीवन का लक्ष्य जो सच्चिदानन्दमय परमात्मा की प्राप्ति है, उसे किसी प्रकार पूरा करने का प्रयत्न करो। संसार के चक्कर में अधिक मत रहो, क्योंकि यह जैसा है वैसा ही चलेगा, व्यर्थ में मृग-तृष्णा बड़ाकर अपने हाथों से अपनी होली मत जलाओ।

अपने घर की सफाई न करके औरों के मकानों में झाड़ू देते फिरो तो यह कहाँ की बुद्धिमानी है। पहले अपना काम बना लो, फिर औरों के काम में मदद करो। पहले वह पूरा कर लो जिसके लिये संसार में आये हो। अपना काम न किया और दूसरों के चक्कर में अपना समय व्यर्थ खोते रहे तो अन्त में पछताना ही पड़ेगा। बुद्धिमानी वही है कि जिससे लोक और परलोक दोनों उत्तम बने। यह तभी होगा जब परमार्थ को अपने जीवन का मुख्य कार्य मानोगे। परमार्थ को मुख्य मानो और गौड़ रूप से संसार का शिष्टाचार चलाओ। समय से भजन, पूजन, ध्यान, आराधन करो और मन से उसे ही अपना मुख्य कार्य मानों। उससे समय निकालकर संसार का शिष्टाचार निबाहो तो कुछ काम बनेगा, नहीं तो धोखा ही धोखा है।

58

First do your own work, then help in the work of others.

There have been very great warriors who were people of character and powerful too, but all have become a morsel of time, there is no sign of any of them now. But this *samsara* (worldly existence) is proceeding, going on and resembling a stream. It is only intelligent that whilst you are here you get on with your own work. The objective of one's life is in acquiring Parmatma who is *sachchidanandamaya* (Truly Blissfully Conscious) - make an effort to complete this by any means. Don't put too much in the wheel of *samsara*, because really it will proceed in the manner it does, there is no purpose of producing a mirage - don't light one's own Holi fire with one's own hand (thus burning oneself).

Where is the intelligence in sweeping the houses of others but not cleaning one's own house? First do your own work, then help in the work of others. Firstly complete the work for which you have come in *samsara* (worldly existence). If you do not perform your own everyday affairs but squander your time to no purpose then in the end you will only fall to regretting. It is really intelligent that both this world and the other are made the best. This will be so when you accept the principal work of one's life is for *paramarth* ('best wealth', salvation). Accept that *paramarth* is the most important and secondarily proceed with proper behaviour in *samsara*. With the time chanting *bhajan*, doing *puja*, doing *dhyaana* (meditation), doing worship, and accept them to be one's principal work. Find time for proper behaviour in *samsara*, then fulfil some desire, if not it is only deception.

५९

मनुष्य-जन्म दुर्लभ है, इसे सार्थक बनाओ

*

अभी तक जो हुआ सो हुआ अब आगे चेत जाओ

*

हीरे को साग के भाव न बेचो

चौरासी लक्ष योनियाँ भोगने के बाद यह दुर्लभ मनुष्य-शरीर प्राप्त हुआ है; इसे व्यर्थ न जाने दो। जीवन का एक-एक क्षण बहुत मूल्यवान है। यदि इसकी कीमत नहीं समझी? तो फिर सिवाय रोने के और कुछ हाथ नहीं रहेगा।

मनुष्य हो, इसलिये विहिताविहित को विचारने की शक्ति है और बड़ा से बड़ा पुरुषार्थ कर सकते हो। अपने को कमजोर और गिरा हुआ मत मानो। अभी तक जो हुआ, उसे समझ लो कि अनजान में हुआ। पर अब सावधान हो जाओ, मनुष्योचित कर्तव्य-पालन में लग जाओ। तुम स्वयं समझते हो कि क्या अच्छा है और क्या बुरा है। अच्छे को अपनाओ और बुरे को छोड़ो।

मनुष्य होकर यदि परमात्मा को न जान पाये तो समझ लो कि हीरे को साग के भाव बेच दिया। परमात्मा के लिये परमात्मा की उपासना नहीं की जाती। अपनी दुःख निवृत्ति, अशान्ति निवृत्ति; अज्ञानता और अल्पशक्ति की निवृत्ति के लिये ही परमात्मा की उपासना की जाती है। परमात्मा सर्वज्ञ है, सर्वशक्तिमान है और अनन्तानन्दमय है। उपासना द्वारा उसकी अनन्त शक्ति पर कब्जा किया जाता है। इस महान् कार्य की सम्पन्नता में ही मनुष्य-जीवन की सार्थकता है। यदि इस ओर कुछ प्रयत्न नहीं हो रहा है तो समझ

लो कि धोखे में पड़े हो।

59

Every moment of life is very precious.

This scarce human body is acquired after eighty-four hundred thousand lives; don't let it go to no purpose. Every moment of life is very precious. If you don't understand the value of it then you will only be crying and have nothing in your hand.

You have become a human being, therefore have the strength to consider what is said in the Scriptures, and then you can do the best *purushartha* ("human wealth" = willpower). Do not think of yourself as weak and fallen. That which was done up to now, understand that this was unintentional. But now be cautious, apply oneself to doing action fit for a human. On your own accord understand what is good and what is bad. Take to doing that which is good and reject that which is bad.

If having become a human being you do not obtain knowledge of Paramatma then understand that it is as if you have sold a diamond for the price of spinach. Worship of Paramatma is not for Paramatma. Worship of Paramatma if for the disappearance of one's suffering, disappearance of unrest and the disappearance of ignorance and weakness. Paramatma is All-Knowing, Omnipotent and Unlimited Bliss. Worship is a way to get a handle on that unlimited strength. The meaning of human life is in accomplishing this work. If no effort is put in this direction then make sure you learn it by heart and understand.

६०

शक्ति चाहते हो तो शक्ति के केन्द्र से संबंध जोड़ो

*

दुःख-सागर संसार में सुख की भावना करना भूल है

अनन्त शक्ति के स्तोत परमात्मा से सम्बन्ध जोड़ो, तभी अन्तःकरण की गरीबी मिटेगी। संसार जानने की वस्तु नहीं, भुलाने की वस्तु है। इस दुःख-सागर कों जितना जानने का प्रयत्न करोगे उतना ही अधिकाधिक दुःख में डूबते जाओगे। संसार को जान कर सुख-शान्ति को आशा करना अँधेरे को अँधेरे से ढूंढकर प्रकाश पाने की इच्छा करना है।

संसार दुःख का सागर है। इस दुःख-सागर के सहारे सुखी होना चाहो तो असंभव है। संसार में प्रेम करना ही दुःख का बीज वपन करना है।

'यत्र स्नेही तत्व दुःख स्नेहोदुःखस्य भाजनम्।'

संसार में प्रेम मत करो, यही केवल व्यवहार चलाना चाहिये।

संसार में व्यवहार ऐसा करो जैसा शत्रु के साथ व्यवहार करते हो। शत्रु जब दरवाजे पर आता है तब मित्र से अधिक उकसा स्वागत किया जाता है, क्योंकि मित्र तो शिष्टाचार को कमी को नोट नहीं करता पर शत्रु थोड़ि भी कभी को बहुत नोट करता है। इसलिये शत्रु का अधिक शिष्टाचार करना होता है। इसी प्रकार संसार में अच्छी तरह से शिष्टाचार करते चलो, पर भीतर से यही समझो कि यह शत्रु ही है। कहीं ऐसा न हो कि इसमें मित्र की भावना बनालो। संसार में इष्ट बुद्धि हुई तो बड़ा लम्बा धोखा होगा। इसको बहुत जानने का प्रयत्न मत करो।

60

To hope for happiness and peace by knowing *samsara* is desiring to search for light in darkness.

Establish a relationship with Paramatma who is the spring of limitedless energy. On this account the poverty of the inner self will be erased. *Samsara* (worldly existence) is not a thing to know, it is a thing to forget.

However much you will make an effort to understand this ocean of suffering that much you will plunge into more and more suffering. To hope for happiness and peace by knowing *samsara* is desiring to search for light in darkness. *Samsara* is the sea of suffering. Desiring to be happy with the help of this sea of suffering then is unreasonable. To love in *samsara* is only to sow the seeds of suffering;

"यस्य स्नेहो भयं तस्य स्नेहो दुःखस्य भाजनम्।"

"yasya sneho bhayam tasya sneho duhkhasya bhaajanam'"

'Attachment/love is the cause of fear and suffering'
[*Chanakya Niti Shastra* 13:6]

Don't love in *samsara*, you should just get going to do your everyday business.

In *samsara* do your daily business in the manner you would do business together with an enemy.

When the enemy comes to the door give him a greater welcome than a friend, because the friend will not *"note"* any lack of good manners whereas the enemy will take great *"note"* of every little thing. Therefore an enemy is to be met with more formality. It is good to proceed with proper behaviour in *samsara*, yet inside understand that this place is the enemy. Do not make a feeling of friendship anywhere in this. If the mind desires *samsara* then it will be a great long deception. Don't make an effort to get much understanding of this.

६१

जिनके लिए हाव-हाव करके मारे-मारे फिरते हो वे ही जवाब देते हैं

निश्चय रखना चाहिये कि संसार से हमें जाना अवश्य है और सब कुछ यहीं छोड़ कर जाना होगा; साथ में कुछ नहीं जायगा यह भी निश्चित है। जब साथ में कुछ ले नहीं जाना है तो जब तक यहाँ रहो निश्चिन्तता से रहो। व्यर्थ की चिन्तायें बना कर अशान्ति मत भोगो।

अपने जीवन-निर्वाह के लिये तो निश्चित ही रहना चाहिये, क्योंकि जो प्रारब्ध-भोग है वह तो अवश्य ही आयेगा - वह स्वयं हमें ढूँढ़ लेगा - उसके लिये चिन्ता करने की आवश्यकता ही नहीं है। और यदि दूसरों के लिये चिन्ता करते हो तो विचार करके देख लो कि जिनके लिये हाव-हाव करके मारे-मारे फिरते हो वे ही मौके पर जबाब दे देते हैं।

संसार में बने के साथी सब हो जाते हैं - 'बने के साले सब बन जाते हैं बिगड़े का बहनोई कोई नहीं बनता' - महर्षि वाल्मीक का पहले का नाम मार्कण्डेय था। वे यात्रियों को लूट-मार कर अपने कुटुम्ब का भरण-पोषण करते थे। एक बार कुछ ऋषी गण वहाँ से निकले। मार्कण्डेय ने उन पर भी छापा मारा। ऋषियों ने कहा कि हम भागेंगे नहीं, पर अपने घरवालों से यह पूछ आओ कि यह जो तुम दूसरों को लूटमार कर पाप कमाते हो वे इस पाप को भी बटायेंगे या नहीं? क्या वे केवल धन ही चाहते हैं? मार्कण्डेय ने जाकर कुटुम्बियों से पूछा। सबने कह किया कि हम तुम्हारा पाप नहीं लेंगे - हम तो धन चाहते हैं, तुम यदि पाप करके धन लाते हो उस पाप के भागी तुम्हीं होगे। कुटुम्बियों का यह उत्तर पाकर मार्कण्डेय को समझ आ गई उन्होंने निश्चय किया कि -

"अभी तक जो भूल हुई सो हुई, अब संभाल जाना चाहिये। जीवन का थोड़ा सा समय है, उसे व्यर्थ नहीं जाने देना चाहिये।"

उसी समय मार्कण्डेय ऋषियों के उपदेशानुसार राम-राम (मरा-मरा) कहते हुये एक आसन से बैठ गये और भगवान् के भजन में इतने तल्लीन हो गये कि उनके ऊपर दीमकों ने बमीठे बना लिए। बाद में जब वे उन बमीठों (बल्मीक) से बाहर लाए गए तो उनका नाम बाल्मीक पड़ा - "बल्मीकोद्यवः बाल्मीकः।"

तात्पर्य कहने का यह कि संसार में दूसरों के लिए जितना हाव-हाव करके अनर्थ सम्पादन करते हो इससे लोक-परलोक दोनों बिगड़ता है। इसलिए सच्चाई के साथ व्यवहार करते हुए शान्ति के साथ भगवान् का भजन करते हुए समय को बिताओ, यही बुद्धिमानी है।

61

Don't suffer unrest by having pointless worries.

You should believe that we will go from *samsara* and be released from everything. Moreover, nothing will go together with us, this is certain. Knowing that nothing is taken with us, then whilst we are here live free from anxiety. Don't suffer unrest by having pointless worries.

It is sure that you should fulfil your own life, because destiny is to be experienced, that will certainly come then - that will search us out by itself - it is not necessary to think about it. If you are worrying on account of others then take a look and consider what those whom you are attracted to making a fuss of would say, given an opportunity to answer.

All become friends of those who have made it in *samsara* - 'All will be the brother-in-law to those who have made it, nobody will be the brother-in-law to the fallen.'

Maharishi Valmiki's name was Markandeya before. He was beating and looting travellers in order to support his family. One time a group of *rishis* appeared there. Markandeya raided them too. The *rishis* said; 'We will not run away, but ask those in your household this, that you earn sin being a bandit, will they take a share of this sin or not? Do they only desire the wealth?'

Markandeya asked the question to his relatives. They all said that 'We will not take your sin - we want the wealth, if you earn sin bringing wealth then that sin you and you only share.'

On getting this answer Markandeya understood and decided; 'Up to now has been an error, now I should keep a watch. There is a little more time in life, that should not be to no purpose.'

At that time, seated in a posture, Markandeya said "Raama Raama" according to the advice of the *rishis*, and became deeply immersed in chanting *bhajan* of Bhagwan, and on him white ants made a *bamitha* (an anthill). Afterwards when he came out of the *bamithon* (ant hills) his name became Valmiki [another name for an anthill is *valmika*] –

"बल्मीकोद्यवः बाल्मीकः ।"

"balmiikodyavah baalmiikah."

The significance of telling this story is that in *samsara*, however much fuss one makes for others; misfortune becomes accomplished. From this, both this world and the other world are spoiled. Therefore pass the time honestly performing everyday business and peacefully chanting *bhajan* of Bhagwan, that is intelligence.

६२

होली में गाली व रंग-गुलाल क्यों?

आज होली का समय है। यह जान लेना चाहिए कि यह क्या

चीज है। प्रहलाद की फुआ अर्थात् हिरण्यकश्यपु की बहन का नाम ढूँढ़ा था (उसे होलिका भी कहते हैं)। उसने तपस्या करके यह वर प्राप्त कर लिया था कि जिसे वह गोद में लेकर अग्नि में बैठ जायगी वह जल जायगा। जब हिरण्यकश्यपु प्रहलाद को कष्ट देते-देते थक गया और प्रहलाद को कुछ भी दुःख न दे सका-पहड़ों से नीचे गिराया तो भी प्रहलाद हँसते रहे, जल में डुबाया तो भी प्रहलाद प्रफुल्लित निकले, अग्नि में डाल दिया तो भी जले नहीं। इस प्रकार जब हिरण्यकश्यपु सब-कुछ करके हार गया और प्रहलाद ने भगवद्भजन नहीं छोड़ा तो ढूँढ़ा ने कहा कि लाओ हम उसे भस्म कर देते हैं। ढुंढ़ा प्रहलाद को गोद में लेकर बैठ गई। चारों ओर से अग्नि लगाई गई। प्रहलाद की भक्ति का प्रभाव हुआ कि ढुंढ़ा जल गई और प्रहलाद हँसते हुए अग्नि से बाहर आ गये।

होली के अवसर पर जो लोग गालियाँ बकते हैं, अश्लील शब्द कहते हैं, वह सब ढुँढ़ा (होलिका) के लिए गाली है। ये गंदे शब्द ही उस दैत्या के लिए स्तोत्र के सामने हैं; क्योंकि आसुरी शक्ति ऐसे ही शब्दों से प्रसन्न होती है। इनके द्वारा लोक में ढुँढ़ा की निष्ठा को जाग्रत रख कर यह स्मरण किया जाता है कि अग्नि आदि तत्वों कों अपने वश में रखने बाली ढुँढ़ा के समान कोई भी कैसा भी शक्तिशाली क्यों न हो, किन्तु जब वह भगवद्भक्त के विरुद्ध उठता है तब उसी की वह शक्ति उसके विरुद्ध होकर उसका संहार करके भक्त की रक्षा करती है। यही होली के अवसर पर (होकिका-दहन के समय) गालियाँ बकने का रहस्य है।

होली के दिन जो रंग-गुलाल आदि के द्वारा व्यवहार होता है वह प्रसन्नता का द्योतक है। परस्पर मिल-भेंट कर इस बात की खुशी मनाई जाती है कि आज के ही दिन भगवदभक्त प्रहलाद को कष्ट देने वाली आसुरी शक्ति स्वयं ही भस्म हो गई थी। "भक्त प्रहलाद से द्रोह करने वाली राक्षसी के भस्म होने की खुशी मनाई जाती है" -

यही होली का माहात्म्य है।

62

Why the insults and the red-coloured powder at Holi?

Celebrating Holi
[*'India and Its Inhabitants'*, Caleb Wright, Brainerd, 1856]

Today is the occasion of Holi. You should understand what this thing is. Prahlad's aunt, that is to say, Hiranayakashyapu's sister, her name was Doondha (she is also known as Holika). She had done *tapasya* (penance, austerity) and from this she had gained a boon, that by sitting in her lap one will be burned in fire. When Hiranyakashyapu became wearied of giving hardship to Prahlad and could not give any more trouble to Prahlad. He threw him from hills, but when Prahlad was laughing he ducked him in water, then also Prahlad emerged cheerful, so he cast him into fire but still he was not burned. When Hiranyakashyapu was defeated this way in everything and Prahlad did not desist from chanting to Bhagwan then Dhoondha said that; 'Bring! We will turn him to ashes.' Dhoondha sat down with Prahlad in her lap. From all four directions fire came. But the effect of Prahlad's devotion was that Dhoondha became burnt and Prahlad came out of the fire laughing.

On the occasion of Holi people jabber abuse, they say vulgar words, all that abuse is for Dhoondha. These dirty words are similar to *stotra* (hymns of praise) for *daitya* (demons); because demoniacal energy rejoices with words like these. In this way we are awakened to the condition of Dhoondha, a memory of someone for whom the elements, fire etc., fulfilled wishes. How could there not be someone possessing the same strength of Dhoondha? But when they rise up contrary to a devotee of Bhagwan then that energy is amassed together against them, for the devotee's protection. This is really the secret of the babbling insulting language at the time of Holi.

The coloured powder etc. on the day of Holi is a way of showing happiness. Meeting one another, this causes them to share the good news that today - on this very day - that having given hardship to Bhagwan's devotee the demoniacal energy became burned to ashes. The celebration is that the ogress that showed malevolence towards the devout Prahlad was turned to ashes. This is the value of Holi.

६३

महा असुर हिरण्यकश्यपु के पुत्र प्रहलाद क्यों भक्त उत्पन्न हुए?

*

एक समय देवताओं के साथ युद्ध में पराजित होकर हिरण्यकश्यपु शक्ति संचय करने के उद्देश्य से तपस्या करने के लिये बन में चला गया। उसकी पत्नी उस समय गर्भिणी थी। इन्द्र ने सोचा कि हिरण्यकश्यपु का पुत्र उससे भी अधिक बलवान् होगा और देवताओं को अधिक परेशान किया करेगा, इसलिये उत्पन्न होते ही उसका बध कर देना ठीक रहेगा। इसी लक्ष्य से हिरण्यकश्यपु की गर्भवती स्त्री को इन्द्र अपने यहाँ उठा ले चला। मार्ग में वह विलाप करती हुई जा रही थी, नारद जी मिल गये। उन्होंने पूछा कि इस अबला को कहाँ लिये जाते हो, क्या उद्देश्य है? इन्द्र ने बताया कि यह हिरणअकश्यपु की स्त्री है, गर्भवती है, इसके गर्भ से उत्पन्न बालक

को तुरन्त मार कर देवताओं का कण्टक दूर करने के लक्ष्य से इसे अपने लोक में ले जा रहा हूँ। नारद ने कहा कि इसके गर्भ से भगवद्भक्त उत्पन्न होगा और अजेय होगा, तुम इसे छोड़ दो। नारद के ये वचन सुन कर इन्द्र उसे छोड़ कर चला गया। नारद उसे अपने आश्रम में ले आये और नित्य उसे भगवान की भक्ति-गाथायें सुनाते रहे।

गर्भवती स्त्री जो बातें सुनती है या जो दृश्य आदि देखती है और जिस वातावरण में वह रहती है, उसका असर गर्भस्थ बालक पर पढ़ता है। प्रहलाद जब पढ़ने जाते थे तो अपने सहपाठियों को ज्ञान-ध्यान की बातें और भगवान की बातें सुनाते थे। उनसे उन लोगों ने पूछा कि आप तो हमारे साथ ही पढ़ते हो, ये बातें तो यहाँ बताई नहीं जातीं और घर में भी दैत्यों के आस-पास ही आप रहते हो, वहाँ भी इस प्रकार की शिक्षा पाने का कोई अवसर नहीं मिलता होगा तो ये सब अच्छी-अच्छी बातें आप को मालूम कैसे हुई जो आप हम लोगों को सुनाते हो?

प्रहलाद ने अपने गर्भकाल की बातें बताईं कि इस प्रकार हमारी माता नारद के आश्रम में पहुँचीं और वहाँ महर्षि नारद उन्हें नित्य ही भगवान की गाथायें जब सुनाया करते थे तो हम माता के गर्भ में सुब सुना करते थे। वहाँ से आने के बाद दैत्यों के बातावरण में माता तो वह सब भूल गई, पर हमको सब याद हैं। वनी हम तुम लोगों को सुनाते हैं।

दैत्यराज महा असुर हिरण्यकश्यपु का पुत्र गर्भावस्था में सत्संग की बातें सुन कर भक्तराज पैदा हुआ। आज भी गर्भवती माताओं को उत्तम धार्मिक भक्तिमान वातावरण में रखा जाय, भगवान् की अच्छी-अच्छी धार्मिक बातें उनको सुनाई जायें तो आज भी भारत में ध्रुव-प्रहलाद उत्पन्न हो सकते हैं। परन्तु आजकल तो सिनेमाओं और गन्दी पुस्तकों के पढ़ने से फुरसत ही नहीं मिलती। यही कारण

है कि उत्पाती और चरित्रहीन सन्तानें पैदा होती हैं और उनके माता-पिता जन्मभर रोते हैं। गर्भवती स्त्री के संस्कार ही गर्भस्थ बालक के संस्कार बनते हैं और वैसी ही उसकी निष्ठा बनती है। पशु के समान सन्तान पैदा कर देना और बात है, किन्तु यदि उत्तम् विचारशील चरित्रवान् सन्तान चाहते हो तो गर्भकाल में स्त्री को पवित्र वातावरण में रखो। विधिपूर्वक गर्भाधान संस्कार के बाद स्त्री को रजोगुणी-तमोगुणी पदार्थों से बचाओ। गर्भिणी स्त्री की उत्तम भावनायें ही गर्भस्थ बालक के उत्तम संस्कारवान होने का कारण है।

प्रह्लाद को यह पुष्ट था कि भगवान् सर्वत्र हैं। उन्हें सर्वत्र परमात्मा का ज्ञान था। जहाँ वे देखते थे अपने इष्ट को ही देखते थे। प्रह्लाद को निर्विवाद पुष्ट था कि सर्वत्र परमात्मा है। जल, थल, अग्नि में सर्वत्र वे अपने राम को देखते थे। यही कारण था कि जल, अग्नि आदि तत्त्व उन्हें कष्ट नहीं पहुँचा सके - यह थी भारत के एक पाँच वर्ष की निष्ठा। भारतीय यदि अपने सिद्धान्तों पर आ जायें तो फिर त्रैलोक्य में कोई भी ऐसी शक्ति नहीं है जो उन्हें कष्ट से सके। परन्तु अपने घर की बात भूल कर सब दरिद्र हो रहे हैं। सर्वशक्तिमान परमात्मा जब अपने अनुकूल हो जाते हैं तो प्रकृति की समस्त शक्तियाँ अपने अनुकूल हो जाती हैं। प्रह्लाद को जिस तत्त्व के द्वारा कष्ट देने का प्रयत्न किया जाता था, वही तत्त्व उनके अनुकूल हो जाता था। प्रह्लाद को जब अग्नि में डाला गया तो वे हणसते हुए कहते हैं -

"रामनामजपतां कुतो भयं
सर्वतापशमनैकभेषजम्,
पश्य तात ममगात्रसन्निधौ
पावकोऽपि सलिलायतेऽधुना ॥"

अर्थात्, राम-राम जपने वाले को कहाँ भय है? यह (राम-नाम)

तो समस्त तापों के (दुःखों के) निवारण की एक औषधि है। हे पिता! देखो मेरे शरीर के पास इस समय अग्नि भी जल का काम कर रही है, अर्थात् ठंडी हो गई है।

बात यह है कि जब तक हम अपने इष्ट को एकदेशीय डिबिया में बन्द करके रखे रहेंगे तब तक जो चाहे हमें दुःख देता रहेगा और अपाहिज की तरह हमें उसके सहन करने के अतिरिक्त और कोई उपाय नहीं है। सर्वत्र व्यापक अपने इष्ट को देखने लगो तो जा समीप आयेगा वह इष्ट बनकर, सहयोगी बन कर आयेगा। यही सिद्धान्त है कि जो जैसा होता है उसके समीप आने वाला भी वैसा ही हो जाता है, यदि निष्ठा पक्की है तो।

योगशास्त्र-कर्ता पतंजलि ने यही लिखा है कि -

"अहिंसा प्रतिष्ठायां तत्सन्निधौ वैरत्यागः।"

जिसकी अहिंसा की निष्ठा पुष्ट है उसके निकट सिंह, व्याघ्र आदि हिंसक पशु भी अपना हिंसक स्वभाव त्याग कर अहिंसक हो जाते हैं। पर हमारा आधार पुष्ट होना चाहिये, परमात्मा का भरोसा पक्का होना चाहिये। ऐसा नहीं कि जिसके हाथ में माटी का लोआ देखा उसी के पीछे हो लिये। धोबी का कुत्ता, न घर का होता है न घाट का। विचार से काम लेना चाहिये, उदर-परायणता से पीछे अपना सर्वस्व गँवा सेना ठीक नहीं। उदर-परायणता तो पशु-पक्षी, कीट-पतंगादि योनियों में भी रहती है। मनुष्य होकर भी यदि उदर-परायण रहे तो मनुष्य-योनि की विशेषता ही क्या? भारतीयों ने पेट को कभी प्रधान नहीं माना। यहाँ आध्यात्म की ही प्रधानता सदा स्वीकार की गई है। महर्षि लोग कन्द-मूल फल खाकर, जल पीकर रहते थे, परन्तु चक्रवर्तियों को भी अपने इशारे पर चलाने का बल रखते थे। हलुवा-पूड़ी, रबड़ी-मलाई खिलाने वाले भक्त लोग उस समय भी रहे होंगे, परन्तु वे समझते थे कि इन लोगों का दिया दुआ

यदि हलुवा-पूड़ी खायेंगे तो बुद्धि भ्रष्ट हो जायगी और पतन हो जायगा। जब भीष्म ऐसे व्यक्तियों की बुद्धि मलिन धान्य खाने से भ्रष्ट हो गई, तो आजकल के लोगों की बात ही क्या! इसलिये बुद्धि की शुद्धि के लिये धान्य शुद्धि पर सदा विचार रखना चाहिये और भगवान् का सहारा लेकर सतोगुणी वृत्ति से जीवन-यापन करने का प्रयत्न करना चाहिये।

Indru, King of the minor Deities

[*'India and Its Inhabitants'*, Caleb Wright, Brainerd, 1856]

63

The *maharshi* people ate roots, tubers and fruits, and were drinking water, but had the power to command emperors.

Why was Prahlad, the son of the great asura Hiranyakashyapu, born a devotee?

One time, having become defeated by the gods, Hiranyakashyapu went to the forest to do *tapasya* (austerity) in order to amass energy. His wife was pregnant at that time and Indra considered that Hiranyakashyapu's son would be even stronger, so the gods became greatly distressed. Therefore they will just kill him at birth. With this objective, Indra proceeded to go near and he took away the pregnant wife of Hiranyakashyapu. She was going along the road lamenting and met with Narada ji. He asked the question 'Where are you going on account of this woman, what is the idea?'

Indra informed him that, 'This is Hiranyakashyapu's wife, she is pregnant with a baby who is a future nuisance to the gods, the aim is that when the baby comes from this womb I beat it and send it going back to it's own world.'

Narada said, 'From this womb will be born a devotee of Bhagwan and he will be unconquerable, you should release her.'

When Indra heard these words of Narada he released her and proceeded to go away. Narada took him [Prahlad, in his mother's womb] to his own ashram and there he continuously heard devotional verses. The words that a pregnant woman hears and the sights she sees, the atmosphere that she lives in, has an influence on the young child in the womb.

When Prahlad was studying, his fellow-students heard his talk of knowledge and meditation, also they heard talk of Bhagwan. The others asked the question that; 'You study along with us; but these words are not instructed here. Also, in the house you are living near *daityon* (demons) so there you do not meet with any opportunity to obtain this kind of instruction, so how have you found out all these good words that we people are hearing from you?'

Prahlad told them of his own time in the womb; 'My mother arrived at Narada's *ashram* (hermitage) and when there she constantly heard Maharishi Narada's stories of Bhagwan, then I heard everything whilst in our mother's womb. After going from there and revering the words of demons, mother then forgot all that, but I remembered everything. In the forest I heard that which I tell you.'

So the son of *daityaraja* (demon king) the great *asura* (demon) Hiranyakashyapu, had heard the words of *satsang* whilst he was in the womb and was born a *bhaktaraja* (devotee king). Today it is also best that pregnant mothers stay in a pious atmosphere, hearing good devout good words of Bhagwan, then today can be born in India a Dhruva or a Prahlad. But nowadays they take no rest from the cinemas and reading dirty books. This is really the cause of [children] being born mischievous and depraved and their mother and father are crying the whole life. The *samskara* (mental impressions) of the mother are the *samskara* of the infant child in the womb and so is his faith created. If the intention is to give birth to a beast then? But if you want the most considerate character then keep the woman in a pure atmosphere. After the *samskara* impressions of the ceremony of *garbhadhana* (a ceremony performed by Hindus when a woman has conceived) then protect her from *rajoguni* (pleasure seeking) and *tamoguni* (impure) things. The chief feelings of a pregnant woman are the origin of the unborn child's chief mental impressions.

Prahlad was certain that Bhagwan is everywhere, he knew Paramatma is everywhere. Wherever he looked he looked he saw his own *ishta* (desired deity). Prahlad was unassailably strong that Paramatma is everywhere. He saw his own Rama everywhere, in water, earth and fire. This was the reason that the elements of water, fire etc. could lead to no harm - this was the faith of a five-year old Indian. If Indians return to their own established truths then no hardship can come from any force in the three worlds. But to forget the talk of one's own birthplace then all are being needy. When Omnipotent Paramatma becomes favourable to oneself then the whole of nature become favourable to oneself. Whatever element was used in an effort to cause hardship to Prahlad, that very element became favourable to him. When he was cast into the fire he laughed saying;

"रामनामजपतां कुतो भयं सर्वतापशमनैकभेषजम्।
पश्य तात ममगान्नसन्निधौ पावकोऽपि सलिलायतेऽधुना ॥"

"ramanamajapatam kuto bhayam
sarvatapashamanaikabheshaja.
pashya tata mamagannasannidhau
pavako api salilayate adhuna.."

That is to say;

'For the one who does Raama, Raama *japa* (silent repetition of the name of a deity), where is fear?
This is one medicine for all afflictions! Look! Near my body fire desires to be water at this time'

That is to say it becomes cool.

The thing is that when we will lock our own *ishta* (favourite god) in a box then we will be given to suffer, and like a cripple we suffer additionally too. There is no remedy. Look at your own *ishta* as being pervasive everywhere, then whatever will come near, this is made into the *ishta* and will come as a helper. This is really the theory that whoever comes near becomes likewise, if the faith is ripe at that time.

Patanjali, the author of *Yoga Shastra*, wrote this;

"अहिंसा प्रतिष्ठायां तत्सन्निधौ वैरत्यागः।"

"ahimsaa pratishthayaam tatsannidhau vairatyaagah."
[*Yogadarshanam* 2:35]

'Whoever has strong faith in *ahimsa* (non-violence), if a lion, tiger etc. comes near it will abandon it's predatory nature and become non-violent.'

Yet we should stay strong, we should be steady in faith of Paramatma. It is not that when we see [someone with] a metal pot in the hand then we follow behind (a *sadhu* often carries a metal pot). The dog of the *dhobi* (washerman) does not belong at home or at the *ghat*. You should act with consideration, it's not okay to waste one's time out of attachment to the stomach. The beast, the bird, the worm and the bird etc. are also births having attachment to the stomach. Becoming a human being, if you are attached to the stomach then what is the specialness of the human birth? Indians never weighed the stomach to be important. Here *adhyatma* (spiritual contemplation) was accepted as superior. The *maharshi* people ate roots, tubers and fruits, and were drinking water, but had the power to command emperors. There were also at that time, devotees who delighted in *halwa-puri* and *rabari-malai (*sweetmeats), but they understood that if they will eat these *halwa-puri* then their wisdom will fall and they will become ruined. When Bhishma's intelligence appeared soiled by eating *dhanya* (grains - food) and he became fallen, then what is there to say of people nowadays? Therefore, for the purity of the intelligence, you should always consider the *dhanya* and with support of Bhagwan you should make an effort to spend life in a condition of *satoguni* (purity).

६४

दीन बनकर दीनदयालु की दयालुता का लाभ उठाओ

*

भगवान् दीनदयालु हैं। जो दीन है उस पर भगवान दया करते हैं। मनुष्य दीन या तो उपासना के द्वारा भगवान को प्रसन्न करने की चेष्टा करे या स्वधर्मानुष्ठान करते हुए अपने कर्म रूपी फूलों से भगवान् की पूजा करे। कर्म और उपासना कुछ न बन पड़े तो कम से कम दीन ही बन जाय। दीन कौन है? जिसके लिए संसार में कोई भी आधार नहीं है वही दीन है। सर्वथा निराधार के आधार भगवान् होते हैं। यही उनकी दयालुता है। जिसका संसार से राग सर्वथा हट गया है - स्त्री, पुत्र, धन, इष्ट-मित्र आदि किसी का भी जिसको सहारा नहीं रह गया है - ऐसे सर्वथा निस्सहाय निराधार के

आधार दीनबन्धु दीनदयालु जगदाधार परमात्मा है। द्रौपदी चीर-हरण के समय दीन हो गई थी, कोई भी उसका रक्षक नहीं रह गया था। ऐसी दीनावस्था में जब उसने भगवान् को पुकारा तो दीनबन्धु भगवान् ने उसकी रक्षा की। कर्म का फल तो सबको भोगना पड़ता है; परन्तु दीन को कुछ ऐसा विशेषा-धिककार मिल जाता है कि उसको पाप का फल प्रायः नहीं भोगना पड़ता। इसलिये कुछ न कर सको तो कम से कम दीन तो बन जाओ।

जब मनुष्य दीन हो जाता है तब उसे संसार ऐसा लगता है जैसा मदारी का रुपया। लाखों रुपये का ढेर लगा हो और कह दिया जाय कि यह मदारी का रुपया है तो यदि कोई कैसा भी लालची-लोभी हो तो भी उसकी दृष्टि उसे रुपये के प्रति नहीं जाती। इसी प्रकार जो दीन हो जाता है वह संसार में किसी भी वस्तु के प्रति राग नहीं रखता। संसार से सर्वथा राग रहित होकर जब मनुष्य दीनावस्था में भगवान् को पुकारता है तब वह दीनबन्धु भगवान् की दयालुता का पात्र होता है। बस, दीन बनने की देर है, दीनदयाल तो तुम्हें उठाने के लिये तैय्यार ही हैं।

सत्संग न होने के कारण भगवान के दीनदयाल स्वभाव से भी लोग फायदा नहीं उठा पाते। लोगों को जो कुछ सत्संग मिलता भी है उसकी बातें उनके अन्तःकरण में टिकती ही नहीं। कारण यह है कि आहार-शुद्धि की कमी है।

जिस प्रकार भोजन के देखने मात्र से क्षुधा की निवृत्ति नहीं होती, उसी प्रकार भगवान के केवल नाम माहात्म्य के पाठ से सुख-शान्ति नहीं मिल सकती। आज-कल गीता का पाठ करने का बड़ा प्रचार है। इस पाठ मात्र से पुण्य तो अवश्य होगा किन्तु पूर्ण सुख-शान्ति की प्राप्ति केवल ऐसे पाठ मात्र से सम्भव नहीं। एक भी श्लोक गीता का मान लिया जाय या एक श्लोक का एक चरण भी मनुष्य मान ले तो उसका कल्याण हो सकता है।

64

If the value of one *shloka* of *Gita* is understood, or even one line of a *shloka* is understood, then there can be happiness.

Having been made humble, take advantage of the proceeds of Dinadayalu's charity.

Bhagwan is Dinadayalu (name of God meaning 'merciful to the humble'). Bhagwan is compassionate on him who is humble. If man is humble or, by means of prayer, desires to please Bhagwan or has been working on his own *dharma* (duty), in the form of offering the fruits of his own actions as *puja* (worship) to Bhagwan. If there isn't any *karma* (action) and *upasana* (devotion) done, then little by little you are made very humble. Who is humble? He who has no support in *samsara* (worldly existence), the very same is humble. Bhagwan is the supporter of he who is altogether without support. This is really his kindness. He whose attachment to *samsara* has completely shifted away - wife, son, wealth, favourite friend etc., who does not have anyone to support them - so Paramatma, who is Dinabandhu (a friend to the humble) Dinadayalu (merciful to the humble) and Jagadadhara (universal protector). He is a support to those who are altogether helpless, a supporter of those without supprt.

Draupadi became humble at the time of the stripping off of her clothes, nobody there was rescuing her. She was in such a plight that when she called out to Dinabandhu (a friend to the humble) then Bhagwan protected her. It befalls to all to endure the fruit of action; but if some specific insult happens to the humble, generally that fruit of sin does not need to be endured. Therefore if you cannot do anything else then little by little become humble!

When man becomes humble then afterwards *samsara* (mundane existence) is similar to the *rupees* of a *madari* (conjurer). The accumulation of hundreds of thousands of *rupees*, but when it is said that, 'These are the *rupees* of a conjurer', then however greedy someone is they will not go towards this money. In this way, if he becomes humble he does not become attached to anything in *samsara*. If he is altogether attached to *samsara*, when man is in a plight and calls out to Bhagwan then he becomes the receiver of Bhagwan's mercy for he is Dinabandhu (a friend to the humble). But, if there is delay in becoming humble, then Dinadayalu (merciful to the humble) is [still] ready to rise up for you.

The reason that people are unable to arise and gain from the merciful nature of Dinadayalu Bhagwan is because of not having *satsang* (company of good people). The words from the little *satsang* that people do get doesn't stay in their conscience. The reason for this is the deficiency of pure food.

In the way that appetite does not disappear by looking at food, in the same way by only reading about the greatness of Bhagwan's name you may not get happiness and peace. Nowadays it is very prevalent that *Bhagavad-Gita* is studied. Certainly, merely from this study you will get *punya* (merit) but perfect happiness and peace is not likely by merely studying alone. If the value of one *shloka* of *Gita* is understood, or even one line of the *satoguni* (purity) is understood, then there can be happiness.

६५

स्वधर्म पालन और भगवान् का स्मरण सदा करते रहो

*

जीव को अपने ही कल्याण के लिये भगवान का स्मरण करना है, भगवान के लिये नहीं। भगवान तो न किसी पर प्रसन्न होने हैं और न किसी पर कुपित। पर जीव अपने कल्याण के लिये ही स्मरण करता है।

भगवान के स्मरण के अनेक प्रकार हैं। अपने-अपने अनुकूल प्रकार को गुरुओं से समझ कर करना चाहिये।

कबीर राम के बड़े भक्त थे। हर समय भगवान् राम का भजन करते रहते थे। अपना ताना-बाना बिनते रहते थे और "राम राम राम" कहते जाते थे। नाम लेते-लेते भगवान के नाम में अटल विश्वास हो गया और नाम सिद्ध हो गया। जब नाम सिद्ध हो जाता है तो क्या होता है, यह बताने के लिये एक बड़ी अच्छी घटना है - "कोई एक कोढ़ी अपनी व्याधि को असाध्य मान कर कबीर के घर पर पहुंचा। क्योंकि जब लोग वैद्य, डाक्टरों से थक जाते हैं तभी महात्माओं के पास जाते हैं। कबीर तो घर में थे नहीं, उनकी स्त्री से उसने अपनी व्यथा कही। स्त्री को दया आ गई तो उसने कहा कि तीन बार राम-राम कहो तो तुम्हारा कोढ़ अच्छा हो जायगा। उसने कहा कि हजारों बार राम-राम कहा है पर कुछ नहीं होता। स्त्री ने कहा कि हमारे कहलाने से तो कहो। उसके तीनबार राम का नाम लेते-लेते उसका शरीर सर्वथा ठीक हो गया। बड़ा प्रसन्न होकर वह लौटा। मार्ग में जो मिले उसी से कबीर के गुण गाये। कबीर भी कहीं से उधर ही आ रहे थे। उन्होंने सुना कि वह यह कहता जा रहा है कि किसी को कोई कष्ट हो तो कबीर साहब के यहाँ चला जाये। कबीर ने यह सुनकर उसे बुलाकर कहा कि हम ही कबीर हैं। अब यदि तुमने किसी से अपने अच्छे होने की बात कही तो फिर तुम्हें कष्ट हो जायगा और फिर कभी अच्छा नहीं होगा। इतना उससे कह कर कबीर घर गये और अपनी मुद्रा उदास बना ली। पति-परायणा पतिब्रता स्त्री सब कुछ सहन कर सकती है, पर अपने पति की उदासी सबन नहीं कर सकती। यही पातिब्रत्य का लक्षण है। स्त्री ने कबीर से उदासी का कारण पूछा। कबीर ने कहा कि - बात यह है कि तुमने भगवान के नाम को बहुत सस्ता कर दिया। एक ही बार भगवान का नाम लेने से वह दिव्यकाय हो जाता, पर तुमने तीन बार उससे क्यों नाम लिवाया। तीन बार लिवाने का कारण यही हो सकता है कि तुम्हें एक बार में विश्वास नहीं था।"

तात्पर्य यह है कि भगवान के नाम में पाप नाश करने की इतनी

शक्ति है कि उतना पाप कोई कर ही नहीं सकता। अग्नि में जलाने की जितनी शक्ति है उतना कूड़ा कोई इकट्ठा नहीं कर सकता।

'हरिर्हरति पापानि दुष्टचित्तैरपि स्मृतः'

दुष्ट चित्त से भी स्मरण करने पर भगवान पापों का श कर देते हैं। इसलिये सत्कर्म करते हुए स्वधर्म पालते चलो और भगवान का सदा स्मरण करते रहो तो पिछले पाप नष्ट हो जायँगे। किन्तु ऐसा नहीं करना चाहिये कि पाप करते चलो और भगवद् नाम लेते रहो। क्योंकि जितना बैङ्क में जमा किया जाय, यदि उतना सब निकाल लिया जाय तो क्या लाभ होगा।

65

There are various methods of remembering Bhagwan. You should understand one's own suitable methods from *gurus*.

For the sake of happiness in life remember Bhagwan, not for the sake of Bhagwan. Bhagwan then is never delighted nor offended, but remember him for the sake of your own happiness in life.

There are various methods of remembering Bhagwan. You should understand one's own suitable methods from *gurus*.

Kabir was a great *bhakta* (devotee) of Rama. Every day he was chanting *bhajan* of Bhagwan Rama. He was weaving on the thread on his loom and was saying, "Raama, Raama, Raama". Taking the *naama* (name), he became steadfast in faith of Bhagwan's name and he became a *"naama siddha"*.

When one becomes a *"naama siddha"* then what happens?

For the purpose of informing about this there is one very good instance:-

Somebody, a leper, who thought that his disease was incurable, arrived at the house of Kabir. Whenever people weary of going to the *vaidya* (vedic physician) and to doctors then they go to *mahatamas* (great souls). Kabir was not then at home, so he told Kabir's wife of his own anguish. The woman became tender and said to him to; 'Repeat "Raama, Raama" three times, then your leprosy will be okay.' He (the leper) said that he had done "Raama, Raama" thousands of times but nothing happened. With impatience the woman ordered, 'Then repeat!' Three times he took the name of Raama and his body became altogether well. Becoming greatly delighted he left. Getting to the road he sang the excellence of Kabir.

Kabir was also coming that way from somewhere. He heard him say; 'If anyone has any suffering then come here to Master Kabir.'

When Kabir heard this he called to him and said, 'I am Kabir, now if you tell anyone this talk of you getting better then again you will become pained and you will not be right again.'

Having said that, Kabir went home and made himself appear dejected. The devoted wife, faithful to her husband, can endure anything, but not the suffering of her own husband. This is the very sign of chastity. The woman asked Kabir the cause of the suffering. Kabir said these words; 'You gave Bhagwan's name little value. By taking Bhagwan's name just once that could have become a heavenly body, so why did you cause him to take the name three times? Can the reason that you caused him to take it three times be because you have no faith in the one time?'

The sense of this is that; in Bhagwan's name is the power to make so much *paapa* (wickedness) fade, so much so that it is not possible to do that much *paapa.* There is so much energy in fire to burn that you cannot accumulate that much rubbish to burn:-

"हरिर्हरति पापानि दुष्टचित्तैरपि स्मृतः"

"harirharati paapaani dushtachittairapi smritah"

'Remembering Bhagwan, even with a wicked mind, grants that those sins fade.'
[*Hari Ashtakam* v1 & *Pandava Gita* v65]

Therefore, do *satkarma* (virtuous action), proceed to cherish *swadharma* (one's own religion) and constantly remember Bhagwan, then later the *paapa* (sin) will be destroyed. But you should not proceed to do *paapa* but take the name of Bhagawad (God, Vishnu). Because, however much is accumulated in the *"bank"*, if you take everything out then, on this account, what advantage will there be?

६६

भगवच्चिंतन और आहार-शुद्धि

*

जब तक चीज अनुभव में नहीं आती तब तक ठीक-ठीक विश्वास नहीं पड़ता; संसार का ही चिन्तन हमेशा होता रहता है। इसलिये परमात्मा का चिन्तन करने में कठिनाई पड़ती है। भगवान ने कहा है:-

"मार्च्चत्ता मद्गत् प्राणः बोधयन्तः परस्परम्।
कथयन्तश्च मां नित्य तुष्यन्ति च रमन्ति च।"

अर्थात्, मुझसे ही अपने चित्त को लगाओ। संसार का चिन्तन न हो, परमात्मा का ही चिन्तन होता रहे। तात्पर्य यह है कि भगवान ने कोई भी समय, कोई भी अवस्था ऐसी नहीं छोड़ी है कि उनके चिन्तन से खाली जाय। अनेक चित्तता होने का प्रधान कारण यही है कि आहार की शुद्धि नहीं है। आहार-शुद्धि के विषय में धनार्जन का प्रकार यह है कि -

"अकृत्वा परसन्तापं, अगत्वा खलमन्दिरम्।
अनुल्लंध्य सताँ वर्त्मं यदल्पमपि तद् बहु॥"

अर्थात्, किसी को कष्ट न देकर दुष्टों से सम्पर्क न रखते हुए

अपनी आत्मा को अधिक उलझन में न डालकर थोड़ा भी मिल जाय तो बहुत है। दुसरे को कष्ट देकर जो धन पैदा किया जायगा वह धन तो पड़ा रह जायगा, परन्तु दूसरे को दिये हुए कष्ट का पाप अपने सूक्ष्म शरीर के साथ जायगा। इसलिये ऐसा न करो कि पाप की गठरी साथ में जाय।

'अगत्वा खलमन्दिरम्' का तात्पर्य यह है कि यदि नीच लोगों के निकट जाओगे तो बुद्धि भ्रष्ट होगी और बुद्धि भ्रष्ट हुई तो पतन निश्चित है। 'बुद्धिनाशात् प्रणस्यति' नीच विषयियों का सम्पर्क साक्षात् विषय से कहीं अधिक पतनकारी होता है। इसी लिये धनोपार्जन की दृष्टि से भी खलों के घर में जाने का निषेध किया गया है।

'अनुलंध्य सताँ वत्म' का तात्पर्य यह है कि सत्पुरुषों के द्वारा जो वेद-शास्त्रानुसार जिस मार्ग का अनुशरण किया गया है, उसका उल्लंधन नहीं करना चाहिये।

यदि व्यवहार में किसी समय खलों का सम्पर्क करना ही पड़े तो इस प्रकार उनके पास जाना चाहिये, जैसे पाखाने में जाते हो - काम किया और चलते हुये। पाखाने में कोई अधिक देर तक नहीं ठहरता। यदि ऐसी बुद्धि रक्खोगे तो नीचों के संपर्क से अधिक हानि की शंका नहीं रहेगी। शुद्ध मन परमात्मा के निकट जाता है और अधुद्ध मन नाना प्रकार की भावनाओं में भटकता रहता है। इसलिये आहारशुद्धि के द्वारा मन को विशेष रूप से शुद्ध बनाने का प्रयत्न करते रहना चाहिये - धान्य-शुद्धि पर बहुत अधिक ध्यान रखने की आवश्यकता है। खान-पान ठीक रक्खोगे, भगवान का चिन्तन करते रहोगे तो अवश्य ही मन शुद्ध हो जायगा। शुद्ध मन से लोक में भी सुख-शान्ति का अनुभव करोगे और परलोक में भी उत्तम गति को प्राप्त करोगे।

66

That the food is not pure is the very reason that many thoughts occur.

Until such time as we perceive a thing, then we don't have proper trust; you always stay thinking of *samsara*. Therefore there is difficulty in thinking of Paramatma.

Bhagwan said;

"माच्चित्ता मद्गतप्राणा बोधयन्तः परस्परम्।
कथयन्तश्च मां नित्यं तुष्यन्ति च रमन्ति च ॥"

"machchitta madgataprana bodhayantah parasparam.
kathayantashcha mam nityam tushyanti cha ramanti cha.."
[*Bhagavad Gita* 10:9]

'With their minds and life totally absorbed in me,
enlightening each other,
also talking about me they are delighted and satisfied.'

That is to say;

'Apply one's own mind to me. Not be thinking of *samsara*, really be thinking of Paramatma.'

The sense is this, that at no time or situation is Bhagwan let go, vacated from their thinking. That the food is not pure is the very reason that many thoughts occur. The way of earning wealth in regard to pure food is;

"अकृत्वा परसन्तापं अगत्वा खलमन्दिरम्।
अनुल्लंध्य सताँ वर्त्मं यदल्पमपि तद् बहु ॥"

"akritva parasantapam, agatva khalamandiram.
anullamdhya satan vartmam yadalpamapi tadbahu.."
[a *subhashita* - a 'wise verse']

That is to say, not giving harm to anyone, not mixing with the unrighteous, not flinging oneself into entanglements, then whatever we get - that is good. The money you earn giving hardship to others, that will be let go of, but the sin of the suffering you give to others will go together with your *sukshama sharir* (subtle body). Therefore don't do thus, that you will go with a bundle of sin.

The meaning of *"agatva khalamandiram"* is this; That, if you will go near stingy people then your mind will be defiled and if the mind is defiled then decline is certain.

"buddhinashat pranasyati" - It is much more ruinous mixing in the presence of anything sordid. Therefore it is prohibited to go into the house of the wicked in the hope of earning wealth.

The purport of *"anullamdhya satan vartma"* is this; Following the path according to the *Veda Shastra* is the way for *satpurushon* (right people). That should not be contravened. If at any time in your day-to-day business you mix with wicked people then you should go near them in this method, in the manner in which you have been to the lavatory - you did the business and were gone. Nobody delays long halting in the toilet.

If you will set the mind after this manner then there will be no fear of excessive loss by mixing with rascals. The mind goes near to Paramatma but the impure mind misleads in various kinds of feelings. Therefore, by means of food, you should continue to make an effort to purify the condition of the mind - it is necessary to put much more attention to the purity of *dhanya* (grains - food). If you will eat well and drink well you will think of Bhagavan, certainly the mind becomes pure. With a pure mind you can experience happiness and peace, also you can obtain the greatest state in the other world too.

६७

गर्भवास में फिर न आना पड़े तभी मनुष्य-जन्म सार्थक

*

एक बार मनुष्य शरीर मिला। फिर गर्भ में आने का अवसर न आये, यही मनुष्य होने की कीमत है। यदि बार-बार गर्भ में आना पड़ा तो मनुष्य होने का कोई लाभ नहीं हुआ। जीव तो अनन्त है। परन्तु योनियों की संख्या चौरासी लक्ष है। इन्हीं चौरासी लाख योनियों में जीव भ्रमण किया करते हैं। ऐसा समझना चाहिये कि एक बहुत बड़ा घेरा है और उस घेरे की दीवाल के किनारे-किनारे चौरासी लक्ष छोटे-बड़े कमरे बने हैं। एक अन्धा उसी घेरे में छोड़ दिया गया है। वह बाहर आना चाहता है। विचार करता है कि कहीं न कहीं तो इस घेरे का फाटक अवश्य होगा। इसलिये दीवाल का सहारा लेकर दीवाल के सहारे वह एक कमरे से दूसरे कमरे में पहुंचता हुआ आगे बढ़ता है।

विचार तो उसका ठीक है कि दीवाल को पकड़े-पकड़े आगे बढ़ेंगे और जहाँ फाटक मिलेगा वहीं से घेरे के बाहर हो जायेंगे। परन्तु जिस समय फाटक पर आता है उस समय उसके शरीर में खुजली होने लगती है; दीवाल छोड़ कर वह दोनों हाथ से खुजली मिटाने की चेष्टा करता है। इसी बीच में फाटक निकल जाता है।

इस दृष्टान्त का रहस्य यह है कि अंधा तो है जीव और चौरासी लाख कमरे हैं चौरासी लाख योनियाँ। "मनुष्य योनि इस घेरे से बाहर निकलने का फाटक है।" जीव जब फाटक पर आता है अर्थात् जब उसे मनुष्य-योनि मिलती है तब स्त्री, पुत्र, धन, इष्ट-मित्र आदि में वह जो सुख मानने लगता है यही सुख-बुद्धि उसकी खुजली है। इसी खुजली में पड़कर वह मनुष्य-जन्म का समय बिता देता है

और भवसागर से पार होने का प्रयत्न नहीं करता। यही है अन्धे का खुजली में पड़कर फाटक को छोड़ देना।

मनुष्य का शरीर दुर्लभ है, यही शास्त्र कहत है। इसका अर्थ यह नहीं कि दुर्लभ शरीर मिला है तो अधिक से अधिक धन एकत्रित कर लिया जाय, अधिक से अधिक पुत्र, पौत्रादि उत्पन्न किये जायँ और अधिक से अधिक विषय-भोग किया जाय, इसमें मनुष्य शरीर की दुर्लभता सार्थक नहीं होगी। मनुष्य शरीर दुर्लभ है इसलिये कि यह कर्म-योनि है और दूसरे पशु-पक्षी, कीट-पतंगादि की योनियाँ भोग-योनियाँ हैं। भोग-योनि में जीव जो कर्म करता है उसका कोई लेखा नहीं रहता। कर्म-योनि अर्थात् मनुष्य शरीर से जीव जो कर्म करता है उसका हिसाब रहता है और प्रत्येक कर्म का उसे फल भोगना पड़ता है। इसी लिये कर्म-योनि (मनुष्य शरीर) दुर्लभ है। चौरासी लक्ष भोग-योनियों के बाद यह प्राप्त होती है और इसको प्राप्त करके ऐसे कर्म किये जा सकते हैं जिसके फल स्वरूप जीव का भटकना बन्द हो जाय और फिर-फिर कर गर्भवास के अनन्य दुखों का सामना न करना पड़े।

शास्त्र कहता है कि मनुष्य यदि देवताओं की उपासना करेगा तो देवलोक में और प्रेतों की उपासना करेगा तो प्रेत-लोक में जायगा।

'भूतानि यान्ति भूतेज्या'

भूतेज्य भूत-योनि को प्राप्त होंगे और देवेज्य देवयोनि को प्राप्त होंगे।

जप-तप करने से देवयोनि मिलती है। परन्तु देवयोनि की प्राप्ति भी मनुष्य का लक्ष्य नहीं होना चाहिए। क्योंकि देवताओं में जो सबसे प्रतिष्ठित देवराज इन्द्र हैं उनमें भी इतनी अविवेक पूर्वक विषय-भोग-वासना पाई जाती है कि स्वर्ग-लोक के विषयों से तृप्ति नहीं हुई तो मर्त्य-लोक में आकर अहिल्या से छल किया। जब

देवलोक के राजा की यह दशा है तो वहां की प्रजा तथा अन्य देवताओं की कैसी वृत्ति होगी। इसलिए ऐसे देवलोक को तो दूर से प्रणाम करना चाहिए।

दूसरी बात यह है कि जीव का देवलोक में निवास भी कुछ ही काल तक रहता है।

'क्षीणे पुण्ये मर्त्यलोकं विशन्ति'

पुण्य क्षीण होने पर पुनः मृत्यु-लोक को प्राप्त हो जाने हैं और देवलोक में रहते हुए भी सब समान रूप से सुखी नहीं रहते। अपने-अपने कर्मों के तारतम्य के अनुसार सुख-सामग्री उपलब्ध होती है। इसलिए देवता लोग अपने से अधिक सुख् - सम्पन्न देवताओं को देख कर जलते रहते हैं। देवलोक में भी ईर्ष्या, द्वेष, मत्सर के कारण वहाँ भी दुःख ही दुःख है। ऐसे लोक में जाने की कभी इच्छा नहीं करनी चाहिये।

देवता भी मनुष्य शरीर को प्राप्त करने के इच्छुक रहते हैं, क्योंकि मनुष्य-योनि सोने के पासे के समान है। शुद्ध सोना है, अभी आभूषण नहीं बना है। जितना अच्छा कारीगर मिल जाय उतना अधिक मूल्यवान् आभूषण बन सकता है। इसकी कीमत इतनी अधिक हो सकती है कि यह अनन्त मूल्यवान हो सकता है। देवता तो आभूषणरूप में हैं; सोना के विशुद्ध रूप में नहीं। जो आभूषण बन गया उसका तो मूल्य निश्चित हो गया, अब उसमें कोई परिवर्तन नहीं हो सकता। मनुष्य-योनि शुद्ध सोने का स्वरूप है। यदि कुशल कारीगर (सुयोग्य गुरु) प्राप्त हो जाय तो मनुष्य अनन्तानन्द स्वरूप साक्षात् परब्रह्म परमात्मा हो सकता है और ऐसा होने में ही मनुष्य-योनि की चरितार्थिता है।

67

The body of a human being is scarce, this is just what the *Shastra* says.

It isn't useful to come and live again in a womb and take birth as a human.

Once you have got a man's body you should not hope of coming in the womb again. This is really the value of being a human. If it befalls you to enter the womb again and again, then there is no advantage in being a human.

Life is limitless, but the number of births is *chauarasi lakh* (eighty-four hundred thousand). In these eighty-four hundred thousand births the spirit has been wandering.

So you should understand that there is one very big enclosure and along the wall of the enclosure, eighty-four hundred thousand rooms are made. A blind man is set free in the enclosure. He wants to go outside. He conjectures that somewhere or other the gate to the enclosure will certainly be found, and so with the support of the wall he goes from one room to another room and keeps going on further. Considering then that this is good he will proceed taking hold of the wall and will be able to go outside wherever he will find the gate. However, when he comes to the gate, at that time his body becomes itchy; letting go of the wall with both hands he scratches the itch. In the midst of this the gate appears.

This secret of this illustration is this, that the blind man is the *jiva* (individual life) and the eighty-four hundred thousand rooms are the eighty-four hundred thousand births. Human birth is the gate to get outside of the enclosure. When the *jiva* comes to the gate that is when he meets with human birth, then he becomes attached to thinking that happiness lies in wife, son, wealth, favourite friend etc. This sense of happiness is to feel an itching sensation. The time of man's life is spent scratching the itch and no effort is made to go to the other side of *bhavasagara* (the sea of feelings). This is exactly the blind man's itching that makes him miss the gate.

The body of a human being is scarce, this is just what the *Shastra* says. The significance of this is not that we get this rare body then collect more and more wealth, more and more children, grandchildren etc. who will be born and more and more things are experienced - this will not be the purpose of this scarce human body. The human body is rare, therefore this is a *"karma-yoni"* (an action birth) and others - births of beast, bird, insect, bird etc. - are *"bhoga-yoni"* (births of experience). In the life of the *bhoga-yoni* none of the actions are counted. The *karma-yoni*, that is to say, life with a human body is that which *karma* (action) is accountable, so you will undergo the fruits of each and every action. Therefore the *karma-yoni* (action birth) is difficult to attain. After undergoing eighty-four hundred thousand births this is gained, and having gained this birth you can do actions, the effects of which avoid the *jiva* being misled, and this can lead to putting an end to the endless suffering of again and again returning to the womb.

Shastra says that if you will worship gods then you will go in Devalok (the world of the gods, paradise) and if you will worship spirits then you will go to the world of spirits.

"भूतानि यान्ति भुतेज्या"

"bhutani yanti bhutejya"
[*Bhagavad Gita* 9:25]

'The *bhutejya* (worshipper of ghosts) will acquire the birth of a *bhuta* (ghost)'

and

'The worshipper of the *deva* (god) will gain birth as a god.'
[*Bhagavad Gita* 9:25]

By doing *japa* (silent repetition of a *mantra*) and *tapa* (penance) you will get birth as a god. But the aim of a human being should not be to gain divine birth because even amongst gods that most celebrated Devaraj (king of the gods - Indra) also had such a lack of discrimination, desiring to experience worldly pleasure. Not finding satisfaction in things of Swargalok (world of heaven) having come to the land of mortals he deceived Ahilya. [Ahilya maintained the appearance of a sixteen-year-old and was seduced by both Indra & Surya, who adopted the human form of her husband Gautama Muni]. When this is the state of the king of paradise then what will be the state the subjects there, the other gods? Therefore you should offer *pranaam* (salutation) from afar to heaven.

Another thing is this that the *jiva* stays only a little time dwelling in Devalok (heaven);

"क्षीणे पुण्ये मर्त्यलोकं विशन्ति"

"kshine punye martyalokam vishanti"
[*Bhagavad Gita* 9:21]

'When *punya* (merit) becomes exhausted you get to the world of mortals.'

But living in Devalok, not all have a similar amount of happiness, for according to the proportion of one's own past actions you enjoy that material welfare there. Therefore those gods who have much happiness and are well off, other gods seeing this are jealous. So even in Devalok there is envy too, hatred and jealousy which are the causes of suffering, really suffering. Thus you should not wish to go there on any occasion.

'The Sonar or Goldsmith'
[*'The Underworld of India'*, Sir George MacMunn, Jarrolds, 1895]

The god stays desirous of gaining a human body, because birth as a human being is similar to having gold. Pure gold! Just now jewellery is not made of it. However, if a good craftsman is got, that much more precious jewellery can be made. The value of this can be increased, this can become priceless. The gods then are in the form of jewellery; not in the form of pure gold. The jewellery has been made, then the price is settled, now you cannot reverse anything. The human birth is of the form of pure gold. If an expert craftsman [*satguru*] is obtained then man's own form can be *anantananda* (limitless bliss) *sakshat parabrahma* Paramatma (in the presence of the Supreme Soul) and as such the human birth is successful.

६८

सर्वत्र भगवान का भाव ही भक्तों का लक्षण

भगवद्भक्ति विभोर सभी भक्त वैष्णव हैं। रात्रि-दिन चोरी, दगाबाजी, भृष्टाचार आदि करते हुये अपने को विष्णु-भक्त वैष्णव मानने से कोई वैष्णव नहीं हो सकता।

शिव, गणेश, सूर्य, शक्ति आदि सब भगवान के अङ्ग हैं। कोई शिव-भक्त कहे कि हमारे शङ्कर ही भगवान हैं, कोई सौर्य कहे कि सूर्य ही भगवान हैं तो यह उसी प्रकार है जैसे सम्पूर्ण हाथी के स्वरूप को न जाननेवाले कुछ अंधों ने हाथी की सूँड पकड़कर कहा कि यह हाथी मूसल के समान है। किसी ने चरण पकड़कर कहा कि हाथी खम्भे के समान है। किसी ने कान पकड़कर कहा कि हाथी ऐसा ही सूप के समान है। बात यही है 'अंधों ने हाथी देख झगड़ा मचाई है' जो हाथी के सम्पूर्ण स्वरूप को जानता है वह कभी नहीं कहेगा कि हाथी सूप के समान होता है या मूसल के समान होता है।

इसी प्रकार जिसने भगवान को ठीक से समझ लिया है वह कभी नहीं कह सकता कि शिव ही भगवान का स्वरूप है या गणेश ही भगवान का स्वरूप है या विष्णु का चतुर्भुजि रूप ही भगवान का

स्वरूप है। जो यथार्थ भगवत्-तत्व से परिचित है वह यही कहेगा कि इन समस्त भिन्न-भिन्न स्वरूपों में वही एक परमात्मा के भिन्न-भिन्न अङ्ग रूप हैं। वास्तव में किसी भी देवता की उपासना भगवान की ही उपासना है। यही शास्त्र का सिद्धान्त है।

68

In truth worshipping any of the gods is really worship of Bhagwan.

The aim of devotees is really to feel Bhagwan everywhere.

All those who are fully absorbed in devotion to Bhagavad (God, Vishnu) are *vaishnava* (devotees of Vishnu). Someone who night and day is stealing, deceitful and doing other bad behaviour etc. yet thinking himself to be a devotee of Vishnu, cannot be a *vaishnava*.

Shiva, Ganesha, Surya, Shakti (Durga, Lakshmi) etc. are the limbs of Bhagwan. Any devotee of Shiva can say 'Our Shankar (Shiva) is really Bhagwan', any follower of Surya can say that 'Surya is really Bhagwan', then this is really like not knowing the whole shape of the elephant. Some blind men took hold of an elephant's trunk and said 'This elephant, it is like a pestle.' Seizing the foot one said it was like a pillar. Taking the ear one said it was like a winnowing basket. The thing is really this, that the blind men having seen the elephant got stirred up in dispute. He who knows the whole form of the elephant will never say that the elephant is similar to a winnowing basket or to a pestle.

In the same way, he who has taken a good understanding of Bhagwan, he can never say that Shiva is the true form of Bhagwan or Ganesha is the true form of Bhagwan or that the four-armed form of Vishnu is really the form of Bhagwan. He who is familiar with the essence of Bhagavat (God) will say that all these several forms are really the separate parts or limbs of Paramatma (God). In truth worshipping any of the gods is really worship of Bhagwan. This is really the established truth of the

Shastra.

GANESA, THE GOD OF WISDOM.

[*'Daily Life and Work in India'*, W J Wilkins, T Fisher Unwin, 1890]

६९

गुरु बदलने में कोई पाप नहीं होता

*

कुछ लोग कहते हैं कि एक गुरु बना लिया तो दूसरा गुरु नहीं बनाना चाहिये। किन्तु यह कोई शास्त्र का सिद्धान्त नहीं है, मन गड़न्त बात है। गुरु किया जाता है कल्याण के लिये। जब तक भगवद् प्राप्ति न हो जाय तब तक गुरु बदले जा सकते हैं। ऐसा तो कोई गुरु-भक्त नहीं देखा गया कि गुरु के बदलने के डर से हमेशा उसी क्लास में उसी गुरु से पड़ता रहे। 'क्लास' के परिवर्तन के साथ गुरु का परिवर्तन स्वाभाविक हो ही जाता है। पिछले गुरु की अवहेलना नहीं की जाती, उनका मान-सम्मान गुरु के रूप में ही

किया जाता है किन्तु आगे की पढ़ाई के लिये नये-नये गुरुओं का शिष्यत्व स्वीकार किया जाता है। व्यास-पुत्र शुकदेव जी ने अपने पिता से ज्ञान प्राप्त किया, फिर शंकर जी से ज्ञान प्राप्त किया और नारद जी से भी ज्ञान प्राप्त किया। अन्त में फिर जनके जी के पास भी शिक्षा लेने गये। इसलिये एक गुरु कर लिया है, दूसरा नहीं करेंगे, यह बिल्कुल रद्दी बात है और कल्याण में बाधक है। इस प्रकार की थोथली बातों को लेकर जीवन को नष्ट नहीं करना चाहिये। अनेकानेक जन्म इसी प्रकार अनेक योनियों में भटकते हुए बीत गये हैं अब तो मनुष्य जन्म पाकर सम्भल जाओ। ऊँचे से ऊँचे गुरु से उपासना का प्रकार समझ कर वेद-शास्त्रानुसार ही कर्मों को करते हुए भगवान का भजन-पूजन करते रहो तो निश्चय ही संसार-सागर से पार हो जाओगे।

69

‘Having taken one *guru*, another you should not’ - this is all rubbish talk and is obstructive to the welfare.

Some people say that having taken one *guru* you should not make another. But this doctrine is not of the *Shastra*, this is [just] the mind’s imagination. The *guru* is gone to for happiness. Up until when Bhagavad (God) is gained - up until then you can go and change *guru*. So then we haven’t seen any *guru-bhakta* (devotee) fearful of shifting, always studying in the very same *“class”* of the very same *guru*. Actually, to transfer *“class”* and to transfer *guru* is natural. It is not disrespectful to the previous *guru*, actually respect has been done the *guru*, but in future you get the promise of discipleship of fresh *gurus*.

Vyasa’s son Shukadeva ji acquired knowledge from his own father, then he gained knowledge from Shankar ji and also gained knowledge from Narada ji. In the end he took instruction from

Janaka ji. Therefore, 'Having taken one *guru*, another you should not' - this is all rubbish talk and is obstructive to the welfare. You should not ruin your life with these kind of empty words. Many lives have been caused to live in births, now then be alert to attain the human birth. Understanding the method of *upasana* (worship) from higher and higher *gurus*, having been doing actions according to *Veda Shastra*, be doing chanting and *puja* of Bhagwan, then it is certain you will cross the sea of *samsara* (worldly existence).

७०

जगत् भर का ज्ञान प्राप्त कर लो पर यदि अपने को न जान पाये तो अज्ञानी ही रहोगे

*

संसार तो कज्जल की कोठरी है। इसका जितना ज्यादा सम्पर्क बढ़ाओगे उतनी ही कालिमा लगेगी। जो वस्तु जैसी है उसको वैसी ही रहने दो। जितना प्रयोजन है उससे काम ले लो, व्यवहार चलाओ, पर संसार में प्रेम मत करो।

संसार के पदार्थ बाधक नहीं, उन्के प्रति अपना प्रेम अपने लिये बाधक है। संसारी-जन राग के पात्र नहीं, परमात्मा में राग बढ़ाओ।

पहले अपने को जानो फिर परमात्मा को जानने का प्रयत्न करो। अपने को न जान सके तो संसार को जान कर भी तो अज्ञानी ही रहोगे। अपने सम्बन्ध में जब अज्ञान बना है तो दूसरे का ज्ञान होकर ही क्या होगा। अपने घर में कूड़ा-करकट भरा रहे और दूसरे के मकानों में झाड़ू देते फिरो, यह तो कोई बुद्धिमानी नहीं है। जिस दिन अपने को जान लोगे उसी दिन मन की सारी गरीबी निकल

जायगी और सुख-शान्ति का अनुभव होने लगेगा।

70

Your own house is full of rubbish and you travel to sweep the house of another, this then is not intelligence at all.

Samsara then is a closet of *kajjal* (soot). However much the association grows, that much more blackness gets stuck to you. Whatever the thing is like, you should only give like that. However much the purpose is, from that take action. Do your daily business, but don't love in *samsara*.

The things of *samsara* are not troubling, one's own love for them is troubling for oneself. The worldly person is not a fitting recipient of attachment, increase attachment in Paramatma.

Firstly know yourself, then make an effort to know Paramatma. If you cannot know yourself yet you know *samsara* then you must be really ignorant. When in relation to yourself you are ignorant then what will come of knowledge of another? Your own house is full of rubbish and you travel to sweep the house of another, this then is not intelligence at all. People, the day you know about yourself, that is the day when all weakness of the mind will be disappear and you will be connected with feelings of happiness and peace.

७१

तुम तो सच्चिदानन्द स्वरूप परमात्मा के अंश हो अपने को भूल कर दुःख-सागर में डूब रहे हो

*

एक बार विचार करके देख लो कि तुम कौन हो। संसार में जितना जो कुछ तुम अनुभव करते हो, वह सब तुम से अलग है। शरीर, मन, बुद्धि, प्राण आदि सब कुछ तुम अपना मानते हो, कहते हो कि हमारा शरीर, हमारा मन, हमारी बुद्धि, हमारा प्राण। स्पष्ट है, जो कुछ अपना मानते हो उसके तुम स्वामी तो हो, पर तुम्हारा अस्तित्व उससे ऐसे भिन्न है जैसे तुम्हारा घर, तुम्हारा मंदिर है। मंदिर तुम्हारा है; पर तुम मंदिर नहीं हो। इसी प्रकार शरीर, मन, बुद्धि, प्राण आदि तुम्हारे हैं, पर तुम वह नहीं हो - तुम उससे भिन्न वस्तु हो। तुम सच्चिदानन्द परमात्मा के अंश हो, परन्तु अविवेक के कारण, अज्ञान के कारण शरीर, मन, बुद्धि, आदि के साथ तुमने अपनी इतनी घनिष्ठता बना ली है कि उसे ही तुम अपना स्वरूप समझने लगे हो।

हस्त-पाद आदि कर्म-इन्द्रियाँ नष्ट हो जाँय तो भी तुम रहते हो, आँख-कान आदि ज्ञानेन्द्रियाँ नष्ट हो जाँय तो भी तुम बहरे-आंधे होकर रहते हो - तुम्हारा अस्तित्व ज्ञानेन्द्रियों के नष्ट होने से नष्ट नहीं होता। जब कभी तुम बहुत भयंकर रोग से पीड़ित होते हो तो यही कह उठते हो कि 'प्राण निकल जाता तो हम सुखी हो जाते' अर्थात् तुम समझते हो कि संसार की समस्त वेदनायें प्राण निकल जाने से समाप्त हो जायेंगी। इस प्रकार प्राण भी तुमसे भिन्न पदार्थ है, तुम प्राण भी नहीं हो। जितना जो कुछ दृश्य है और अनुभव हो सकता है, उस सबसे तुम भिन्न हो। समझ लो, जहां तक जिन-जिन पदार्थों का तुम त्याग कर सकते हो वहां तक उन-उन पदार्थों से

तुम भिन्न हो - तुम्हारा स्वरूप वही है जिसका तुम कभी भी त्याग नहीं कर सकते। सबका अनुभव करने वाले सबके साक्षी तुम शुद्ध-बुद्ध-मुक्त चेतन-स्वरूप सच्चिदानन्द सनातन परमात्मा के अंश हो। अपने स्वरूप को समस्त जगत् और शरीर्, इन्द्रियाँ, प्राण आदि सब से अलग अनुभव कर लो तो फिर संसार में रहते हुए भी दुःख-शोकादि से मुक्त हो जाओगे।

अपने स्वरूप का अनुभव करने के लिये वेद-शास्त्र पर विश्वास करके सद्गुरुओं के बताये अनुसार उपासना विधान का सहारा लेकर उपासना करते चलो।

71

Take a look and consider one time, who are you?

Take a look and consider one time, who are you? However much you experience in *samsara*, you are separate from all that - body, mind, intelligence, breath etc. - all that you regard to be your own. It is said; 'Our body. Our mind. Our intelligence.' It is clear that to some extent you think that you are the owner, but your existence is separate from this, in the manner of your house, your temple. The *mandir* (temple) is yours; but you are not the temple. In this manner, the body, the mind, the intelligence, the breath etc. are yours, but you are not them - you are a separate thing from that. You are a part of the Paramatma *sachchidananda* form, but because of *aviveka* (absence of discrimination) and because of *agyaan* (ignorance), you have made such a close association with the body, mind, intelligence, breath etc. that you have become attached to understanding this form as yourself.

If a hand, foot etc. or an organ of the senses is destroyed then you will stay living. If an organ of perception such as the eyes or the ears etc., is destroyed then you become deaf or blind. Your existence is not destroyed with the destruction of the sense of perception. On some occasion when you are sick with a very dire illness then you say this, that really; 'If the breath will stop then we are happy', that is to say that you understand that the whole of *samsara's* agonies will be terminated with the stopping of the breath. In this manner the *prana* (breath) is also a thing separate from you, you are also not breath. However much is visible and can be experienced, you are separate from that. Understand, whatever things you can relinquish, you are separate from these things. Your real form is that which you can never relinquish. The experiencer of all, the witness of all, you are a part of the perfectly awake liberated human form of *sachchidananda* (Truth, Consciousness, Bliss) Eternal Paramatma.

Experience one's own form as separate from body, senses, breath etc. and all of the world, then again you will be released from pain and distress etc. of living in *samsara*. In order to experience one's own true self, trust on the *Veda Shastra* and with support provided according to the instructions of *sadgurus* (genuine *gurus*) proceed with *upasana* (worship, service).

७२

विधि के साथ भगवान् का नाम जपो

*

समय तो किसी न किसी रूप में लोग उपासना के लिये देते ही हैं परन्तु विधान के बिना जाने उसका फल विपरीत ही होता है, अनुकूल नहीं होता। पहले तो इसका ज्ञान होना चाहिये कि कहाँ से उपासना का प्रकार सीखा जाय। ऐसा नहीं कि जहाँ से जो मिलता देखो वहीं से लेलो, पर जहाँ से शास्त्र लेने को कहता है वहीं से लेना चाहिये।

सन्तान चाहते हो तो ऐसा नहीं कि जहाँ भी पड़ी मिले वहीं से उठा लो। विधि पूर्वक विवाह करो, विधाना-नुसार गर्भाधानादि सस्कार कराओ, तब जो सन्तान होगी वह काम की होगी।

इसी प्रकार कोई भी काम किया जाय, यदि विधान से किया गया तो उसका फल उत्तम होगा। यह पक्ष बिल्कुल अनर्थकारी है कि -

"उत्तम विद्या लीजिये, यदपि नीच पर होय।"

यह कहावत तभी से चली है जब से कुम्हार, तेली आदि सब शिक्षक होने लगे हैं। पहिले तो उत्तम विद्या नीच में जा ही नहीं सकती और यदि आ भी गई तो वह नीच नहीं रह सकता। उत्तम विद्या और नीचता दोनों एक साथ कैसे रह सकती हैं - प्रकाश जहाँ जाता है वहाँ अंधकार नहीं रहता।

गंगाजल पीना है तो नाबदान से क्यों पियें, धारा का क्यों न पियें। सन्तान ही चाहना है तो वैध सन्तान क्यों न उत्पन्न करें। उत्तम विद्या ही लेनी है तो उत्तम स्थान से क्यों न ली जाय।

72

To drink Gangajal (water from the River Ganga) why will you drink from the gutter?

'A Carrier of the Ganges Water'
[*'India and Its Inhabitants'*, Caleb Wright, Brainerd, 1856]

Arrange to do *japa* of the name of Bhagwan.

At this time people give worship one way or another, but without arrangement the results are negative, are not favourable. Firstly, where should you get knowledge of where you can learn this kind of *upasana* (worship, service)? We do not take it from wherever we see it, but we take it from where the *Shastra* says we should take it from.

If you desire offspring then you do not pick up whichever from wherever. First, you get married, you get suitably pregnant, then there will be progeny, then this desire will be fulfilled. In this way, fulfil any other desire. If it is done by arrangement then the effects will be the best.

This defence is entirely absurd that; 'You ought to take high knowledge, although it is from low.' This dictum proceeds from this account, from when the potter, the oilman etc. are all applying to be teachers. In the first place the high knowledge cannot go in the low and if it came then this cannot stay low. High knowledge and lowness, how could they both be together? Wherever light goes, there no darkness stays.

To drink Gangajal (water from the River Ganga), why will you drink from the gutter? Why not drink from the current of water? If you desire progeny then why not have a legitimate birth? If you take high knowledge then why not take it from a high place?

'The Sick brought to the Ganges'
[*'India and Its Inhabitants'*, Caleb Wright, Brainerd, 1856]

७३

ॐकार का जप

बहुत लोग शास्त्र-विधान देखकर और अधिकार-अनिधिकार का विचार न करके केवल यहाँ-यहाँ से महात्म्य पढ़-सुनकर ही उपासना में प्रवृत्त हो जाने हैं। कुछ लोग ॐकार को बहुत महत्वशाली मानकर उसी का जप करने लगते हैं। गीता में भगवान् ने कहा अवश्य है कि प्रणव मैं हूँ। किन्तु यदि ऐसी कारण भगवान् का स्वरूप मान कर भगवान को अपनाते हो तो उसो प्रकार सिंह को भी क्यों पकड़ कर नहीं रखते, क्योंकि वह भी तो (ओंकार के समान) भगवान का स्वरूप ही है। भगवान श्री कृष्ण चन्द्र ने कहा है कि -

'मृगानां मृगेन्द्रोऽहं।'

ॐकार के महात्म्य से प्रेरित होकर जो लोग केवल ॐकार का ही जप करते हैं उनकी क्या दशा होती है, यह हम अपने अभी तक के अनुभव से बताते हैं, सुनो -

दो, चार, दस, बीस बार नित्य ॐकार जप से तो कोई विशेष बात नहीं होती। परन्तु यदि दो-चार हजार जप नित्य होता रहे तो थोड़े ही समय में लौकिक परिस्थिति कमजोर हो जायगी। संखिया मारक है, परन्तु थोड़ा-थोड़ा खाया जाय तो उसका असर उतना शीघ्र नहीं होता। यदि थोड़ी भी मात्रा अधिक हो जाय तो मारक तो है ही। इसी प्रकार केवल ॐकार का जप विशेष रूप से करने वालों की लौकिक व्यवस्था अवश्य कमजोर हो जाती है; रोजी-रोजगार में कमी हो जाती है; स्त्री-पुत्र आदि अस्वस्थ रहते हैं और मर भी जाते हैं।

पाँच-छः वर्ष पहिले हम लक्ष-चण्डी यज्ञ के समय लखनऊ गये

थे। उस समय एक व्रिद्धा हमारे पास आई और दो-चार लोग भी उसके साथ आये। उन लोगों ने कहा कि माता जी बड़ी भक्ता हैं, दिन भर भजन-पूजन में लगी रहती हैं, पर अभी थोड़े ही दिन हुए कि इनके दो पुत्र युवावस्था में मर गये। इसके उत्तर में हमने उनसे पूँछा कि 'ॐकार का जप करती हो क्या?' उसने कहा कि महाराज! वही तो हमारा आधार है, दिन भर जप किया करती हूँ। हमने कहा कि अच्छा हुआ आपने संसार को तो जप डाला, अब न छोड़ना। परन्तु उसके लगाव से वह चीज ही नष्ट हो जायगी, यही ॐकार के जप का फल है। या तो कहीं प्रेम न करो और यदि प्रेम करोगे तो वह प्रेमास्पद पदार्थ ही ॐकार के जप के प्रभाव से नष्ट हो जायगा। इसी लिये गृहस्थों को केवल ॐकार के जप का अधिकार नहीं है। शास्त्र जो अधिकार नहीं देता वह कल्याण की दृष्टि से नहीं देता। यदि ॐकार जप से गृहस्थों को लाभ होता तों कोई कारण नहीं था कि शास्त्र उनके लिये निषेंध करता। मन्त्रों के आगे जों ॐकार जोड़ देते हैं वह माङ्गलिक अर्थ में होता है। दूसरी बात यह है कि स्त्रियों कों ॐकार युक्त मन्त्र के जप का निषेध है। जहाँ पुरुषों के मन्त्र के प्रारम्भ में 'ॐकार' लगाया जाता है वहाँ स्त्रियों के मन्त्र के आगे 'श्री' लगाया जाता है।

भगवान् शङ्कर ने पार्वती कों उपदेश करते हुए कहा है कि ॐकार-सहित मन्त्र का जप स्त्रियों के लिये विष के समान होंता है और ॐकार-रहित मन्त्र के जप से ही स्त्रियों का कल्याण होता है। विचार करना चाहिये कि शङ्करजी अपनी पत्नी को ज्ञान का उपदेश कर रहे हैं, परन्तु ॐकार को बचा रहे हैं। यदि स्त्री जाति के लिये ॐकार लाभदायक होता तो अपनीं अर्द्धाङ्गिनी कों उपदेश करते हुये शङ्करजी ॐकार का उपदेश क्यों न करते।

73

Some people set great measure by the magnificence of the *japa* of ॐ *OM*.

Many people have not done the work of consulting the *Shastras* in order to determine what is authorised and what is not. They look here and there and from this they understand what they should do to engage in worship. Some people set great measure by the magnificence of the *japa* of *OM*.

"AUM"

'OM'

In *Bhagavad Gita*, Bhagwan certainly said that 'I am the *pranava*.' But if the purpose is to attain Bhagwan's special form, then why not use the method of grasping the lion as well, since he is also that too? Bhagwan Shri Krishna Chandra said that:-

"मृगानां मृगेन्द्रोऽहं"

"mriganam mrigendro aham"
[*Bhagavad Gita* 10:30]

'Amongst beasts I am the lion'

What actually happens to those who proclaim the greatness of using only *"OMkara ka japa"*, our experience up until recently we are informing, listen; 2, 4, 10, 20 times constantly repeating *OM* then no particular effect there will be. But if 2, 4 thousand unceasing repetitions then in a short time [one's connection with] the worldly surrounding will become weak. Arsenic is a destroyer, but taking a little, then the effects will not be very rapid. If some excessive dose is taken then it actually kills. Those who use the method of *"OMkara ka japa"* alone, taking it to be the special form, find that their worldly discipline certainly weakens; working and regular meals go into decline; wife and son etc. become unhealthy and also die.

Five, six years ago, we had gone to Lucknow for the occasion of Laksha Chandi Yagya. On that occasion one old woman came to us and 2, 4 people came along too. These people said that Mataji was a great devotee, all day long she would remain in prayer and worship. However, only very recently her two sons, who were in the prime of life, had died.

To this we asked; 'Were you practicing *OMkara ka japa?'*

She answered to Maharaj! 'The very same is our basis, all day long I did do *japa*.'

We said that, '*Achchaa* (Okay), you have been casting *japa* for your *samsara* (life), not to quit now.'

However, by that connection the thing becomes destroyed. Right here is the effect of *"OMkara japa"*.

This then is done somewhere without love and if love's work is being done then the meaning and the object of love will be annihilated by the influence of *"OMkara ka japa"*.

For this reason *grihasthon* (householders) are not authorised to do *"OMkara ke japa"* alone. *Shastra* with a view to grant good fortune does not give authority. If there were any benefit to be derived by *grihasthon* by using *"OMkara japa"* there would be no reason for the *Shastra* to prohibit.

Mantras [sometimes] contain a mixture [of sounds including] *OM* that are given for auspicious purposes. Another thing is this that women are prohibited from practising *japa* with a *"OMkara-yukta mantra"* (a *mantra* conjoined with *OM*). Wherever at the beginning there is the *purusha* (male) *mantra "OM"* then instead women should apply the sound *"shree"*.

"shri"

'Shree'

Bhagwan Shankar (Lord Shiva) giving instruction to Parvati on *japa* explained that for women *"OMkara-sahita mantra ka japa"* (*OM* connected *mantra*) can be like poison and for happiness they should only do *japa* without *OMkara*. Due consideration should be given that Shankarji gave this information to his own wife. If *OMkara* is beneficial for a woman to do, why would he instruct his own wife against the practice?

७४

क्षत्रिय, वैश्य, शूद्र और स्त्री जाति के लिये गुरुत्व नहीं

शास्त्रों में स्त्री जाति के लिये गुरुत्व कहीं नहीं बताया। स्त्रियाँ गुरु नहीं हो सकतीं। गार्गी, चुड़ाला, सुलभा आदि स्त्रियाँ ज्ञानी और योगी भी हो गई हैं। परन्तु यह कहीं भी नहीं मिलता कि उन्होंने किसी को अपना शिष्य बनाया हो।

भगवान का भजन पूजन करते हुए साधन सम्पन्न होकर ज्ञान की प्राप्ति तो सब कर सकते हैं, भगवान की भक्ति में सब का अधिकार है, परन्तु गुरु सब नहीं बन सकते। गुरुत्व केवल ब्राह्मण ही को है। ब्राह्मण के अतिरिक्त क्षत्रिय, वैश्य, शूद्र, शिष्य तो हों सकते हैं, पर गुरु नहीं। स्त्रियों को भी गुरु बनने का अधिकार नहीं है।

जनक-राज विदेह इतने बड़े ज्ञानी थे, परन्तु क्षत्रिय होने के नाते उन्होंने गुरु बनने का प्रयत्न कभी नहीं किया। जिस समय शुकदेव जी को व्यास जी ने जनक जी के पास ज्ञान की शिक्षा लेने के लिये भेजा, उस समय जनक जी ने पूछा कि आप किस लिये पधारे हैं? शुकदेव जी ने कहा कि आपसे ज्ञान को शिक्षा लेने के लिये पिता जी ने भेजा है। जनकजी ने कहा कि आप ब्राह्मण हैं, हम क्षत्रिय हैं, आपको उपदेश करने का अधिकार हमें नहीं है। इसलिये शास्त्र विरुद्ध हम आपको कैसे उपदेश करें।

शुकदेवजी ने कहा कि आप क्षत्रिय हैं तो दान देना तो आप का धर्म ही है। शास्त्र आपको दान देने की आज्ञा तो देता ही है; आप हमें ब्रह्मविद्या का दान दे दें। यह सुन कर जनकजी ने शुकदेव जी को उच्चासन पर बैठा कर उनका पूजन किया और दान रूप में उन्हें ब्रह्म-विद्या दी। पर शिष्य बना कर जनक जी ने उपदेश नहीं किया। यह है समर्थ लोगों का शास्त्रीय मर्यादा-पालन का आदर्श। आजकल कायस्थ, वैश्य, तेली, कलवार भी कपड़ा रंग-रंग कर साधू

का वेश बना लेते हैं और लोगों को अपना शिष्य बनाने के लिये लालायित रहते हैं। इस प्रकर के गुरु और शिष्य दोनों ही पतन को प्राप्त होते हैं। जो बातें हम कहते हैं वह शास्त्रानुकूल ही कहते हैं, अपनी मनगढ़न्त बात हम कुछ नहीं कहते।

74

Kshatriya, vaishya, shudra and female sex are not for the purpose of position of *guru.*

Kshatriya, vaishya, shudra and female sex are not for the purpose of position of *guru*.

There is no mention anywhere in the *Shastras* of the female sex being *gurus*. Women cannot be a *guru*. Gargim, Chudala, Sulabha etc. were women who had become yogis and possessed of Self-Knowledge. But it is not met with anywhere that they made their own disciples.

Having been doing *puja*, worship and chanting, accomplishing the *sadhana*, then all can gain knowledge, all have the right of devotion in Bhagwan, but not all can be made a *guru*. Actually, really only *brahmanas* are in the position to be a *guru*. In addition to *brahmanas, - kshatriyas, vaishya* and *shudras* can become *shishya* (disciples), but not a *guru*. Women also have no right to be made a *guru*.

Raja Janaka Videha was a very great *gyaani* (knowledgeable), but being a *kshatriya* he never attempted to become a *guru*. The time that Vyasa ji did send Shukadeva ji to Janaka ji to take *shiksha* (instruction) of *gyaan* (knowledge), at that time Janaka ji asked; 'What are you coming for?'

Shukadeva ji said; 'Pita ji (father) sent me to learn knowledge from you.'

Janaka ji said that; 'You are *brahmana*, we are *kshatriya*, we have no right to give advice to you. Therefore as it is contrary to the *Shastra*, how can we teach you?'

Shukadeva ji did say that; 'You are *kshatriya*, then to give charity is your *dharma* (duty). The *Shastra* commands for you to give charity, then truly give; give us as charity the *brahmavidya* (theology taught in the *Upanishads*)'

After hearing this, Janaka ji sat Shukadeva ji on a higher seat, did *puja* to him and in the form of a donation gave him the *brahma-vidya* (knowledge pertaining to Brahma). But Janaka ji did not make him *shishya* (disciple) and give *upadesha* (advice). This is the model of demarcation of capable people preserving the *Shastra*.

Nowadays *kayastha, vaishya, teli* (oilman), and also *kalavara* (seller of spirits) are taking to wearing the colours of the *sadhu* (holy man) and are eagerly wishing to make *shishya* (disciples) of their own. Actually both these kind of *guru* and *shishya* (disciple) are to get their downfall. Actually this speech we are saying coincides with the *Shastras*, it is not something of our own that we have made up.

A SANYASI AND A SANYASIN, WITH THEIR COMPANIONS.

[*'The Mystics, Ascetics & Saints of India'*, John Campbell Oman, T Fisher Unwin, 1903]

७५

स्त्री-समाज को केवल पति परायण ही रह कर कल्याण

*

स्त्रियों में स्वभाव से ही रजोगुण अधिक रहता है। इसलिये अधिकांशतः ध्यान-समाधि की ओर वे सफलता पूर्वक अग्रसर नहीं हो सकतों। इसीलिये उन्हें एक पति-परायण रहने का विधान है। निरन्तर पति-परायण रहकर स्त्री अन्त काल में पति का स्मरण करती हुई ही शरीर त्याग करेगी, जिससे उसका जन्म पुरुष-योनि में होगा। क्योंकि यह सिद्धान्त है कि जिस-जिस भाव से जीव शरीर छोर्ड़ता है उसी-उसी भाव को प्राप्त होता है -

यं यं वापि स्मरन भावं,
त्यज्यन्ते कलेवरम्।
तं तमेवेति कौन्तेय।
सदा तद्भाव भावितः॥ - "गीता"

स्त्री यदि भगवान का चिन्तन करती हुई शरीर त्यागे तब तो भगवान में मिल ही जायगी, इसमें सन्देह नहीं। परन्तु स्त्री-प्रकृति रजोगुण प्रधान होने के कारण उनमें चाञ्चल्य अधिक होता है। इसलिये भगवान स्वरूप में उनकी वृत्ति टिकना कठिन रहती है। साथ ही यह भी बात है कि पुरुष-चिन्तन का स्वभाव स्त्री का स्वाभाविक हुआ करता है। इस लिये पति-परायण होकर सदा पतिभावापन्न रहना हि उनके लिये शास्त्र में श्रेयस्कर बताया गया है। पति-परायण रहेगी तो अन्त काल में भी पति का स्मरण करती हुई शरीर त्याग कर पुरुष-योनि को प्राप्त हो जायगी और अगले जन्म में भगवत् परायण होकर भगवान में मिल जायगी।

स्त्री-योनि महा कष्टकारी योनि है, गर्भ-धारण और प्रसव-काल में तो मरण के समान महा भयंकर दुःख होता है। उसकें वाद भी सन्तान के पालन-रक्षण आदि में जों कष्ट होते हैं, वह स्त्रियाँ ही जान सकती हैं; दूसरा कोई इसकी भयंकरता का अनुमान भी नहीं लगा सकता। इस प्रकार अत्यन्त कष्टदायिनी स्त्री-योनि से जीव को मुक्त करके पुरुष-योनि में लाने के लिये ही पातिव्रत्य का इतना विधान शास्त्र में किया गया है। यह सब स्त्रियों के कल्याण के लिये ही है।

75

The welfare of women is really only in the attachment to husband.

The welfare of women is really only in the attachment to husband.

By nature there is more *rajoguna* (the passion of love and pleasure) in women. Therefore the majority of them cannot be thriving and getting ahead in the direction of *dhyaana* and *samadhi*. Therefore, their *vidhana* (arrangement, method) is their dedication to husband. Being dedicated to the husband, at the end time (time of death) the woman who has been thinking of the husband will abandon the body, and from that will be born as a male being. This is because of the principle that; whatsoever you are feeling when you let go of the body, that existence the soul will gain.

"यं यं वापि स्मरन भावं त्यज्यन्ते कलेवरम्।
तं तमेवेति कौन्तेय सदा तद्भाव भावितः॥"

"yam yam vapi smarana bhavam tyajyante kalevaram.
tam tameveti kaunteya sada tadbhava bhavitah."
[*Bhagavad Gita* 8:6]

'Whosoever he is remembering when the body comes to an end, O Kaunteya (Arjuna) he goes to that being that is always being thought of.'

If a woman is thinking of Bhagwan then she will get to Bhagwan - in this there is no uncertainty. But, because they are chiefly *rajoguna,* there is more fickleness in them. Therefore, it is difficult for them to stop their *vritti* (flow of mental activity) in the true form of Bhagwan. There is really this statement too that; 'Thinking about a man is the natural disposition of a woman.' Therefore constantly being devoted to the husband, it is said to be propitious in the *Shastra*. She will be devoted to the husband then, in the end time, whilst abandoning the body she will also be remembering the husband and gain the body of a man, and in the next life, by being devoted to Bhagavat will go and get Bhagwan.

The birth as a woman is the source of great suffering - accepting pregnancy and the time of childhood then are similar to the horrific suffering of death. After all that, there is also the hardship in nourishing and protecting etc. the offspring. Only women can really know that; none can guess of the ghastliness of this to another. From life as a female, with this kind of enormous suffering etc. liberation is carried over into the birth as a male, *Shastra* has given so much rule of chastity for this purpose. This is really for the welfare of all females.

७६

भगवान् के आज्ञारूप वेद शास्त्र के अनुसार चलिये

धनवान व पुत्रवान होने के लिये तो सब लोग प्रयत्न करते हैं, परन्तु आचार्यवान होने के लिये वे अधिक प्रयत्न नहीं करते। आचार्यवान होना ही समस्त सुख-शान्ति को प्राप्त करना है। किसी को गुरु मान लेने से वह आचार्य नहीं कहा जा सकता, जिसमें आचार्य के लक्षण हों वही आचार्य कहा जा सकता है। आचार्य ही किसी को आचार्यवान बना सकता है।

श्रुति-स्मृति ममैवाज्ञे,
यस्तोंल्लंघ्य वर्तते।
आज्ञोच्छेदी ममद्रोही,
मद्रभक्तोभपि न मे प्रियः॥

अर्थात्, श्रुति-स्मृति मेरी आज्ञा है। उसका उल्लंघन जों कोई मरता है वह चाहे मेरा भक्त ही क्यों न हो, वह मुझे प्रिय नहीं लगता।

इसलिये भगवान की आज्ञा-रूप श्रुति-स्मृति [वेद-शास्त्र] की ही प्रधानता मानी जाती है।

हम वेद-शास्त्र की ही बात सुनाते हैं, अपनी कोई मन-गढ़न्त बात नहीं कहते। हमने कभी नहीं कहा कि हमारी बात मानो। क्योंनंकि हमारी व्यक्तिगत बात मानोगे तो शङ्कराचार्य की बात मानने की आदत पड़ जायेगी। फिर यदि कोई नालायक भी इस गद्दी पर आ गया तो उसकी भी बात मानोगे। किसी के भी व्यक्तिगत विचारों से कल्याण नहीं होगा, कल्याण तो वेद-शास्त्र की बातें मानने से होगा। इसलिये हम कहते हैं कि शङ्कराचार्य की व्यक्तिगत बात मानने की आदत मत डालो, वेद-शास्त्र के अनुसार जो कहें वही मानो। शास्त्र कहता है कि वेद-शात्र भगवान् की आज्ञा है।

भगवान् के भक्तों को तो अवश्य ही भगवान् की आज्ञा रूप वेद-शास्त्र का पालन करना चाहिये। जब तक भगवान मिले नहीं हैं तभी तक उनकी आज्ञा का पालन करना आवश्यक है। जब भगवान से मिल जावगे तब तो भगवद्रूप ही हो जाओगे; उस समय आज्ञा-पालन का कोई प्रश्न ही नहीं रह जायगा।

76

The *Shastra* is said to be the command of Bhagwan.

To be wealthy or to possess sons, then all people make an effort, but not much effort is made to get an *acharya* (teacher). Only from getting an *acharya* do you gain all happiness and peace. By accepting anyone as a *guru* he cannot be said to be an *acharya*, only he who has the characteristic qualities of an *acharya* can be called an *acharya*. Only an *acharya* can make anyone an *acharyavan* (one who has an *acharya*).

"श्रुति-स्मृति ममैवाज्ञे यस्तोंल्लंध्य वर्तते ।
आज्ञोच्छेदी ममद्रोही मद्रभक्तोभपि न मे प्रियः ॥"

"shruti-smriti mamaivagye yastomllamdhya vartate.
agyochchedi mamadrohi madrabhaktobhapi na me priyah."
[*Vishnudharma Purana* 76:31]

That is to say that;

'*Shruti* and *smriti* are my commands, he who contravenes is the destroyer.
That he really desires to be my devotee. Why not? He is not beloved to me.'

Therefore the commands of Bhagwan are pre-eminently thought to be in the form of the *shruti* and *smriti*.

We are hearkening only to the *Veda Shastra*, we are not telling our own mental construction. We never say to accept our words; because if you will accept our own personal statement then you will be in the habit of accepting the words of the Shankaracharya. Then if anyone unfit is coming on the throne then you will accept his words too. From any personal notions there will be no welfare, welfare then will be from accepting the words of the *Veda Shastra*. Therefore we say; 'Don't get the habit of accepting the personal views of the Shankaracharya, accept what is said according to the *Veda Shastra*. The *Shastra* is said to be the command of Bhagwan.'

The devotees of Bhagwan then certainly should only protect the commands of Bhagwan in the form of the *Veda Shastra*. Whilst you have not met with Bhagwan, then up until then it is necessary to preserve his commands. When you will have met with Bhagwan then you will really be the form of Bhagavad (God); at that time there will really be no question of preserving commands.

७७

सद्गुरु किसे कहते हैं?

*

"तद्विज्ञानार्थं सद्गुरुमेवाभिगच्छेत्।

समित्पाणिः श्रोत्रियं ब्रह्मनिष्ठम्।"

प्रत्येक शब्द के दो अर्थ हैं, एक वाच्यार्थ और दूसरा लक्ष्यार्थ।

इस श्रुति में तत् पद का वाच्यार्थ है "मायोपाधि चैतन्य देव ईश्वर" भगवान राम, कृष्ण, शक्ति आदि साकार ब्रह्म। और तत् पद का लक्ष्यार्थ है मायातीत पूर्ण ब्रह्म-निर्गुण निराकार परमात्मा जो चराचर में रमा हुआ है। प्रयोजन यह है कि तत् पद वाच्य सगुण साकार परमात्मा तथा तत् पद लक्ष्य निर्गुण निराकार परब्रह्म है। किसी के भी जानने की इच्छा हो तो गुरु के पास जाना चाहिये। गुरु के पास रिक्त हस्त न जाय। हाथ में कुछ पत्र-पुष्प लेकर जाना चाहिये।

श्रोत्रिय ब्रह्मनिष्ठ गुरु के पास जाना चाहिये। श्रोत्रिय का अर्थ है वेद-वेदार्थ का ज्ञाता और ब्रह्मनिष्ठ उसे कहते हैं जो वेद-वेदार्थ द्वारा निरुपित परब्रह्म परमात्मा का रसास्वादन करता हो। ये दो विशेषण जिसमें हों, वही गुरु और आचार्य पदवाच्य हो सकता है।

गुरु ही भवसागर से पार उतारने वाली नौका है। संसार में सदगुरु मिलना ही दुर्लभ है और सब कुछ तो यहाँ सुलभ ही है। मंत्र तो वेद-शास्त्र में भरे पड़े हैं, मंत्रों की कमी नहीं है। परन्तु पुस्तकों के मंत्र तो ऐसे हैं जैसे कारतूसों का ढेर। पचासों प्रकार की कारतूसों का ढेर लगा हो और बन्दूक भी पास में रखी हो, परन्तु जब तक कोई यह बताने वाला न हो कि किस नम्बर का कारतूस किस जानवर को मारने के लिए ठीक है, तब तक कारतूसों का ढेर सामने रहते हुए भी बेकार सा ही है। जिस प्रकार कुशल शिकारी शेर, हाथी, हिरण आदि के शिकार के लिये अलग-अलग नम्बर के कारतूसों से काम लेता है, उसी प्रकार अनुभवी गुरु लोग साधकों की शक्ति-प्रवृत्ति आदि को देखकर उनके अधिकार के अनुसार ही लाभदायक मंत्रों का निर्णय करते हैं और उन्हीं से साधकों को लाभ होता है।

कहीं भी शास्त्रों में विधान नहीं है कि गुरु लोग शिष्यों के यहाँ जायँ। गुरु को मोटर-गाड़ी भेज कर अपने पास बुलाने का कहीं भी विधान नहीं है, शिष्य को स्वयं गुरु के पास जाना चाहिये, यही मर्यादा है। परन्तु जब से शिष्यों के सहारे पेट लग गया तभी से गुरुत्व की मर्यादा मिट्टी में मिल गई। राजगुरु क्या होते हैं? राज-गोरू होते हैं - गोरु कहते हैं पशु को। राजा की तरफ से गाँव - इलाका लग गया, मोटर चढ़ने को मिल गई, बस मानो स्वर्ग का सारा सुख मिल गया, अब आगे कोई पुरुषार्थ नहीं। शिष्य के कल्याण की चिन्ता नहीं, चाहे वह नरक में ही क्यों न चला जाय। तुलसीदास जी ने ठीक ही लिखा है -

हरै शिष्य धन, शोक न हरई।
मौ गुरु घोर नरक मंह परई॥

शोक कैसे निवृत्त होता है? इसके लिये श्रुति कहती है -

'तरति शोकमात्मवित्'

आत्मज्ञानी ही शोक-सागर को पार करता है। इसीलिये शिष्य श्रोत्रिय ब्रह्मनिष्ठ के पास जाकर आत्म-ज्ञान प्राप्त करै - यह श्रुति का आदेश है।

यदि गुरु शिष्य को आत्मज्ञान या भगवद्दर्शन न करा सका और उसके धन का बराबर उपयोग करता रहा तो निश्चय ही उसे घोर नरक प्राप्त होगा। हम जब किसो को शिष्य करते हैं तो प्रयत्न करते हैं कि इसे स्वरूप-ज्ञान या भगवद्दर्शन हो जाय। यदि उसकी अपात्रता के कारण ऐसा न हो सका तो उसके कारण हम तो नरक से बचे रहें, यही सोच कर किसी भी शिष्य से कभी किसी प्रकार की आर्थिक सेवा नहीं लेते।

एक समय हम कुम्भ में प्रयाग में थे। वहाँ किसी सभा में हमने कहा कि हम तो समझते थे कि हमारी दूकान नई है, परन्तु चली खूब। यह सुनकर कुछ साधुओं ने विचार किया कि ये तो कुछ लेते-देते नहीं। हमीं लोगों पर यह व्यङ्ग बोला गया है। यह सोचकर कुछ लोग हमारे पास आये और पूछा कि महाराज! दूकान में तो लेना-देना होता है पर आप तो कुछ लेते-देते नहीं - तो यह किस अभिप्राय से कहा गया है? इस पर हमने कहा कि हम भी लेते-देते हैं, पर हमारे लेने-देने की चीज आपसे भिन्न है। आप लोग रुपया-पैसा लेते हो, परन्तु हम उससे अधिक कीमती चीज लेते हैं। आप समझते हो कि जब दो रईस परस्पर मुकद में - बाजी करते हैं तो अपना सर्वस्व बेचकर लड़ने को तैयार रहते हैं, पर एक दूसरे के सामने विनीत नहीं होते। कोई कुछ भी करे पर अपना सर झुकाने के लिये तैयार नहीं रहते। वही सिर जो अपना सर्वस्व नष्ट करके भी नहीं झुकता, हमारे सामने आकर जमीन पर लग जाता है। जिसने अपना मस्तक हमारे सामने झुका दिया, उसके पास उससे बड़ी हमें देने के लिये और कोई चीज नहीं है। इस प्रकार मनुष्य की हम

सबसे बड़ी चीज लेते हैं और उसके बदले में देते हैं "उसके कल्याण का मार्ग"। यही हमारे यहाँ का लेना-देना है। सिर का झुकना कितनी बड़ी बात है, यह वही समझ सकता है जिसका सिर कहीं न झुका हो। जिनका सिर इधर-उधर झुकता ही रहता है उनके सामने सिर का क्या मूल्य! वे तो सिर की अपेक्षा रुपये को अधिक मूल्यवान् मानते हैं। सिर झुकना अपने अहंकार, अपने अस्तित्व का समर्पण है। उससे अधिक मूल्य रुपया-पैसा का मानना उचित नहीं। हम लेते है लोगों का अहंकार और देते हैं उनके कल्याण का मार्ग, इसलिये यही लेना-देना हमारे यहां होता है।

77

Bowing the head is to surrender one's own *ahamkara* (ego)

"तद्विज्ञानार्थं सद्गुरुमेवाभिगच्छेत्
समित्पाणिः श्रोत्रियं ब्रह्मनिष्ठम् ।"

"tadvigyanartham sadgurumevabhigachchet.
samitpanih shrotriyam brahmanishtham."
[*Mundaka Upanishad* 1:2:12]

'For that learning, with firewood in hand, one ought to approach a *sadguru* (a good *guru*) who is *shrotiyam* (well-versed in *Vedas*) and *brahmanishtham* (possessing knowledge of immortal self.'

There are two meanings of each sound - one is *vachyartha* (the clear meaning expressed in words) and the other is *lakshyaartha* (the metaphorical meaning or significance). In this *shruti* (Scripture) the *vachyartha* (the clear meaning) of the word *"tat"* (as in *"tat vigyanartham"*) is;

"मायोपाधि चैतन्य देव ईश्वर"

"mayopadhi chaitanya deva ishvara"
'The Lord in the condition of *maya* as the conscious god'

Bhagwan Ram, Krishna, Shakti, etc. are Brahman taking form, and the *lakshyaartha* (metaphorical) meaning of the word *"tat"* (that) is *mayatita* (beyond *maya*), *purna* (perfect), *brahma-nirguna* (Brahma, without qualities), *nirakara* (without form) - Paramatma (the Supreme Self) that plays in the world of the animate and inanimate. The intention is this - the word *"tat"* expresses Paramatma having form and endowed with qualities, and the *lakshya* (metaphorical) meaning of the word *"tat"* is Parabrahma (the Supreme Soul), without quality and without form. Any who also wish to understand should then go beside a *guru*, not go to the *guru's* side empty-handed. You should go and take some flowers and foliage in the hand.

You should go towards a *guru* who is *shrotriya* and *brahmanishtha*. The meaning of *shrotriya* is one who knows the

Vedas and we say that he is *brahmanishtha* who by means of discovering the *Vedas* gets appreciation of Parabrahma (the Supreme Soul) Paramatma (the Supreme Being). Wherein these two attributes occur, he is a *guru* and can be expressing the word *acharya*.

The *guru* is really a boat to get across the ocean of life. In *samsara* (worldly existence) it is very rare to obtain a *sadguru* (good *guru*). The *Veda Shastra* are full of *mantra*, there is no shortage of *mantron* (*mantras*). But books of *mantras* are similar to a pile of cartridges. There are piles of cartridges of different kinds by the fifties and to be put in the gun, but until someone is telling which *"number"* cartridge is fit to kill the beast, the pile of cartridges will really be next to useless. In the manner that an expert hunter desires several *"number"* of cartridges for hunting tiger, elephant, deer etc., that kind of experienced *guru,* observing the *shakti-pravritti* (energy and inclination) of those people devoted to spiritual achievement, in accordance to their right, deduces the beneficial *mantron* according to their entitlement and which would be of benefit to them, the *sadhakon* (spiritual seekers).

Nowhere in the *Shastras* is there a rule where the *guru* goes to the disciples. Nowhere is there a rule that they send a motor car and invite the *guru* to their place. The *shishya* (pupil) should personally go to the *guru*, this is the rule. However, since they have become attached to the pupils for the support of the stomach, for this reason the decorum of the position of *guru* has been mingled in the dirt. What is it to be a *"rajaguru"* (spiritual preceptor of a king)? They are become *"raja-goru"* - *"goru"* is said to be *pashu* (brute, beast, cattle).

By the side of the *raja* (king) he has tenure of several villages, gets to clamber into a *"motor"* (car). Admit it, he gets all the pleasure of Swarg (heaven), now, in future there is no *purshartha* (efforts to fulfil life). No desire of thought for the welfare of the pupil. Why does he not go to hell?

Tulasidas did properly write:-

"हरइ शिष्य धन शोक न हरई ।
सो गुर घोर नरक महुँ परई ॥"

"harai shishya dhana shoka na harai.
so gura ghora naraka mahun parai."
[*Shri Ramacharitmanasa - Uttarakand* 99:3]

'He who takes the wealth of the *shishya* (disciple) but does not take away the sorrow,
that *guru* will be sent to *ghora narak* (horrible hell).'

How can *"shoka"* (distress, sorrow, grief) be got rid of?
For this it is said in the *shruti*;

"तरति शोकमात्मवित्"

"tarati shokamatmavit"
[*Chandogya Upanishad* 7:1:3]

'The knower of *atman* crosses over sorrow'

'The *atmagyaani* (the knower of the self) crosses the ocean of sorrow.' Therefore, going to one who is *shrotriya* (thoroughly well versed in the *Vedas*) and *brahmanishtha* (one possessing knowledge of the immortal Self), *atma-gyaan* (self-knowledge) is gained. This is the instruction of the *shruti*.

If the *guru* cannot give the pupil *Bhagavadadarshana* (sight of God) or *atmagyaan* (self-knowledge) and continually avails himself of his wealth, then certainly he will gain *ghora narak* (horrible hell).

When we accept any pupil then we make an effort, and by this he comes to knowledge of the Self or comes to see God. If the reason can be that he is not fit, then if it is this cause then we will escape hell - this very thought - we never accept any kind of economic service from any pupil.

One time we were at the Kumbha (Mela) in Prayag (Allahabad). In a meeting there we said that we were thinking that; 'Our shop is new, but it is going well.' Having heard this, some *sadhus* (hermits) reasoned that; 'There is no give and take (buying and selling). This is telling a joke on us people.'

Considering this some people came near to us and asked; 'Maharaja, in a shop there is giving and taking, but you then are not giving and taking, then what is the idea of this?'

About this we said that, 'We also give and take, but our giving and taking is different from yours. You people are taking *rupees* and *paisa*, but we take a more valuable thing from him. You understand that when two wealthy people are in litigation with one another then they are ready to sell their entire property in order to fight, but not be courteous face-to-face with one another, they will do anything else but are not ready to bow their own head. This very head that they will not bow even if they are to lose their entire property, to come before us and goes on the floor. Who does this bowing of the head face-to-face with us, he has nothing greater, nothing more to give? From this kind of person we take the greatest and in exchange we give him the route to *kalyana* (happiness, welfare, benediction, prosperity). This is really the give and take here. How great is the meaning of bowing of the head? This can only be understood by he who does not bow anywhere. What cost to bow the head to him whose head is bowed on this side and on that side? They consider *rupees* more valuable than bowing the head.

Bowing the head is to surrender one's own *ahamkara* (egotism, arrogance, conceit, empty pride, vanity), one's own existence. It is not proper to regard *rupees* and *paisa* as more valuable than this. We take people's egotism and give then the path to *kalyana* (welfare, happiness, benediction). Therefore this is really the give and take we are doing here.'

७८

जगद्गुरु किसे कहते हैं?

*

संसार में आस्तिक व नास्तिक दो श्रेणी के लोग हैं:-

नास्तिक जगत् के तो कोई गुरु होते नहीं। आस्तिक जगत् का जो गुरु हो उसे ही जगद्गुरु कहना चाहिये। आस्तिकों में दो प्रकार की निष्ठा पाई जाती है - कुछ लोग साकार ब्रह्म में निष्ठा रखते हैं और कुछ की निष्ठा निराकार में होती है। जो साकार-वादियों और निराकार-वादियों दोनों का गुरु होने की क्षमता रखता हो, वही जगद्गुरु कहा जा सकता है। तात्पर्य यह है कि साकार देवताओं में जो पंच-देवता वैदिक हैं, अर्थात भगवान विष्णु, शिव, शक्ति, सुर्य और गणेश, इन सब की उपासना का प्रकार समझाने वाला जो हो और जो इन पंच-साकार देवताओं में निष्ठा न करके निर्गुण निराकारवादी है उसको भी जो उपदेश कर सके वही जगद्गुरु है। एक-एक देवता की उपासना का प्रकार समझाने वाले लोग उसी प्रकार हैं, जैसे एक-एक रोग की दवा की एक-एक शीशी रखने वाले टुटपुंजिया वैद्य लोग जो कम्पा-उन्डर की भी हैसियत नहीं रखते और कहते हैं अपने को सिविल सर्जन। कोई अपने पुत्र का नाम 'राम' रखले तो कौन रोक सकता है। परन्तु नाम मात्र से तो वह राम नहीं हो जाता। कोई अपने नाम के आगे जगद्गुरु लिखने लगे तो उसे रोके कौन? किन्तु जब जगद्गुरु के लक्षण पूछने लगते हो तो लक्षण-युक्त जगद्गुरु वही है जिसके दरवाजे से किसी भी देवता में निष्ठा रखने वाला निराश होकर न लौटे। आधुनिक सम्प्रदायों ने शिव, शक्ति, विष्णु आदि की उपासनाओं के सम्बन्ध में जो बटवारा किया गया है वह अनुचित है। पंच-देवताओं में कोई

छोटा-बड़ा नहीं है। सभी देवता अपने भक्त का समान रूप से कल्याण करने में समर्थ हैं जितने उपासक हैं सभी वैष्णव हैं; क्योंकि सभी देवता भगवान के ही अंग हैं। भगवान का स्वयं कथन है कि -

"ज्ञानं गणेशो मम चक्षुरर्कअः,
शिवो ममात्मा ममशक्तिराद्य।
विभेद बुद्धया मयि ये भजन्ति,
ममाङ्गहीनं कलयन्ति मन्दाः॥"

अर्थात् गणेश जी भगवान के मस्तिष्क हैं, सुर्य भगवान के नेत्र हैं, शिव भगवान की आत्मा, आद्या भगवती भगवान की शक्ति है। इसलिये इन पण्चदेवों को एक ही भगवान के भिन्न-भिन्न अङ्ग न मान कर जो इनमें परस्पर भेद-भावना मान कर इनमें से किसी एक की उपासना करते हैं, वे भगवान की उपासना नहीं करते बल्कि उनका अङ्ग-छेदन करते हैं।

स्पष्ट है कि जो गणेश का खण्डन करता है वह चाहे विष्णु-भक्त हो, किन्तु भगवान विष्णु के मस्तिष्क का छेदन करने वाला होता है। कोई विष्णु-भक्त यदि शिव का खण्डन करता है तो वह भगवान विष्णु की आत्मा का छेदन करता है। इसी प्रकार देवी का खण्डन करने वाला भगवान को शक्तिहीन करता है। इसलिये आज-कल के साम्प्रदायिक लोग जो परस्पर एक दूसरे से ईर्ष्या-द्वेष करते हैं और अपने को वैष्णव कहते हुए भगवान शिव का या अपने को शैव कहते हुए भगवान विष्णु का खण्डन करते हैं, वे न शैव ही हैं और न वैष्णव ही, वे केवल दम्भी है। वैष्णव वही है जो भगवान विष्णु का भक्त है।

'विष्णौरतः वैष्णवाः' 'ऊर्ध्वपुंड्वत्वं वैष्णवत्वम्'

'ऊर्ध्वपुंछ्र वाले को वैष्णव कहते हैं' - यह कोई सिद्धांत नहीं है।

जो भगवान विष्णु की उपासना करता है वह तो वैष्णव है ही। परन्तु सभी देवता भगवान के भिन्न-भिन्न अंग होने के कारण किसी भी देवता की उपासना करने वाला भी वैष्णव कहा जा सकता है जिस समय किसी देवता की उपासना कर रहे हो, उसी समय वैषव हो। समस्त आस्तिक-जगत् वैष्णव है।

केवल ऊर्ध्व-पुंड्र लगा कर अपने को वैष्णव और दूसरे को अवैष्णव कहने वाले वास्तविकता से अपरिचित हैं। वे भगवान विष्णु का अपमान करते हैं। कोई शिव भक्त या शक्ति उपासक यदि अपने को वैष्णव नहीं मानता है तो यह भी उसकी भूल है। कोई भी संसार में ऐसा नहीं है जो वैष्णव नहीं। संप्रदाय-वादियों की फिरकेबाजी न उनके काम की चीज है और न दूसरे की ही।

78

What do we say is a *jagadguru*?

In *samsara* there are two sorts of people - *astika* (religious) and *nastika* (unbeliever) - in the world of the atheist there isn't any *guru*. Of the world of the *astika* (religious) that *guru* should really be called *"jagadguru"*. Amongst the religious there are two kinds of believers. Some folk are setting their belief in a *sakara* (form) of Brahma and some in the *nirakara* (formless). The one who holds the ability to be *guru* to both, those who are speakers of the *sakara* (form) and those who are speakers of the *nirakara* (formless), the very same can be called a *jagadguru*.

The meaning of this is that; of the *sakara* deities there are five Vedic deities, that is to say; Bhagwan Vishnu, Shiva, Shakti, Surya and Ganesha. There are different instructions for worship of all of these and for those who do not believe in the five deities he can also give instruction, the same is really a *jagadguru*. The person who instructs in the method of worship for *devata* (deities) is similar to the lowly paid *vaidya* (physician) who sets phials of medicine for all diseases, without also having the status of a *"compounder"* but calls himself a *"civil surgeon"*.

Anybody can name their own son Rama. Who can stop them then? But merely from a name he does not become Rama. Then who stops anybody writing *jagadguru* in front of his own name? But when you ask the mark of the *jagadguru* then the proper indication really is this that nobody with faith in any deity goes away from the door disappointed. Recently *sampradaya* (sects) have allotted a relationship of worshipping Shiva, Shakti, Vishnu etc., this is improper. In the five deities there is not any inferiority or superiority. Every deity is similarly capable of dealing with the welfare of their own devotees, however much a worshipper they are, all are *vaishnava*, since all deities are parts of Bhagwan. Bhagwan states that:-

"ज्ञानं गणेशो मम चक्षुरर्कंअः
शिवो ममात्मा ममशक्तिराध्य ।
विभेद् बुद्धया मयि ये भजन्ति
ममाङ्गहीनं कलयन्ति मन्दाः ॥"

"gyaanam ganesho mama chakshurarkamah
shivo mamatma mamashaktiradhya.
vibheda buddhaya mayi ye bhajanti
mamangahinam kalayanti mandah."

That is, Ganesh ji is the head of Bhagwan, Surya are the eyes of Bhagwan, Shiva is the *atma* of Bhagwan, Adya Bhagavati is the *shakti* of Bhagwan.

'The Hindu Goddess Durga'
[*'India and Its Inhabitants'*, Caleb Wright, Brainerd, 1856]

Therefore these five gods are several equal parts, which cannot be measured and split from one another, and they are to be worshipped as equals. [If not] then worship is not being done but [instead] the cutting off of parts is being done.

It is clear that denying Ganesha in desiring to be a devotee of Vishnu, but he one who is cutting off Bhagwan Vishnu's head. If any devotee of Vishnu denies Shiva then he is cutting off the *atma* (soul) of Bhagwan Vishnu. This is really the manner of someone denying Devi (goddess) making Bhagwan powerless. Therefore, nowadays sectarian people have ill-will and malice towards one another but call themselves *vaishnava* (devotees of Vishnu) or of Bhagwan Shiva, has been calling himself *shaiva* (a devotee of Shiva), denying Bhagwan Vishnu, They are not really *shaiva* and not really *vaishnava*, they are merely hypocrites. A *vaishnava* is really he who is a devotee of Bhagwan Vishnu - *"vishnauratah vaishnavah"*

"विष्णौरतः वैष्णवाः"

"ऊर्ध्वपुंड्वत्वं वैष्णवत्वम्"

"urdhvapundvatvam vaishnavatvam"
'Those who possess a *urdhavapund* (perpendicular marking on the forehead) are said to be *vaishnava*.'

This is not a rule.

He who worships Bhagwan Vishnu, he then is really a *vaishnava*. But also because all deities are different parts of Bhagwan, the worshipper of any deity can be called a *vaishnava*. At the time one is worshipping any deity, really at that time he is a *vaishnava*. The whole religious world is *vaishnava*. Those who say that only those who have perpendicular marking on the forehead are *vaishnava*, and who call others non-*vaishnava*, are unacquainted with reality. They are a disgrace to Bhagwan Vishnu. Any devotee of Shiva or worshipper of Shakti, if they do not accept themselves as *vaishnava*, then they are also in error. Anyone else in *samsara* (worldly existence) after this manner he is not *vaishnava*. Those sects who voice sectarian arguments do not achieve anything for themselves nor for others either.

७९

सत्संग की बातों का मनन करना आवश्यक

*

शुकदेव जी ने भागवत सुनाया, हजारों लोगों ने सुना, परन्तु उसके प्रभाव से मोक्ष केवल परीक्षित को ही हुआ। गोकर्ण से भी बहुतों ने सुना, परन्तु मोक्ष केवल धुंधकारी को हुआ। इस पर यह प्रश्न उठता है कि वृष्टि व्यापक हो और तृप्ति एक मनुष्य को हो - यह कैसी बात है! बात यह है कि मोक्ष का सम्बन्ध मन से है। जिसका मनन किया जाता है उसी का संस्कार दृढ़ होता है और संस्कारों की दृढ़ता पर ही जीव का बन्धन या मोक्ष निर्भर करता है। श्रुति और स्मृति (अर्थात् वेद् और शास्त्र) दोनों का यही सिद्धान्त है -

"मन एव मनुष्याणां कारणं बन्धमोक्षयोः।"

-श्रुति।

"ध्यान एव मनुष्याणां कारणं बन्धमोक्षयोः॥"

- याज्ञवल्क्य स्मृति।

जो सिद्धान्त या जो भगवत्-सम्बन्धी वार्ता सत्संग में सुनी जाय, उस पर भली प्रकार विचार करके उसको मनने करते रहना चाहिये।

सत्संग की बातें सुनने से कर्ण तो पवित्र होंगे। परन्तु यदि उन पर कुछ विचार नहीं किया गया, कुछ मनन नहीं किया गया, तो वह सब कर्ण तक ही रह जायगा और एक कर्ण से होकर दूसरे से बाहर निकल जायगा। सत्संग की सारी बातों का प्रयोजन मन (अन्तःकरण) को पवित्र करना है। मन ही प्रधान वस्तु है। मन यदि

अपवित्र रहा तो इसी के कारण जन्म-मरण का चक्र चलता रहेगा और यदि मन पवित्र हो गया तो उसी से मोक्ष हो जायगा। महर्षि याज्ञवल्य जी ने ध्यान को ही बंधन या मोक्ष का कारण बताया है। ध्यान मन ही करता है। मन पवित्र हुआ तो भगवान् का ध्यान करता हुआ मनुष्य मोक्ष प्राप्त करेगा और यदि मन अपवित्र रहा तो नाना प्रकार की वासनाओं में फण्सा रह कर अनर्थ चिन्तन करता हुआ, अनावश्यक वस्तुओं का ध्यान करता हुआ, संसार-चक्र में मन उसे घुमाता रहेगा।

79

Meditating on insignificant things, the mind remaining in the cycle of *samsara*, he will continue to be giddy in the head.

Shukadava ji spoke the Bhagavat (Purana) and thousands of people heard. However, by it's influence only Parikshita obtained *moksha* (liberation). Many also heard from Gokarna, but only Dhundhakari (Gokarna's brother) obtained *moksha*. But this question arises; if wide-spread rain occurs and gratification comes to only one man, what is this news? This information is that *moksha* is connected with the mind. Whatever thought you are thinking, the *samskara* (mental impression) becomes resolute and the bondage or freedom of an indivual life depends on the strengthening of the *samskaras*. This is the doctrine of both the *shruti* (information heard from the *Veda*) and *smriti* (remembered, from the *Shastra*).

"मन एव मनुष्याणां कारणं बन्धमोक्षयोः।"

"mana eva manushyaanaam kaaranam bandhamokshayoH."
[*shruti – Amrita Bindu Upanishad* v2]

'Only the mind causes bondage, or *moksha*'

"ध्यान एव मनुष्याणां कारणं बन्धमोक्षयोः ॥"

"dhyaana eva manushyaanam kaaranam bandhamokshayoh.."
[*Yagyavalkya Smriti*]

'Only *dhyaana* (meditation) causes bondage or *moksha.*'

That doctrine or information relating to Bhagavat (God) we hear in *satsang*, on that kind of thought you should set good store.

With the words of *satsang* the ears then will become pure. But if on those [words] there is no consideration, there is no thought, then they will be going up to the ears and going in to one ear and appearing out from the other.

The purpose of all the words of *satsang* is to purify the mind. The mind is really the chief thing. If the mind is staying impure, then this is really the cause of remaining going in the cycle of life and death, and if the mind becomes pure then from this you will become liberated. Maharishi Yagyavalya pointed out that; '*Dhyaana* (meditation) is the cause of bondage or *moksha* (liberation).' Meditation is really performed by the mind. If the mind becomes pure then *dhyaana* of Bhagwan is done, man will gain *moksha.* But if the mind is impure then thinking will be contrariwise, the mind will be ensnared in thinking about all kinds of desires. Meditating on insignificant things, the mind remaining in the cycle of *samsara* (worldly existence), he will continue to be giddy in the head.

८०

घरमें रहते हुए ही महात्मा बनो

*

जो जहाँ है, वह वहाँ रहते हुए ही महात्मा बन सक्ता है। गेरुअ वस्त्र या तिलक-छाप से कोई महात्मा नहीं होता। वेश कल्याणकारी नहीं, निष्ठा से कल्याण होता है। मन की वृत्ति में महत्मापन होता

है। इसलिए यहाँ हो, वहीं रहते हुए मन की धारा को बदलो-संसार का चिन्तन भीतर से कम करो और परमात्मा का चिन्तन बढ़ाओ।

आजकल अचिन्त्य को चिन्त्य मान लिया गया है। मुख्य चिन्त्य परमात्मा ही है। उसका चिन्तन न करके अचिन्त्य संसारी पदार्थों का चिन्तन किया जाता है। इसलिए सुख-शान्ति का अनुभव नहीं होने पाता। यदि प्राणों का रक्षण केवल सांसारिक कार्यों और विषय-भोगों के लिए है तो वह लुहार की धौंकनी ही है। अतः प्राण का पोषण करो और उसे परमात्मा में लगाओ।

पहले श्रद्धा उत्पन्न करो। धन में श्रद्धा है, तभी तो धन का चिन्तन करते हो। जब परमात्मा में श्रद्धा हो जायगी तो उसी का चिन्तन होने लगेगा। विचार करो कि धन आदि समस्त सांसारिक पदार्थ यहीं पड़े रह जाँयगें और आगे की यात्रा अकेले ही करनी पड़ेगी। उस आगे की यात्रा के लिए अभी से कुछ तैयारी कर लो - परमार्थ में श्रद्धा बढ़ाओ, नित्यानन्द स्वरूप परमात्मा से प्रेम बढ़ाओ। जो चीज यहीं पड़ी रह जाने वाली है उसमें, अर्थात् जगत् की व्यावहारिक चीजों में केवल शिष्टाचार बनाओ और मुख्य श्रद्धा परमार्थ में करो, जो साथ जायगा।

एक बार भी निश्चय हो जाय कि वह रुपये क ढेर मदारी का बनाया हुअ है, तो फिर चाहे कोई कितना भी लालच देगा पर उसमें प्रेम नहीं हो सकता। मदारी के क्षणिक रुपये के समान ही संसार के समस्त पदार्थ और सम्बन्ध क्षणिक ही हैं। इसलिए इनसे व्यवहार तो करो और ऊपर से शिष्टाचार पूरा रखो। मन के भीतर इनका स्थान मत बनाओ। मन में नित्य अविनाशी आनन्द-स्वरूप परमात्मा को स्थान दो। मन में हमेशा भगवान् का स्मरण बना रहे और मर्यादा का उल्लंघन न हो - यही महात्मापन है।

80

One does not become a *mahatma* from clothes dyed in ochre or the mark of a *tilak*.

Be a *mahatma* living at home wherever that is, he can become a *mahatma* wherever he is living. One does not become a *mahatma* from clothes dyed in ochre or the mark of a *tilak* (a mark on the forehead as an emblem of a sect). Benediction does not come from costume, welfare comes from faith. In the *vritti* (fluctuations, activity) of the mind the state of *mahatma* exists. Therefore be here, staying there alter the flow of the mind a little from thinking inside of *samsara* and think more of Paramatma.

Nowadays people value *chintya* (contemplation) of *achintya* (the unthinkable, incomprehensible). The topmost *chintya* (thinking) is really Paramatma. Not thinking thereof, thinking of incomprehensible worldly things, therefore they do not experience happiness and peace. If you only look after the *pranon* (the five vital airs) for working and experiencing things in worldly activity then really that is the blacksmith blowing the bellows. Therefore cherish the *prana* and apply that on Paramatma.

First gain *shraddha* (faith, veneration, reverence). There is faith in wealth, for this reason you are thinking of wealth then. When you will have faith in Paramatma then your thinking will be really applied to him. Consider that wealth etc. and all worldly things will be left here and the *yatra* (journey) will really be taken alone. For the journey ahead make a little preparation, at present increase faith in Paramatma, increase love with the *nityananda* (always happy) form of Paramatma. Someone who knows lets things fall in this place, that is to say make only proper behaviour in usual things of the world and place the main faith in Paramatma, which will go together.

Once more become certain that a conjurer has made the heap of *rupees*. Then again to want any, then how much desire and ambition you will give on this, in you there can be no love. Really like the conjurer's passing *rupees*, all the things of the mundane existence and connection are really transitory. Therefore, with all these dealings then do and complete with good behaviour on the outside. Don't make a place for these things inside of the mind. In the mind give a place to the *nitya* (eternal) *ananda-swaroop* (bliss form) of Paramatma. In the mind, always be remembering Bhagwan and not be contravening the *maryada* (propriety of conduct) - this is really the state of being a *mahatma*.

८१

धन-संग्रह से अधिक प्रयत्न बुद्धि शुद्ध करने के लिए करो

*

सन्तान के लिए धन-संग्रह करने में आप लोग जितना प्रयत्न करते हैं उसका आधा प्रयत्न भी यदि बुद्धि-शुद्ध करने के लिए करें तो बहुत लाभ हो।

बुद्धि शुद्ध रही तो धन कम रहते हुए सन्तान सुख-शान्ति का अनुभव कर सकती है। पर यदि बुद्धि दूषित रही तो अनन्त धन-धान्य रहते हुए भी दुर्वासनाओं में पड़कर सन्तान दुःख और अशान्ति ही भोगेगी। इसलिए प्रथम बुद्धि शोधन के लिए प्रयत्न करो, पश्चात् धन-संग्रह करो।

81

Take more effort in purifying the mind than in collecting wealth.

Take more effort in purifying the mind than in collecting wealth. The effort you people put in collecting wealth for progeny, if you put a half of that effort for purifying the mind, it would be a great advantage. If the mind is clear then even if wealth is little the progeny can experience happiness and peace. But if the mind is defiled then even with unlimited wealth, they will fall into evil habits, be distressed and only suffer anxiety. Therefore, first make an effort to cleanse the mind, afterwards collect wealth.

८२

बिना ज्ञान के न भक्ति हि हो सकती है और न मोक्ष ही

*

जितने कर्म मनुष्य एक जन्म में करता है उसका फल इतना अधिक होता है कि कई जन्मों में भी भोग कर समाप्त नहीं किय जा सकता। यही कारण है कि संचित कर्मों की अनन्त राशि प्रत्येक जीव के लिए भोगने को पड़ी है। उसको भोगने के लिए अनन्तानन्त जन्म-धारण करना पड़ेगा। यदि उसे भोग कर समाप्त करना है तो जब तक संचित कर्म नष्ट नहीं होंगे तब तक जन्म-मरण के चक्कर से छूटोगे नहीं। कर्म-राशि को समाप्त करने के लिए ही ज्ञानाग्नि उत्पन्न की जाती है। जो अपनी संचित कर्म राशि को ज्ञानाग्नि से भस्म कर देता है उसी को बुधजन 'पंडित' कहते हैं -

"ज्ञानाग्नि दग्धकर्माणं तमाहः पंडितं बुधाः!"

कोई मनुष्य एक मिनट में किसी को कत्ल कर दे तो उसे यदि फांसी न हुई तो आजन्म काला-पानी या बीस वर्ष की सजा अवश्य ही होगी। इसी प्रकार और भी कार्यों के उदाहरण से यही मालूम होता है कि २-२, ४-४ मिनट में किये हुए कर्मों का फल वर्षों भोगना पड़ता है तो जीवन भर में किये हुए कर्मों का फल कितने जन्मों तक भोगना पड़ेगा, इस का कुछ ठिकाना नहीं। इसीलिये ज्ञान का महत्व है कि ज्ञान हो जाने पर समस्त संचित कर्म नष्ट हो जाते हैं।

यथैधांसि समिद्धोग्निर्भस्मसात्कुरुतेऽर्जुन।
ज्ञानाग्नि सर्वकर्माणि भस्मसात्कुरुते तथा॥

अर्थात्, जैसे प्रज्वलित अग्नि इंधन को भस्म कर देती है, उसी प्रकार ज्ञानाग्नि समस्त (संचित) कर्मों को भस्म कर देती है। इसलिये ज्ञानाग्नि से वंचित को नष्ट करो और प्रारब्ध को शान्ति-पूर्वक भोग डालो।

अपने संचित कर्मों को नष्ट कर्नें के लिए ज्ञान की प्राप्ति करना ही सबसे बड़ा कार्या है। ज्ञान-प्राप्ति के बाद फिर कोई कर्तव्य शेष नहीं रह जाता। यथा -

ज्ञानामृतेन तृप्तस्य कृतकृत्यस्य योगिनः।
नैवास्ति किंचित्कर्तव्यं अस्ति चेन्नस तत्त्ववित्॥ स्लोक

ज्ञानी के लिए लिखा है कि यदि उसका मनोराज्य किसी कार्य के लिए हो तो उसे ॐकार का जप करता चाहिये -

बुद्ध तत्वेन धी दोष शुन्येनेकान्तवासिनः।
दीर्घ प्रणवमुच्चार्य मनोराज्यं विलीयते॥

ज्ञान हो जाने के बाद विदेह मोक्ष तो होता है, पर जीवन्मुक्ति के लिए उसे भी अहंग्रहोपासना का सहारा लेना पड़ता है।

पहले अपरोक्ष ज्ञान होता है अर्थात् शास्त्र और गुरुओं के द्वारा यह निश्चय होता है कि एक अद्धितीय परमात्मा सर्वत्र चराचर में परिपूर्ण है, वह सच्चिदानन्द अखण्ड ज्ञान्स्वरूप है। ऐसा निश्चयात्मिक, संशय विपर्यय रहित बोध ही अपरोक्ष ज्ञान है।

प्रहलाद को पहले से ही यह ज्ञान था कि हमारा राम सर्वत्र परिपूर्ण है। ऐसा उन्हें निश्चय था, इसलिये वे अहर्निश भगवान का चिन्तन करते रहते थे। जब तक भगवान् को कोई जानेगा नहीं, तब तक उनकी भक्ति ही क्या करेगा। भगवान् को सर्वत्र चराचर में जान लेना ही ज्ञान है और उनकी सेवा-पूजा करने लगना भक्ति है भक्ति के द्वारा उन्हें एक देश में प्रकट करके उनका साक्षात्कार करना ही विज्ञान है और विज्ञान के बाद उसी भाव में तल्लीन हो जाना परा भक्ति है।

82

By the fire of knowledge one's own mass of *karma* becomes ashes.

Without *gyaan* (knowledge) there cannot be *bhakti* (devotion), indeed nor can there be *moksha* (final liberation). However much *karma* (action) man does in one lifetime, these much more effects thereof cannot be completely experienced in several lifetimes. This is really the reason for the *jiva* to have to endure interminable collected *karmon* (actions), for him to undergo acceptance of birth for ever and ever. If he is to completely endure, then until when the collected *karma* will be destroyed, then you will not abandon the cycle of birth and death. For the termination of the mass of *karma* the fire of knowledge is to be gained. By the fire of knowledge one's own mass of *karma* becomes ashes. The *budhajana* (wise) call him a *pandit:–*

"ज्ञानाग्नि दग्धकर्माणं तमाहः पंडितं बुधाः ॥"

"gyaanagni dagdhakarmanam tamahah panditam budhah."
[*Bhagavad Gita* 4:19]

In a minute, if any man commits murder then if he hasn't been executed then there is life sentence *"Kala Pani"* ('Kalapani' or 'Black Water' - the island prison of freedom fighters in the Andamans) or certainly it will be a penalty of twenty years. This is the method and also by way of illustration it becomes obvious that if the effects of actions lasting two to four minutes are suffered for years, then the effects of the *karmas* of an entire lifetime will be endured for how many lifetimes? This is not limited! Therefore, this is the greatness of knowledge, that on gaining knowledge the whole collected *karma* becomes destroyed.

"यथैधांसि समिद्धोऽग्निर्भस्मसात्कुरुतेऽर्जुन ।
ज्ञानाग्निः सर्वकर्माणि भस्मसात्कुरुते तथा ॥"

*"yathaidhamsi samiddhognirbhasmasatkurute arjuna.
gyaanagni sarvakarmani bhasmasatkurute tatha."*
[*Bhagavad Gita* 4:37]

That is to say;

'Just as *agni* (fire) turns fuel into ashes, by this kind of fire of knowledge all karmas are turned to ashes.'

Therefore, cheated by *gyaan agni* (the fire of knowledge), destroy the destiny and cast it off before it is endured. It is the greatest work to gain knowledge for the purpose of destroying one's own accumulated *karmas* (actions). There is nothing remaining to be done after gaining knowledge. As for example:-

"ज्ञानामृतेन तृप्तस्य कृतकृत्यस्य योगिनः ।
नैवास्ति किंचित्कर्तव्यं अस्ति चेन् न स तत्त्ववित् ॥"

*"gyaanamritena triptasya kritakrityasya yoginah.
naivasti kinchitkartavyam asti chen na sa tattvavit.."*
[*Shrijabaladarshana Upanishad* 1:23 / *Kubjikamata Tantra* 25:171]

'The yogi is satisfied, having drunk the *amrit* (nectar) of *gyaan* (knowledge), the most perfect of endeavours.

If there is yet a little to be done, then he has not realised the truth.'

For the *gyaani* (realised) it is written that, for any work in *manorajyam* (the realm of the mind) he should do *"OMkara ka japa"* - '*japa* of the OM syllable':-

"बुद्धतत्त्वेन धीदोष शून्येनैकान्त वासिना ।
दीर्घं प्रणवम् उच्चार्य मनोराज्यं विजीयते ॥"

*"buddhatattvena dhidosha shunyenaikanta vasina.
dirgham pranavam uchcharya manorajyam vijiyate.."*
[*Panchadashi* 4.62]

'One who has intellectually understood the nature of the secondless Brahman and who is free from defects of intellect, should live in solitude, and over a long period practice the *japa* of OM and thus control the vagaries of the mind.'
[*Panchadashi* - translation by Swami Swahananda, Sri Ramakrishna Math]

After becoming realised, then become *videha moksha* (*moksha* without a body). But for *jivanmukti* also accept the help of *ahamgrahopasana* (service of holding onto oneself).

First there is *aparoksha gyaan* (tangible knowledge), that is *Shastra* and by means of *gurus* [comes] this faith of the One beyond comparison, Paramatma, everywhere, perfect in the animate and inanimate, this is *sachchidananda* (Truth, Consciousness, Bliss) *akhanda* (entire) *gyaanswaroop* (form of knowledge). Such determination, without feeling devoid of hostility and uncertainty, is really *aparoksha gyaan* (direct knowledge).

Prahlad had this knowledge from the first, 'Our Rama is everywhere perfect.' He was so certain. Therefore, day and night he was thinking about Bhagwan. Whilst you do not have any understanding of Bhagwan then how can you really perform *bhakti* (devotion)? To accept and understand that Bhagwan is everywhere, animate and inanimate, and serve and worship him is *bhakti*. The way of *bhakti* is to meet with Him in one place, this is really *vigyaan*, and after *vigyaan*, becoming immersed in this feeling is *para bhakti* (the best devotion).

८३

अच्छे कार्यों को जल्दी करो

संसार का अनुभव जीव अनेक जन्मों से करता चला आ रहा है। संसार की ओर उसकी प्रवृत्ति स्वाभाविक हो गई है। इसको संसार से हटाकर परमात्मा की ओर लगाने में ही प्रयत्न करना है। पुरुषार्थ वास्तव में मन को संसार से रोकने के लिए करना है। भगवान का भजन-पूजन, चिंतन-कथन आदि होता रहे, इसी में मन घूमे तो कुछ समय में संसार से स्वतः हट जायगा।

व्यवहार में यह नीति रखनी चाहिये कि अच्छे कर्मों को, भगवत्संबन्धी कार्यों को तो जल्दी से जल्दी पूरा करने की कोशिश रहे और यदि कोई बुरा संकल्प उठे तो उसको उसी समय टालना चाहिये कि कल कर लेंगे या परसों कर लेंगे - इस प्रकार बराबर उसे टालते रहना चाहिये।

83

To withdraw from *samsara* and to apply oneself in the direction of Paramatma takes effort.

The *jiva* (individual soul) has been coming to experience *samsara* (worldly existence) for several lifetimes, so it becomes natural that the inclination of the mind is to the direction of *samsara*. To withdraw from *samsara* and to apply oneself in the direction of Paramatma takes effort. In essence *purushartha* (efforts to fulfil life, willpower) is for the purpose of keeping back the mind from *samsara*. Really in this chanting and worship of Bhagwan, thinking and talking etc., in some time the wandering mind will spontaneously get out of the way of *samsara*. In the day-to-day business you should insert this guidance; that to good *karmas* (actions) - to tasks relating to Bhagavat (God) - then quickly, quickly attempt to fulfil and if any bad intention arises then you should put it off, 'I will do it tomorrow or I will do it the day after tomorrow', in this manner you should continually put it aside.

८४

भगवान् से लाभ उठाना चाहते हो तो उपासना करके उन्हें एक-देश में प्रकट करो

*

व्यापक निराकार भगवत्सत्ता से कोई कार्य नहीं हो सकता, वह तो साक्षी मात्र है। वह जब माया का सहारा लेकर एक-देश में आती है तभी माया के त्रिगुणात्मक व्यवहारिक जगत् में कुछ कार्य करती है। जैसे निराकार अग्नि काष्ठ में सर्वत्र व्यापक होते हुए उस काष्ठ को नहीं जलाती और न उससे कुछ कार्य ही लिया जा सकता है। किन्तु जब उसे घर्षण करके काष्ठ को भी जल सकती है और इच्छा-अनुसार उससे कार्य लिया जा सकता है। इसी प्रकार व्यापक भगवत्सत्ता जब उपासना द्वारा एक-देश में प्रकट की जाती है तभी वह व्यवहारोपयोगी हो सकती है।

उपासना ही ऐसा सोपान (सीढ़ी) है जिससे भक्त भगवान के पास पहुँचता है और भगवान् भक्त के पास आते हैं। उपासना ही के द्वारा सर्वत्र चराचर में एक-रस रमी हुई भगवान् की सत्ता एक-देश में प्रकट होकर भक्त की इच्छानुसार कार्य करती है। निर्गुण निराकार सत्ता जब सगुण साकार होती है तभी कुछ व्यावहारिक कार्य होते हैं। इसलिए भगवान से लाभ उठाना चाहते हो तो उपासना करके उन्हें अपने हृदय में या बाहर कहीं भी प्रकट करो। एक बार भगवान का उद्घाटन हृदय में हो जाय तो फिर जन्म की सारी गरीबी मिट जायगी।

84

But when the wood is rubbed then it can be lit and can be used according to our wishes.

No work can be done by the pervasive, incorporeal essence of Bhagavat (God). He is merely a witness. When with the support of *maya* He comes to one place, on account of the usual three *gunas* (qualities) of *maya* (*sattva*, *rajas*, *tamas*), he does some work in the world. In the manner that formless *agni* (fire) is everywhere in wood but it cannot light the wood and can do no work. But when the wood is rubbed then it can be lit and can be used according to our wishes. By this manner, when by means of worship, the extensive essence of Bhagavat (God) manifests in one place then there can be proper business.

Upasana (worship, service, devotion) is really like a staircase by which the devotee arrives at Bhagwan's side and Bhagwan comes near to the devotee. Really, *upasana* (prayer, worship, service, devotion) is the way that the essence that pervades everywhere in the world, the power of Bhagwan manifests in one place according to the desire of the devotee. When the shapeless Absolute, without qualities, takes a form endowed with qualities then it can do some usual work. Therefore if we desire advantage from Bhagwan, then by worship he manifests in one's own heart or somewhere outside too. Once Bhagwan becomes released in the heart then afterwards poverty is erased the whole lifetime.

८५

सुख चाहते हो तो सुख-सागर की ओर चलो

*

जो वस्तु जहाँ होती है वहीं से वह प्राप्त की जा सकती है। धन चाहते हो तो धनिकों के पास मिलेगा, विद्या चाहते हो तो विद्वान् के पास जाना होगा। यदि हीरा-मोती खरीदना है तो सराफा में जाने

से मिलेगा, साग के बाजार में ढूँढ़ने से हीरा नहीं मिलेगा चाहे जितना परिश्रम करो। इसी प्रकार सुख-शान्ति चाहते हो तो सुख-स्वरूप व शान्ति-स्वरूप परमात्मा के पास जाने से ही सुख-शान्ति की प्राप्ति हो सकती है। इधर-उधर चाहे जितना सिर पीटते रहो, संसार में चाहे जितना परिश्रम करो, सुख-शान्ति से भेंट न होगी।

जितना-जितना संसार में परिश्रम करके, धनार्जन करके या मान-प्रतिष्ठा प्राप्त करके सुख-शान्ति प्राप्त करने के लिए करोगे, उतना-उतना दुख और अशान्ति ही हाथ लगेगी। सुख मान लेना तो दूसरी बात है - मान लो कि अमुक वस्तु मिल जाय तो मैं सुखी हो जाऊँगा; और वह वस्तु मिल गई तो ऐसा मानो कि मैं सुखी हो गया। इस प्रकार मान लेना तो दूसरी बात है। परन्तु विचार करो तो यहाँ की किसी भी वस्तु में न सुख है, न शान्ति है।

संसार की चकाचौंध में पड़कर अनन्त आनन्द स्वरूप परमात्मा को भूल गये हो। ईश्वर के विमुख होने से ही दुःख आया है, और वह दुःख उसी के सामने से जायगा। संसार की बाहरी चीजों में इतना भूल गये हो कि स्वयं अपने सम्बन्ध में ही भ्रम हो गया है - यही पता नहीं है कि हम हैं कौन!

जो इतना बावला हो गया हो कि स्वयं को भूल गया हो, अपने ही स्वरूप को न पहचान पाता हो, उस पागल को क्या कहा जाय। वह तो ऐसा कर ही सकता है कि प्रकाश पाने की इच्छा से किसी अँधेरी गुफा में घुस जाय। संसारी पदार्थों से सुख-शान्ति की इच्छा करना इसी प्रकार है जैसे प्रकाश की इच्छा वाले का अँधेरी गुफा में प्रवेश करना।

सुख चाहते हो तो सुख-सागर जो परमात्मा है उसकी ओर चलो। परमात्मा की ओर चलोगे तभी सुख-शान्ति मिलेगी और लौकिक-पारलौकिक ऐश्वर्य भी मिलेगा। जिस प्रकार प्रकाश से

विमुख होने पर अँधकार घेर लेता है, वैसे ही परमात्मा से विमुख रहोगे तो दुःख और विपत्तियाँ घेर लेंगी।

85

By searching in the vegetable bazaar you will not get a diamond, no matter how much you want and try.

If you desire to be happy, then go in the direction of the ocean of happiness. Wherever that thing is, from that very place that can be obtained. If you desire wealth then you will meet with those who have riches, if you want knowledge then you will go to the learned man. If you are to buy diamonds and pearls then you will get them from going in the *sapha* (banking, money changing business). By searching in the vegetable bazaar you will not get a diamond no matter how much you want and try. In this way, if you wish to be happy and peaceful, then you can gain happiness and peace only from Paramatma, the real form of happiness and the real form of peace. However much you look here and there, you beat your head looking in *samsara,* however much you labour you will not meet with happiness and peace.

However much you exert yourself in *samsara* obtaining wealth or gaining respect and reputation, if you will do this for happiness and peace only that much pain and anxiety will attach to the hand. You get a measure of happiness then here is another thing - if you stick to the measure that; 'If I get such and such thing then I will be happy'; and having got that thing then after this manner you profess 'I have become happy.' To accept this kind of standard then is another thing. But consider then, happiness in not in things here, nor is *shaanti* (peace).

By falling for the dazzling effects of light on the eyes of *samsara*, the limitless *ananda* (bliss) of the real from of Paramatma is forgotten. Really, by being indifferent to Ishwar (God) you have come to suffer, and that suffering will go away by being in front of Him. As much as you have forgotten yourself in the world of external things, your connection has become confused. This is only not knowing who we are!

He who becomes so crazy that he forgets himself, his own

identity he does not know. What to say, that he is crazy? Such he is then, that desiring to obtain light he goes to any dark cave. Desiring happiness and peace from worldly things, this is like someone desiring light entering a dark cave.

If you desire happiness, then go in the direction of Paramatma, that ocean of happiness. You will go in the direction of Paramatma and for this reason you will get happiness and peace and you will also get wealth both worldly and ultramundane. In this way, by being indifferent to the light, you are surrounded by darkness. Really, if like that you are indifferent to Paramatma then you will become surrounded by pain and calamities.

८६

भगवान का भजन अवश्य करो मन लगे या न लगे

दुष्ट चित्त से, मलिन चित्त से भी भगवान् का स्मरण किया जाय तो भी वे पापों का नाश कर देते हैं, जैसे कि बिना इच्छा के भी यदि अग्नि को छू लिया जाय तो भी वह जला ही देती है। भगवान् में प्रेम बनाना तो कठिन है क्योंकि अनेक जन्मों का बिगड़ा हुआ मन है, सहसा भजन के लिए बैठो अवश्य। मन भगता है तो भागने दों, पर तुम उसके साथ मत उठकर भागने लगो। भजन करने बैठो और मन बाहर जाय तो चिन्ता नहीं, वे मन के ही माला फेरते बैठे रहो - ऐसा नहीं कि मन हटा और तुम उठ खड़े हुए। धीरे-धीरे मन भी लगने लगेगा, घबराना नहीं चाहिये। परन्तु एक बात अवश्य ध्यान देने की है कि भगवान् का भजन तो करो, पर पाप से अवश्य बचते रहो। ऐसा मत सोचो कि कि भगवान के भजन से पाप कट ही जायेगा तो क्यों न थोड़ा और कर ले। यदि पाप करने लगोगे तो फिर पाप ही तुम्हें भगवान के भजन से भी हटा देंगे - यह भी निश्चय रखो।

86

Chant worship of Bhagwan - whether the mind is attached or not attached.

Chant worship of Bhagwan - whether the mind is attached or not attached. With a bad *chitta* (faculty of reasoning), even with a filthy *chitta,* remember Bhagwan, then the sins they fade, in the manner that if you touch fire then it will burn even if you don't desire it to. To build a love of Bhagwan is difficult then, because for many lifetimes the mind has become spoiled. Certainly sit for chanting prayer at once. If the mind runs away then let it run, but don't arise and runaway with it! Sit chanting prayer and if the mind is outside then don't worry. Indeed with that mind sit turning the *mala* (rosary) - not such that the mind shifts and you rise standing. Slowly, slowly the mind becomes attached, you should not be perplexed. But one thing is certain, giving *dhyaana* (meditation), chanting worship of Bhagwan, but certainly refrain from *paapa* (sin). Do not consider that; 'By chanting the worship of Bhagwan, *paapa* is destroyed, then why not do a little more (sin).' If you become attached to sinning then afterwards the sin will take you away from chanting worship of Bhagwan - this also is certain.

८७

'ज्ञान से भगवान् के दर्शन का भाव रखना ठीक है या प्रत्यक्ष का?'

*

यह दोनों प्रकार से होता है। जिस प्रकार से वे सामने आयें, जिस रूप में वे सामने आये, उसी रूप में देखो, हठ नहीं करना चाहिये। साकार रूप में आयें, तो उसी रूप में देखो और निराकार रूप में रहें तो वैसी ही निष्ठा बना लो। परन्तु नित्य के अपने अभ्यास के लिये एक आधार बनाकर नियम बना लेना चाहिये। साकार में वृत्ति टिकने का आधार स्पष्ट ही है। निराकार में निष्ठा करनी हो तो मन को नेत्र बनाकर देखना चाहिये। यह अवश्य है कि नियम बना लेना चाहिये। अभ्यास करते-करते, ध्यान करते-करते, इष्टदेव में प्रेम बढ़ जाता है और जहाँ प्रेम बढ़ा कि इष्ट का साक्षात् हो जाता है।

87

Is it best to experience the *darshan* of Bhagwan by knowledge or with the sight?

Is it best to experience the *darshan* of Bhagwan by knowledge or with the sight? By both kinds this is done. By that method He will come in front of you. In that appearance He will come before you, see Him in that very form, you should not be stubborn. If He will come in a *sakara* (concrete) form then see that very form and if *nirakara* (shapeless) form then indeed build your faith in That. However, you should regularly practise one exercise, accept *niyama* (prescribed practices) as your basis. Clearly the *vritti* (flow of mental activity) stops in the *sakara* (gross form). If you have faith in *nirakara* then you should make the mind's eye to see. Certainly this is so, that you should accept and make *niyama*. Doing the *abhyasa* (practice), doing the *dhyaana* (meditation), the love for the *ishtadeva* (desired form of God) grows and wherever the love grows the meeting with the *ishta* occurs.

८८

भक्ति और ज्ञान, निराकार और साकार के झगड़ों में न पड़ो

*

भक्ति और ज्ञान के सम्बन्ध में परस्पर लोगों में बहुत सी बातें चला करती हैं। किसी के मत से ज्ञान बहुत बड़ा है और किसी के मत से भक्ति बहुत बड़ी है। जिनको न भक्ति का कुछ बोध है और न ज्ञान को ही कुछ समझते हैं, वे लोग ही भक्ति और ज्ञान सम्बन्द्ध में भेद मानकर परस्पर झगड़ा मचाते हैं। इस सम्बन्द्ध में यह बात कही जा चुकी है कि परमात्मा को जान लेने का नाम ज्ञान है और जान कर सेवा करने का नाम भक्ति है।

जिसको जानोगे नहीं, उसकी सेवा क्या करोगे। इसलिये स्पष्ट है कि बिना ज्ञान के भक्ति नहीं हो सकती। जो ज्ञान का खण्डन और ज्ञान का समर्थन करते हैं, वे दोनों ही नहीं समझते, दोनों अन्धे हैं। अन्धों की बात का क्या विश्वास करना - आँखों वाला कोई बात कहे तो मानी भी जाय।

कई लोग साकार निराकार का भेद मान कर बड़ा विवाद उठाते हैं। परमात्मा को यदि सर्व शक्तिमान् मानते हो तो फिर कैसे कह सकते हो कि वह साकार नहीं होता या निराकार ही रहता है। परमात्मा को सर्व शक्तिमान् मानते हुए यह कहना कि वह निराकार हो है, साकार नहीं होता, सर्वथा असंगत बात है। जब उसे सर्वतन्त्र

स्वतन्त्र कहते हो तो फिर वह क्या नहीं हो सकता और क्या नहीं कर सकता भगवान के निर्गुण और सगुण रूप से समझने के लिये हम एक उदाहरण देते हैं - अग्नि सर्वत्र परिपूर्ण है। जल में भी अग्नि है, थल में भी अग्नि है, काष्ठ में भी अग्नि है, ऐसा कोई स्थान नहीं है जहाँ अग्नि न हो। यह निर्विवाद सिद्ध है कि अग्नि व्यापक है। अग्नि के समान ही परमात्मा सर्वत्र व्यापक है।

लकड़ी के चैले में जो अग्नि है वह निराकार रूप से उसमें स्थित है। यदि चैले को चूल्हे में डाल कर प्रार्थना करो कि अग्नि जल जाय, परन्तु प्रार्थना करने से अग्नि जलेगी नहीं। निराकार अग्नि से जब तक साकार अग्नि प्रकट नहीं होगी तब तक कुछ काम नहीं हो सकता। निर्गुण अग्नि रह जायेगी, परन्तु तुम्हारे काम नहीं आ सकती। इसी प्रकार अग्नि के समान ही निर्गुण, निराकर परब्रह्म परमात्मा सर्वत्र चराचर में पूर्णतया व्याप्त होते हुए भी वह तुम्हारे किसी काम का नहीं है। जब कुछ काम होगा तो साकार ब्रह्म से ही होगा। यदि गुरु मिल जायें तो चैले को धर्षण करके उसी में से साकार अग्नि प्रकट कर सकते हैं और मन-चाहा काम ले लेते हैं। जब तक निराकार से साकार रूप में भगवान प्रकट नहीं हो जाते, जब तक जरूरत का कोई कार्य नहीं बनता। इसी भाव को लेकर गीता में कहा है -

यदा यदा हि धर्मस्य ग्लानिर्भवति भारत।
अभ्युत्थानमधर्मस्य तदात्मानं सृजाम्यऽहम्॥

'आत्मानं सृजामि' अर्थात मैं निराकार रूप से साकार होता हूँ। कब? जब धर्म घटता और अधर्म बढ़ता है तब। किस लिये भगवान को निराकार से साकार होना पड़ता है, यह बताते हुए कहते हैं -

परित्राणाय साधूनां, विनाशाय च दुष्कृताम्।
धर्म संस्थापनार्थाय संभवामि युगे युगे॥

साधुओं के कल्याण के लिए और दुष्कृतियों के संहार के लिए मैं प्रकट होता हूँ और धर्म की स्थापना करता हूँ। साधु शब्द से गेरुआ तिलक छाप या कंठी-माला वालों को न समझ लेना। साधु शब्द का अर्थ है - अच्छे साधु वृत्तीय पुरुष जो अच्छे स्वभाव वाले हैं, जो वेद शास्त्र की मर्यादा मानने वाले हैं, स्वधर्म-पालन में जिनकी निष्ठा है, उन्हीं के कल्याण के लिये भगवान् का अवतार होता है।

यदि साकार रूप में भगवान् न आयें तो जगत् की व्यवस्था नहीं कर सकते। जो जैसी चीज होती है उसी रूप में उसकी व्यवस्था हो सकती है। जैसे हम यहाँ बैठे हैं, आप लोगों ने हमारे सामने लाउड-स्पीकर लाकर रख दिया तो यदि हम मौन बैठे रहें तो आपको क्या लाभ होगा। निराकार का ऐसा ही स्वरूप है कि हम सर्वथा निश्चेष्ट मौन बैठे रहें। हमारे मौन बैठे रहने से आप लोगों को क्या लाभ हो सकता है? निराकार भगवान् से कोई लाभ नहीं होता, जब तक साकार रूप में न आयें। जो बात जैसी है, हम वैसी हो कहते हैं। हमें आप लोगों को वेद-शास्त्र के सिद्धान्तों को ही बताना है, अपनी तरफ से कोई बात नहीं कहनी है। हमको स्पष्ट रूप से सिद्धान्त का विवेचन करते हैं। इसकी हमें परवाह नहीं कि इसको सुनकर कौन प्रसन्न होगा, कौन नाराज होगा। हमें न किसी का रञ्जन करना है और न किसी को प्रसन्न करने के लिये कुछ कहना है। निराकारवादियों हम पूछते हैं - वैसे तो हम भी निराकार को मानते हैं परन्तु जो केवल निराकार को मानते हैं और साकार को नहीं मानते, ऐसे ही लोगों की निराकारवादी कहा जाता है, ऐसे ही लोगों से हम पूँछते हैं - कि क्या लकड़ी के चैले में जो निराकार अग्नि है उससे क्या कोई लाभ उठाया जा सकता है? निराकार अग्नि से कोई रोटी बनाकर दिखाये। निराकार रूप तो केवल सत्ता मात्र है।

निराकारवादी जो निराकार का ध्यान करते हैं, उस सम्बन्ध में हम उनसे पूँछते हैं कि क्या निराकार का ध्यान किया जा चकता है? कोई ध्येय बनाया जायगा तभी उसमें वृत्ति टिकेगी। पर जो निराकार है उसको ध्येय कैसे बनाया जा सकता हैं?

निराकार का ध्यान नहीं बन सकता। यदि कोई कहता है कि निराकार का ध्यान होता है तो उसका कथन उसी प्रकार है जैसे कोई कहे कि बन्ध्या के पुत्र की बारात में जा रहे हैं। बन्ध्या के पुत्र ही नहीं होता तो उसकी बारात कैसी? निराकार की जब कोई रूप-रेखा ही नहीं तो उसका ध्येय कैसे बनेगा? वृत्ति को जमाने के लिये कुछ तो आधार चाहिये। जिसका आधार लोगे वही साकार होगा।

निराकार-तत्व, ध्याता, ध्यान ध्येय, और ज्ञाता, ज्ञान, ज्ञेय आदि त्रिपुटी से परे है। निराकार का ध्यान विडम्बना मात्र है। निराकार तत्व को न समझने वाले लोग ही निराकार के ध्यान की बात कर सकते हैं। निराकार तत्व केवल मानने के लिए हैं; सिद्धान्त रूप से वह स्वीकार किया जाता है; केवल उसकी सत्ता मात्र है, उससे जगत् का कुछ उपकार नहीं हो सकता। क्या कोई निराकार लड़के से लाभ उठा सकता है? निराकार स्कूल में जाकर, कोई पढ़ सकता है? निराकार कुर्सी पर कोई मिनिस्तर बैठ सकता है? निराकार औषधि से कोई रोगी अच्छा हो सकता है? निराकार भोजन से किसी की तृप्ति हो सकती है? निराकार बिलकुल बेकार चीज है, उससे कुछ भी काम नहीं हो सकता। इससे केवल निराकारवाद सर्वथा अमान्य है, सर्वथा बेकार है।

निराकार चीज बीज के समान है, उसको उसी रूप में रखे रहो। बीज पेटी में बन्द पड़ा रहे, तो किस काम का? तक उसे बोओगे नहीं, खनन-सिंचन नहीं करोगे और जब तक वह पल्लवित पुष्पित नहीं होगा, तब तक उस बीज से क्या लाभ है?

निराकार परमात्मा ब्यापक रूप से है, सर्वत्र है। फर्नीचर कमरे में भरा है और फर्नीचर के काष्ठ में निराकार अग्नि है, पर उस कमरे का अंधकार उस व्यापक निराकर अग्नि से नहीं हटता। यदि किसी फर्नीचर को रगड़ कर निराकार अग्नि को साकार रूप में प्रकट कर लिया जाय तो तुरन्त ही कमरे का अंधकार दूर हो सकता है। परन्तु जब तक अग्नि प्रकट नहीं होगी, वह निराकार रूप में साकार जगत् के व्यवहार में नहीं आ सकती। निराकार से जब वह साकार होगी तभी जगत् का कुछ उपकार उससे हो सकता है।

यदि परमात्मा साकार नहीं हो सकता तो क्या वह तुम्हारा पशु है कि जैसा चाहो उसको बनाओ - वह परम स्वतन्त्र है। वेद कहता है: -

'सोऽक्षरः परम स्वराट्'

अर्थात, वह अक्षर अविनाशी है।

परमात्मा परम स्वतन्त्र है। इसलिए 'वह निराकार ही है, साकार नहीं हो सकता या वह साकार ही है, निराकार नहीं है।' ऐसा मानने वाले परमात्मा-तत्व के सिद्धान्त को नहीं समझते, केवल एक पक्ष बनाकर झगड़ा मचाते हैं। साकार-निराकार के झगड़े में नहीं पड़ना चाहिये। जो साकार है वही निराकार होता है। निराकार केवल मानने के लिए है और साकार जगत् का कल्याण करने के लिये।

निराकार परमात्मा जब साकार रूप में प्रकट होता है तभी उसके निराकार रूप की प्रत्यक्ष सिद्धि होती है। काष्ठ को धर्षण करने से जब व्यापक निराकार अग्नि साकार रूप होकर एक वेष में प्रकट हो जाती है तभी प्रत्यक्ष रूप से यह निश्चय होता है कि काष्ठ में अग्नि थी। उसी प्रकार निर्गुण निराकार परमात्मा का संशय विपर्यय रहित बोध तभी होता है जब वह सगुण साकार रूप में प्रकट हो जाते हैं। जिसने काष्ठ को धर्षण करके अग्नि प्रकट कर लिया है, वही दावे के

साथ निर्भ्रान्त रूप के कह सकता है कि काष्ठ में अग्नि रहती है। साकार रूप में अग्नि प्रकट हो जाने पर ही निराकर अग्नि का काष्ठ में अस्तित्व सिद्ध होता है। यदि काष्ठ से साकार अग्नि प्रकट न हो तो उसमें निराकार अग्नि का अस्तित्व ही प्रत्यक्ष रूप से नहीं कहा जा सकेगा। जब साकार रूप में भगवान् प्रकट होते हैं, तभी यह निश्चय होता है कि निराकार रूप में भी बे हैं। साकार से ही निराकार की प्रत्यक्ष सिद्धि होती है - नहीं तो निराकार को कौन कैसे जान सकता है। जैसे अग्नि निर्गुण से सगुण होती है उसी प्रकार परमात्मा भी निर्गुण से सगुण होता है। यह बात सर्वथा अमान्य है कि निर्गुण से सगुण नहीं होता। निर्गुणवादियों के द्वारा ही समाज में अधिक पाप फैलता है क्योंकि ये लोग साकार भगवान को तो मानते नहीं और निराकार के लिये सोचते हैं कि वह तो कुछ देखता-सुनता नहीं, मन-चाहा किया करते हैं; उन्हें पाप-पुण्य से कोई मतलब नहीं।

88

Can anybody who is unwell become healthy from formless medicine?

Don't fall into disputes about *bhakti* and *gyaan*, *nirakara* and *sakara*. People talk a lot about the connection between *bhakti* and *gyaan*. Neither *gyaan* is greater nor is *bhakti* greater. Those who have little feeling of *bhakti* and who really have little understanding of *gyaan*, those people squabble with each other in differentiating between *bhakti* and *gyaan*. In this connection this is said; that to know Paramatma is termed *gyaan* (knowledge) and to serve having known (Paramatma) is termed *bhakti* (devotion).

He whom you do not know, how will you serve him? Therefore it is clear, that without *gyaan* (knowledge) there cannot be *bhakti* (devotion). The one who denies *gyaan,* and he who is supporting *gyaan*, both of them do not understand, both are blind. Why have faith in the words of the blind? Any words said by someone with sight has meaning at that time.

A few people are getting up and having a big argument to measure and distinguish *sakara* and *nirakara* separately. If you accept Paramatma is All-Powerful then how can you say afterwards that he is not with form or that he is really shapeless? If you have been accepting that Paramatma is All-Powerful, it is improper to say that he is *nirakara* (formless), that he is not having form. When he is said to be free and independent then what can he not be and what can he not do? Bhagwan is *nirguna* (without qualities) and *saguna* (endowed with qualities).

For example we give *agni* (fire), who is complete everywhere. *Agni* is also in water, *agni* is also in dry land, *agni* is also in wood, so there is no place where *agni* is not. This is valid and undeniable, that *agni* is pervasive. Like *agni*, Paramatma is pervasive everywhere.

In that sliver of firewood *agni* is situated in that *nirakara* aspect. If you throw the sliver into the fireplace and pray *agni* to burn, but by prayer *agni* will not burn. Whilst *nirakara* (formless), *agni* cannot manifest, *agni* cannot do a little work until it is *sakara* (with form). *Agni* will stay *nirguna* (without qualities), but cannot do your work. In a similar way to *agni* being *nirguna* (without quality), so Paramatma is *nirakara* (formless). Parabrahma (Supreme Soul) is everywhere, in the animate and inanimate, completely pervading everywhere, also is not doing any of your work. When there will be some work then will be *sakara* (having form) with Brahma. If you get a *guru* then the *agni* can manifest, rub the sliver of wood inside and accept the mind's desire. Until the *nirakara* is *sakara* then Bhagwan cannot be manifest, of necessity He cannot do any work. This quotation is said in the *Gita*:-

"यदा यदा हि धर्मस्य ग्लानिर्भवति भारत ।
अभ्युत्थानमधर्मस्य तदात्मानं सृजाम्यऽहम् ॥"

"yada yada hi dharmasya glanirbhavati bharata.
abhyutthanamadharmasya tadatmanam srijamya aham.."
[*Bhagavad Gita* 4:7]

That is to say;

'I become *sakara* (with form) from the *nirakara* (the formless).'

When?

At whatever time *dharma* declines and *adharma* grows. Then!

For what does Bhagwan become *sakara* (with form) from being *nirakara* (without form)? We tell you; this has been told:-

"परित्राणाय साधूनां विनाशाय च दुष्कृताम्।
धर्म संस्थापनार्थाय संभवामि युगे युगे॥"

"paritranaya sadhunam vinashaya cha dushkritam.
dharma samsthapanarthaya sambhavami yuge yuge.."
[*Bhagavad Gita* 4:8]

'For the welfare of *sadhus* and for the destruction of the wicked I am manifest and for the estsablishment of *dharma* I am manifest.'

By the word *"sadhu"* don't understand it to be the ones who have red-brown *tilak* marking, or *mala* of beads around the neck. The meaning of the word *"sadhu"* is 'good', the person who has a good disposition, that man exists as a *sadhu*. That man accepts the code of conduct of the *Veda Shastra*, whose faith is in tending his own religion. Really, for the welfare of them, Bhagwan becomes the *avataar* (incarnation).

If Bhagwan will not come in *sakara* form then he cannot regulate the world. The regulation of a thing can only be done in a similar form. In the way that we are sitting here, if you people bring a *"loudspeaker"* and place it in front of me then and I will sit *maun* (silent) then what will be the advantage to you? The *nirakara* (formless) is really a similar form as me sitting completely motionless in silence. From our remaining in *maun* what will be the advantage for you people? From *nirakara* Bhagwan there is not any advantage until he will come in the *sakara* form. That statement is such as it is. We are telling it like that. We are informing you people the standpoint of the *Veda Shastra*, not telling any speech from my own side. I am making a clear impression by investigation of the doctrine. This is not our concern whether those who listen enjoy, or who will be displeased. We are not doing anything to gladden and not saying anything to please. Those people of the *nirakara* - Such it is that we also accept the *nirakara* but not that *nirakara* alone and not accepting *sakara*. Really in this way those who are people of *nirakara*, really we would ask from those very people, 'Can there be any profit from *agni*, shapeless in a sliver of firewood?' Show how to make any *roti* (flat bread) from shapeless *agni*. The *nirakara* form then is merely only existence.

That person who meditates on the formless, in that connection we ask how did you meditate on *nirakara*? If you are to make contemplation then you will continue the *vritti*, but how can you make a meditation of the *nirakara* (formless)? You cannot make meditation of *nirakara*. If anyone says that they meditate on *nirakara* then it is like stating that there is a son of a childless woman is going in a marriage procession. There is not really a son of a barren woman, then of what kind is the marriage procession? When there is not any mark or form of the *nirakara* then how is meditation of it made? You should have some basis to consolidate the *vritti* (fluctuations of the mind). That which is the basis, that really will be *sakara* (having form).

The *nirakara-tatva* (formless essence) - to meditate, contemplative meditation and *gyaata* (one who knows), knowledge fit to be known etc., the above is *triputi* (knower, known & knowledge). Meditation of *nirakara* is merely a mockery. Those who do not understand the theory of *nirakara* can speak of *dhyaana* (meditation) of *nirakara*. Only to accept the theory of *nirakara*; by that fashion of theory; that has been accepted; alone that is merely existence, from that there isn't any benefit for the world.

What benefit arises from a formless son?

Can anyone study who goes in a formless *"school"*?

Can any *"minister"* sit on a formless chair?

Can anybody who is unwell become healthy from formless medicine?

Can there be any satisfaction from formless food?

The formless is a wholly useless thing, nothing can be done with it. From this the belief of only *nirakara* is completely invalid, is altogether useless.

The *nirakara* is like a seed thing, is kept in that form. Putting a seed in a box then what can be done with it? Until is is sown, tended with digging and watering it will not produce fresh foliage and blossom, until then what advantage is there in the seed?

The *nirakara* (formless) Paramatma is of a pervasive aspect, is everywhere. The room is full of *"furniture"* and in the wood of the *"furniture"* is formless *agni* (fire), but the darkness of the room is not dispelled by the pervasive formless *agni*. If any furniture is rubbed the formless *agni* will manifest as a form, then at once the darkness of the room can go away. But until *agni* will be manifested, that formless aspect cannot come into the use of the world. When the *nirakara* (formless) becomes *sakara* (with form) then it can be of some use to the world.

If Paramatma may not be a form then why desire him to be like your cattle?

He is Supreme and free. *Veda* tells:-

"सोऽक्षरः परम स्वराट्"

"so aksharah parama svarat"
[*Narayana Suktam* v12]

That is, 'He is *akshara* (permanent) everlasting.' Paramatma 'is Supreme and free.'

Therefore, [in saying] 'He is really *nirakara*, cannot be having form' or 'He is really *sakara*, is not shapeless'; such people that profess thus have not understood the essence of Paramatma, have made a quarrel with a one-sided argument. You should not fall into dispute about *sakara* and *nirakara*. That *sakara* is the very same as *nirakara*. The *nirakara* is only for accepting, and *sakara* is for the welfare of the world.

When formless Paramatma manifests as a form then that formless aspect becomes perfectly evident. By rubbing timber, when the pervasive shapeless *agni* (fire) becomes form it becomes apparent in activity. For this reason it becomes evident that the form of *agni* (fire) was in the wood. Really that kind of uncertainty, about the shapeless Paramatma without qualities, changes when that form with attributes becomes manifest. The *agni* manifests by rubbing the wood, really one can say without doubt, of the form along with the wood-fire, the fire lives in the wood. The *agni* becomes manifest in the aspect of form, this is proof that the *nirakara* aspect of *agni* dwells in wood.

If the form of *agni* does not manifest from wood then you will not be able to say that the form of the existence of *agni* is really visible. When Bhagwan becomes manifest in the aspect of *sakara* (having form), at the same moment He is certainly in the shapeless aspect too. By the *sakara* the *nirakara* is successfully perceived - if not then who and what *nirakara* is, cannot be known. In the manner that *agni*, from being without qualities becomes endowed with qualities, in a similar way Paramatma also becomes *saguna* (endowed with qualities) from being *nirguna* (without qualities). This speech, that *saguna* does not come from *nirguna*, is altogether unacceptable. The way of the group of those who believe in *nirguna* [alone] spreads more wickedness, because these people do not accept the manifest form of Bhagwan and suppose that the *nirakara* cannot see or hear. So they do their mind's desires; they have no concern for what is wicked and what is sacred.

८९

अपने किये का फल तो भोगना ही पड़ेगा।

*

चाहे आज या दस बरस के बाद या दस जन्मों के बाद, कभी न कभी अवश्य ही किये हुए कर्म का फल भोगना पड़ेगा। कोई भी कार्य छोटा हो या बड़ा, जो किया जायगा उसका फल होकर ही रहेगा। यह अवश्य है कि

अत्युग्र पुण्यपापानां, इहैव फलमश्नुते।

अत्यन्त उग्र पुण्य किया जाय या पाप किया जाय, अति प्रभावशाली कोई भी कार्य किया जाय तो उसका फल यहीं इसी जन्म में, जल्दी ही मिलता है। सामान्य पुण्य-पापों का फल कालान्तर में जाकर मिलता है। पर ऐसा नहीं हो सकता कि किसी कार्य का फल न मिले।

जो कर्मों के फल देने वाला है, वह सर्वज्ञ है। कर्म तो जड़ होता है और कर्म का फल भी जड़ ही होता है। जड़ कर्मों के फलों का नियामक चेतन पर्मात्मा सर्वान्तर्यामी है, सर्वज्ञ है, व्यापक है। वह सबके सब कर्मों का ठीक हिसाब रखता है। जिसका जैसा कर्म होता है, उसको वैसा ही फल देता है। मनुष्यों की आँख बचाकर तो आप कोई कार्य कर सकते हो, पर परमात्मा के नेत्र में धूल नहीं झोंक सकते। उसकी आँख बचा कर कोई कार्य नहीं किया जा सकता। इसलिये ऐसा कार्य मत करो जिसको तुम पाप समझते हो। यह नहीं भूलना चाहिये कि पाप कर्मों का फल दुःख होता है। जो कर्म करोगे उसका फल तो भोगना ही पड़ेगा। अच्छे कर्म करोगे तो सुख होगा और बुरे करोगे तो दुःख मिलेगा - यह निश्चय है। बबूल का वृक्ष लगाओगे तो उसमें कांटे ही होंगे, आम नहीं फलेंगे।

89

If you will grow an acacia tree then you will really have a thorn in you, no mango will be grown.

You will endure the fruits of your own actions. Today or after ten years or after ten lifetimes, really, certainly, at sometime or other, the fruits of *karma* will be endured. Any other action, be it small or big, the fruit of that which you do will stay with you. This is certain.

"अत्युग्र पुण्यपापानां इहैव फलमश्नुते ।"

"atyugra punyapaapanam ihaiva phalamashnute."
[*Hitopadesha* 1:84]

'If you have done very powerful *punya* (merit) or *paapa* (sin)',
any other actions of extra influence,
'then the fruit thereof is quickly met with in this lifetime.'

Generally the fruit of *punya* and *paapa* is met with at a later time, but it cannot be such that the fruit (effect) of action is not met.

The one who gives the fruit of the *karmas*, He is All-Knowing. The *karma* then is unfeeling and truly the fruit of *karma* is also unfeeling. The superintendent of those fruits of unfeeling *karmas* is the living Paramatma who is All-Pervasive, is All-Knowing. He makes an accurate calculation of all the *karmas* of all. According to the *karma*, the exact fruit is given. If you escape the eyes of people then you can do anything, but you cannot throw dirt in the eye of Paramatma. Nothing can escape His eyes. Therefore don't do actions that you understand to be *paapa* (sin, immoral, evil). This you should not forget, that you suffer the fruit of sinful actions. If you will do that *karma* then you will endure the effect. If you will do good *karma* then there will be happiness and if you will do bad then you will get suffering - this is certain. If you will grow an acacia tree then you will really have a thorn in you, no mango will be grown.

९०

जैसा मन में हो, वैसा ही कहो और वैसा ही करो

जिन दिनों में हम जंगलों में एकान्त में रहते थे, एक समय रीवां के पास किसी जंगल में नदी के किनारे एक मन्दिर था, उसी में ठहरे। कुछ दूर पर एक गाँव था। वहाँ का एक आद्मी आया और उसने मन्दिर में पूजन किया और हमसे आकर पूँछा कि महाराज! ज्ञानी लोग तो अपने ज्ञान के बल पर मोक्ष प्राप्त कर लेंगे, भक्त लोग अपनी भक्ति के कारण तर जायेंगे, और जो पतित हैं उनको पतित-पावन भगवान् का सहारा है तो फिर नरक में कौन लोग जाते हैं? हमने कहा कि इसका उत्तर कल सबेरे देंगे।

सबेरे वही आदमी आया। मन्दिर में जाकर भगवान् के सामने प्रार्थना के रूप में कहने लगा -

पापोऽहं पापकर्माऽहं, पापात्मा पापसम्भवः।

इसी प्रकार के वाक्य बहुत देर तक कहता रहा, अर्थात् मैं पापी हूँ, पापात्मा हूँ, पाप कर्म करने वाला हूँ। - यह सब कह कर जब वह हमारे पास आने लगा, तो हमने ब्रह्मचारी से कहा कि हटाओ यह पापी सबेरे-सबेरे कहाँ से सामने आ गया, इसका मुख देखने लायक नहीं है। हटाओ इस पापी को जल्दी से दूर करो।

हमारे सामने से हटकर उसने ब्रह्मचारी से कहा कि इतने पापी तो हम नहीं हैं जितना महाराज जी हमको समझ रहे हैं। यह सुनकर हमने उसको बुलवाया और कहा कि हम तुम्हें पापी नहीं कह रहे हैं, तुम्हारे कल के प्रश्न का उत्तर दे रहे हैं।

तुमको हमने पापी कहा तो तुमको बुरा लगा, इससे मालूम पड़ता है कि तुम भीतर से अपने को पापी नहीं मानते। परन्तु, सबेरे-सबेरे आकर भगवान् के सामने यही कहते हो कि - पापोऽहं, पापकर्माऽहं

– मैं पापी हूँ, पाप करने वाला हूँ। ऐसा तो भगवान् के सामने कहते हो, परन्तु अपने मन में अपने को पापी नहीं मानते। ऐसे ही 'मनसि अन्यत् वचसि अन्यत्' लोग नरक में जाते हैं कि जो मन में कुछ और रखें और ऊपर से कुछ और कहें। यही तुम्हारे प्रश्न का उत्तर है। मनुष्य को भीतर बाहर एकसा रहना चाहिये, जैसा मन में हो वैसा ही कहो और वैसा ही करो तो किसी दूसरे को भी तुम्हारे द्वारा धोखा न होगा और तुम भी सुख-शान्ति का अनुभव करोगे।

90

Which people go to hell?

In those days I was living alone in the jungles, one time there was a temple on the bank of a river in a jungle near Rewa, right there we stayed. A little way off was a village.

A man came there and did *puja* and asked of us; 'Maharaj, the *gyaani* person gets *moksha* on the strength of his own *gyaan* (knowledge) then, for the *bhakta* person the *bhakti* (devotion) is the cause that they will cross over (attain salvation), and the one who is fallen obtains the support of Bhagwan. Then again, which people go to hell?'

We said that; 'The answer to this I will give tomorrow.'

At dawn the very same man came in the temple praying before Bhagwan saying:

"पापोऽहं पापकर्माऽहं पापात्मा पापसम्भवः।"

"paapo aham paapakarma.aham paapatma paapasambhavah."
[*Pradakshina*]

This kind of sentence he said for a very long time, that 'I am a sinner, I am a wicked soul, I am the doer of evil *karma*.'

When he had said all this he comes to me, then I said to a *brahmachari*; 'Remove this evil one. Where has he come from this morning to be before us? His face is not fit to be seen. Quickly drive away this evildoer far away.'

Getting out of my way he told to the *brahmachari* that 'I am not such a sinner as Maharaja is understanding.'

Hearing this I called to him and said that; 'We are not calling you a sinner, we are giving an answer to your question of yesterday. We called you a sinner, then you felt bad. From this it is obvious that inside yourself you don't consider yourself to be evil. However, you come every morning in front of Bhagwan saying this *"paapo aham, paapakarma aham"* - 'I am evil, I am an evil doer.' So you are saying this then in front of Bhagwan, but in your own mind you don't consider yourself to be evil. Thus it is really;

"मनसि अन्यत् वचसि अन्यत्"

"manasi anyat vachasi anyat"
'Thinking one thing but saying another'

Such people go to hell that have something in their mind and yet outwardly say something else. This is the answer to your question. You should be identical on the inside as the outside. According to that which is in the mind, you speak that and like that indeed do, then you will not deceive any other, and you will also experience happiness and peace.'

९१

मन को ससार में अधिक न फँसाकर भगवान् कीं तरफ लगाओ

*

संसार में मन को अधिक फँसा देना ठीक नहीं। विचार से काम लेने की आवश्यकता है। तन, मन, धन तीन ही हैं। यदि इन तीनों का ठीक-ठीक उपयोग करते बन जाय तो फिर अन्त समय में पछताना नहीं पड़ेगा। पहले की जो बिगड़ी सो बिगड़ी, पर ऐसा करो कि अब तो न बिगड़ने पाये। वेद-शास्त्र का सहारा लेकर चलोगे तो पतन से बचे रहोगे। एक दिन यहाँ से जाना अवश्य है अतः चलते समय के लिये कुछ पूंजी इकट्ठी कर लो जो परलोक में सहायक हो।

वस्तु का सदुपयोग करना ही बुद्धिमानी है। मन का सदुपयोग यही है कि उससे भगवान् का चिन्तन किया जाय। संसार का चिन्तन करना मन का दुरुपयोग है।

किसी के परोपकार में शरीर को लगाना, भगवान् के भजन-पूजन में लगाना, शरीर का सदुपयोग है। दूसरे को कष्ट देना, चोरी करना, ये सब शरीर का दुरुपयोग है।

इसी तरह अच्छे कार्यों में धन को लगाना, यही उसका सदुपयोग है और बुरे कामों में लगाना दुरुपयोग है। 'दानं भोगो नाशः' धन की तीन ही गति हैं - या तो दान में खर्च होगा या भोग में या नाश हो जायगा - यही इसकी अन्तिम गति है।

जो धन न भोगा जायगा, न दान दिया जायगा तो उसकी तीसरी गति होगी ही अर्थात् नाश हो जायगा।

दान भी तीन प्रकार का है - सात्विक, राजस, तामस। सात्विक दान का उत्तम फल है। भोग का अर्थ यह नहीं हैं जैसा आजकल लोग भोगते हैं। अत्यन्त विलासी जीवन ठीक नहीं। भोग भी मर्यादापूर्वक होना चाहिये। मन की तो कभी भी विषयों से तृप्ति नहीं हो सकती और न तृप्त होने की आशा ही रखनी चाहिये। इन्द्रियाँ शिथिल हो जायँ किसी काम की न रह जायँ तो भी मन तृप्त नहीं हो सकता। भोग से किसी की तृप्ति होनी असम्भव है। थोड़ा सा अनुभव कर लो, तब भी वही बात है और दिन-रात उसी में लिप्त रहो, तब भी वही बात। मदिरा एक कप पियो या दस बोतल पियो बात एक ही है।

नशा करना है तो ऐसा नशा करो जो कभी उतरे नहीं, ऐसा नशा किस काम का कि धन भी गया और नशा भी उतर गया।

भगवान् की प्राप्ति ही ऐसा नशा है जो एक बार आकर फिर नहीं उतरता। नशा तो वही करना चाहिये, जो कभी उतरे नहीं और उसी नशे में शरीर छूट जाय।

मनुष्य जीवन में कोई काम करना हो तो सोच-समझ कर करो। ऐसा नहीं कि जो सामने आया, जैसे संगी-साथी मिल गये, वही करने लगे। अपना हानि-लाभ देख कर काम करना चाहिये। कुछ लोग सत्संग में इसलिये नहीं जाते कि उनका मद्य-मांस छूट जायगा। इस डर से सत्संग में न जाना, इससे भारी प्रमाद और क्या हो सकता है। स्वयं यदि उसे छोड़ने में असमर्थ हो तो संग अच्छा बनाओ। सम्भव है, सत्संग से ही लाभ हो जाय! अन्धकार को हटाना है तो प्रकाश का सहारा लो। प्रकाश के सामने अन्धकार अपने आप हट जायगा। प्रकाश के लिये चेष्टा करनी चाहिये। इसलिये संसार से मन को हटा कर पर्मात्मा में लगाना चाहिये, और वेदशास्त्र, साधु-महात्माओं की बात पर विश्वास करना चाहिये।

हम तो कहते हैं, पहले संसार को भज लो, फिर भगवान् को भजो तो संसार वाधक नहीं होगा। संसार का भजना यही हे कि इसके स्वरूप को जान लो। पहले संसार ही गुरु बनता है। कहीं कुटुम्बियों ने अपमान किया, कहीं पुत्र के द्वारा अपमान हुआ तो संसार से वैराग्य हो गया।

इसलिये पहिले से ही सचेत होकर भगवान की ओर मन लगाने का अभ्यास करना चाहिये।

जब तक हम धन संग्रह में समर्थ हैं तभी तक संसारियों का प्रेम है। हमेशा तो शक्तिशाली रहेंगे नहीं, एक दिन वृद्धावस्था आयेगी ही, तो जो कुट्म्बी लोग आगे चल कर हमारे साथ करेंगे वह हम आज ही क्यों न जान लें।

अभी हम उनको अपना प्रेमास्पद मानते हैं। जिस समय हमारी वह अवस्था आयेगी तो पछतायेंगे। फिर यही कहेंगे कि लड़का कहा नहीं मानता, बहू कहा नहीं मानती, जिसके लिए हमने इतना सब किया अब वही हमारा अपमान करते हैं। तो ऐसा क्यों करो जिसके लिये अन्त में रोना पड़े। अभी के उसके लिए सावधान हो जाओ। संसार में कोई किसी का नहीं है। सब अपने-अपने स्वार्थ के साथी हैं। जब तक जिसका स्वार्थ सिद्ध होता है तभी तक उसका प्रेम है। इसलिए इन लोगों की अश्रद्धा होने के पहले ही भगवान् की तरफ झुक जाओ। यदि अभी से भगवान् का भजन् पूजन करते रहोगे, तो कुटुम्बियों के अपमान की परवाह नहीं होगी। प्रेमास्पद तो परमात्मा ही है, उससे ही प्रेम करो तभी सुखी रह सकते हो।

91

Don't get the mind excessively involved in *samsara*, apply it towards Bhagwan.

Don't get the mind excessively involved in *samsara*, apply it towards Bhagwan. In *samsara,* don't get the mind excessively trapped in *samsara*, it is not right. It is necessary to take action considerately. The body, the mind, the wealth - these are indeed the three. If these three are made use of properly then you will not repent at the end time (the time of death).

If that [thing] is spoiled therefore it is spoiled, but now do such that nothing gets spoiled. If you take support from the *Veda Shastra* then you will escape from falling. One day you will certainly go from here, therefore for the time of going accumulate some assets that will assist you in the other world.

It is prudent to make good use of a thing. Good use of the mind, that is really thinking of Bhagwan. Thinking of *samsara* (worldly existence) is a misapplication of the mind. To apply the body in any benevolence, to engage in worship of Bhagwan, to chant and to do *puja*, is the proper use of the body. Giving suffering to another, to do theft, these are all misapplications.

This really means; to apply the wealth in good works, this is really the proper use, and to engage in bad works is a misapplication;

"दानं भोगो नाशः"

"danam bhogo nashah"

'donation – indulgence - destruction'

There are three conditions of wealth; whether it is disbursed as a *"dana"* (charitable gift) or in *"bhoga"* (indulgence) or it will be *"nasha"* (destroyed), that is the final condition. That wealth which is not enjoyed, not given as charity then that will be the third condition, that is to say, it will diminish.

There are also three kinds of *"dana"* (charity) - *satvika*, *rajasa* and *tamasa*. *Satvika* charity has the greatest effect.

The meaning of *"bhoga"* (the experience of pleasure or a pain) - it is not like people are experiencing. A life which is extremely sensual is not proper. Also, you should be indulging within proscribed limits. The mind is not satisfied with anything perceived by the senses and you should not trust that you will be satisfied. Even if the senses become inert then the mind still cannot be satisfied. It is impossible to get any satisfaction from *bhoga* (sense enjoyment). Getting some experience, afterwards it is the very same statement and even if you are engrossed day and night, then also it will be the very same news. Alcohol - drink one "cup" or ten "bottle", it is just the same! Getting intoxicated, then get intoxicated and never come down, so this intoxication which is desired [from alcohol], when it is gone so is the wealth.

Actually gaining Bhagwan is similar to getting an intoxication that you should never come down from, and in that intoxication there is also freedom from the body.

In the human life, if you are to do any action, then think and understand. Thus we are against meeting with that in the manner of friends, the very same you are attached to act (out of habit). You should do an action seeing your own loss and gain.

Until they will take a break from their alcohol and meat, some people do not go to *satsang*. From this fear they do not go to *satsang*. What can be done about this big mistake?

If they are unable to let go by themselves then make excellent *sanga* (association, friendship). It is probable that indeed there will be an advantage from *satsang*! To drive away the darkness then, take the help of light. Face-to-face with light, darkness will get out the way by itself. You should try for the light. Therefore, to get the mind out of the way of *samsara* you should apply it to Paramatma, and *Veda Shastra*, you should trust in the words of *sadhus* and *mahatmas*.

We say then; 'Firstly worship *samsara* (worldly existence), afterwards worship Bhagwan then there will be no argument.'

Worship of *samsara*? This is really understanding the real form of it. In the first instance *samsara* is really a *guru*. If a relative makes an insult, if through the son there is dishonour then you become detached from *samsara* (wordly existence).Therefore, actually before this, become mindful! You should routinely engage the mind in the direction of Bhagwan.

Whilst we are supporting, in collecting wealth, up until then there is the love of worldly people. You will not always be strong. One day you will come to old age. Then why not understand what those relatives will do with you afterwards then?

Just now we suppose that we are an object of love to them. At that time, when that state will come, then we will regret. Afterwards, this we will say, that; 'The son doesn't speak, the daughter-in-law doesn't speak, those for whom we have done so much are now being irreverent.' So why do such that will end in tears? Right now become cautious. In *samsara* nobody belongs to any other. All are companions for their own self-interest. As long as there is self-interest to be accomplished, for this reason there is love. Therefore before you become distrustful of these people go bow in the direction of Bhagwan. If from right now you will chant and worship Bhagwan, then the dishonour of relatives will not be a concern. The object of love then is Paramatma, love him, then you can remain happy.

९२

भगवान् के पास पहुँचना है तो उनके नाम का सहारा लो

*

हनुमान भगवान् राम के अनन्य भक्त थे। उन्होंने भगवान् की इतनी सेवा की। परन्तु उसके बदले में कुछ चाहा नहीं - यह अनन्यता है। उच्च कोटि के सेवक के लिये कहना नहीं पड़ता; यह भाव को जानकर काम करता है। भगवान् राम ने हनुमान को सीता की खबर लाने के लिये ही भेजा था - इतनी ही आज्ञा थी कि पता लगाकर चले आओ। परन्तु हनुमान ने लंका को भी जलाया और रावण को लड़ने की चुनौती भी दी; क्योंकि वह जानते थे कि रावण

का विनाश करना है - इसमें भगवान् प्रसन्न होंगे।

भगवान् तो कहते हैं कि -

दुराचाररतो वामि मन्नामभजनात्कपे।
सालोक्यमुक्तिमाप्नोति न तु लोकान्तरादिकम्॥

अर्थात्, दुराचारी भी यदि हमारा भजन करता है तो वह अन्य लोक-लोकान्तरों में न जाकर हमारे सालोक्य मोक्ष को प्राप्त करता है।

सालोक्य मोक्ष में भगवान् में लीन होने में कुछ विलम्ब तो होता है, परन्तु गर्भवास से तो मुक्त हो ही गया। फिर इस संसार में वह लौटकर नहीं आता। दुराचारी मनुष्य जब भगवान् का भजन करने लग जाता है, तो वह भी धर्मात्मा हो जाता है। इसका अर्थ यह नहीं हे कि दुराचार-पापाचार भी करते चलो और भगवान् का भजन भी। भगवान् का भजन करनेवाला दुराचारी कैसे रह सकता है?

भगवान् के पास पहुँचना है, तो उन्के नाम का सहारा लो। भगवान् तो अपनाने के लिये तैयार हैं, हमारी ही तरफ से कमी है। भगवान् तीन हाथ से तो जगत् का कार्य करते हैं परन्तु एक हाथ खाली रखते हैं। उसाहरण है - जैसे स्त्रियाँ जब पानी भरने जाती हैं, तो दो घड़ा एक के ऊपर एक सर पर रख लेती हैं और एक हाथ में रस्सी व डोल, परन्तु एक हाथ खाली रखती हैं। बच्चा जब माता की गोद में आने के लिये रोता है तब वह कहती है कि मेरा चरण पकड़ ले तो मैं एक हाथ से उठा लूँ। उसका कोई व्यापार बन्द नहीं होता। उत्पत्ति, पालन, संहार यही घड़े हैं - इन तीनों कामों को करते हुए भी भगवान् अपना एक हाथ भक्त के लिये खाली रखते हैं। परन्तु उपाय यही है कि भगवान् का चरण पकड़ लो तभी वह उठा सकते हैं, ऐसे नहीं। भगवान् की सेवा-पूजन करना, उनका भजन करना, यही भगवान् का चरण पकड़ना है। भगवान् को अगर

अपना लिया तो भगवान् भी तुम से दूर नहीं रह सकते। भगवान् का भजन करते-करते शरीर छूट गया, तो फिर जन्म-जन्म की दरिद्रता मिट जायगी।

92

To reach towards Bhagwan, then take the assistance of his name.

Huneman.

[*'India and Its Inhabitants'*, Caleb Wright, Brainerd, 1856]

Hanuman was endlessly devoted to Bhagwan Rama. He did so much service of Bhagwan, but desired nothing in exchange - this is endlessness. The high-class servant does not need to be told; the work is in knowing the temperament. Bhagwan Rama sent Hanuman for news of Sita - this much only was the command, that he discovered her whereabouts. But Hanuman also set fire to Lanka and further challenged Ravana to make war; because he understood that Ravana is to be destroyed - in this Bhagwan will be pleased. Bhagwan then says;

"दुराचाररतो वापि मन्नामभजनात्कपे ॥
सालोक्यमुक्तिमाप्नोति न तु लोकान्तरादिकम् । "

*"duraachaararato vaapi mannamabhajanaatkape.
saalokyamuktimaapnoti na tu lokaantaraadikam."*
[*Muktika Upanishad* 1:1:18 & 19]

That is to say;

'If even a wicked person chants and worships us then he is not going to another world, he gains *"salokya moksha"*.'

In *salokya moksha* then there exists some delay in being absorbed in Bhagwan, but one becomes set free from inhabiting a womb. Again, there is no return to this worldly existence. When a wicked man chants worship of Bhagwan then he also becomes a *dharmatma* (a righteous soul). To this meaning, this is not that you do wickedness and sinful conduct and also chant worship of Bhagwan. How can someone who chants adoration of Bhagwan be wicked?

To reach towards Bhagwan, then take the assistance of his name. Bhagwan then is ready for to make our own, the deficiency is from our side. With three hands Bhagwan does the work of the world but one hand is kept empty. That is to carry - in the manner that women go to carry water, then two jars, one above, one put on the head and in one hand is a rope and bucket. so when the child cries to come to the lap of mother then she says; 'Take hold my foot then with one hand I will lift you.' None of the activity is interrupted. Creation, sustaining, destruction - these are really jars - these three (hands) are doing the actions, also Bhagwan keeps one hand empty for the devotee. However this not a means for him to catch hold of the foot of Bhagwan then he can get up, it is not like this. The service of Bhagwan is:- doing *puja*, chanting *bhajan*, this is really seizing hold of Bhagwan's foot. If you make Bhagwan your own then Bhagwan can not keep away from you too. Chanting *bhajan* of Bhagwan, there is freedom from the body, then afterwards the poverty of many lifetimes will be erased.

९३

दुःख की प्रातिभासिक सत्ता है, वास्तविक नहीं

*

आजकल चारों ओर लोग अशान्त और दुःखी दिखाई देते हैं। इसका कारण यथार्थ ज्ञान का अभाव है। विवेक पूर्वक विचार करने से यह स्पष्ट हो जाता है कि बाहरी परिस्थितियाँ हमें तब तक प्रभावित नहीं कर सकतीं, जब तक हम दृढ़ता पूर्वक उनसे अप्रभावित रहने के लिये उध्योग-शील रहते हैं। जब हम अपने मन से बाह्य परिस्थितियों को सुखद या दुःखद मान लेते हैं, तभी वे हमें सुखी-दुःखी बनाती हैं। यदि निरन्तर यह भाव बना रहे कि हम स्थूल, सूक्ष्म और कारण-शरीर, इन तीन शरीरों से परे शुद्ध सच्चिदानन्दमय आत्मा हैं, तो किसी भी परिस्थिति में दुख की अनुभूति नहीं हो सकती।

प्रारब्ध-भोग टाला नहीं जा सकता। ज्ञानी भी उसे भोगना है और अज्ञानी भी। अन्तर केवल यह है कि ज्ञानी तो प्रसन्नतापूर्वक अच्छा-बुरा सभी प्रकार का प्रारब्ध भोगता है और अज्ञानी रोते हुये भोगता है। जब यह निश्चित है कि प्रारब्ध अवश्य भोगना पड़ेगा, तब उसे प्रसन्नता के साथ ही क्यों न भोग लिया जाय। दुःख यथार्थ में है ही नहीं। उसकी तो प्रातिभासिक सत्ता है जो केवल भ्रम के कारण दिखाई देती है। जैसे किसी कमरे में पड़ी हुई रस्सी को अन्धकार में देखने वाला सर्प का अनुमान करके भय से काँपने लगता है, परन्तु जिसने सुर्य के आलोक में उस रस्सी को देखा है वह न तो कम्पित होता है और न व्याकुल। यद्यपि वह उन्हीं लोगों के बीच में है जो रस्सी में सर्प को कल्पना करके भयभीत हो रहे हैं। इसी प्रकार से ज्ञानी भी आपके बीच में रहता है, परन्तु दुःख उसे विचलित नहीं कर सकते।

आप लोग विचार कर देखिये कि रज्जु तो सबके लिये समान था, परन्तु जो प्रकाश में उसके यथार्थ स्वारूप को देख चुका था वह अंधेरे में उसका देखकर कम्पित नहीं हुआ। जो उसके स्वरूप को नहीं जानते थे वे हो भ्रम से उसे सर्प मानकर भयभीत और दुःखी हुये। यदि किसी प्रकार उन लोगों का भ्रम दूर हो जाता तो फिर उनके लिये दुःख का अस्तित्व ही नहीं रहता। इसका निष्कर्ष यही है कि दुःख का कारण है भ्रम। भ्रम की निवृत्ति हो सकती है, इसीलिये दुःख की भी निवृत्ति हो सकती है। यदि दुःख भ्रम-मूलक न होता और पारमार्थिक सत्तावान् होता तो उसकी निवृत्ति विधाता भी न्हीं कर सकते थे; क्योंकि सत् वस्तु का अभाव कभी भी नहीं होता।

भ्रम-नाश दो प्रकार से होता है। इसे समझने के लिये उसी रज्जुवत् सर्प के दृष्टांत को ले लीजिये। दीपक लेकर रज्जु के वास्तविक स्वरूप को देख लेने पर उसमें सर्प का भ्रम मिट सकता था। रस्सी से तो कोई भयभीत होता नहीं, केवल सर्प की कल्पना ही भय-कम्प का कारण थी। अतः अधिष्ठान का प्रत्यक्ष ज्ञान होने पर उसका अस्तित्व ही नहीं रहता। भ्रम-नाश का दुसरा उपाय है - जानने वाले की बात पर विश्वास करना। जिसने उस रज्जु को दिन के प्रकाश में ठीक-ठीक समझ लिया है, उसकी बात पर विश्वास करके भी भय को मिटाया जो सकता है।

विवेक, वैराग्य, षट्-सम्पत्ति, मुमुक्षुता इत्यादि साधनों से सम्पन्न होकर ज्ञानी समाधि के द्वारा जगत् और ब्रह्म के यथार्थ स्वरूप का प्रत्यक्ष ज्ञान प्राप्त करता है। वह जानता है कि आत्म और अनात्म सभी रूपों में एक परमात्मा ही व्याप्त है। अतः जगत् में रहते हुए भी वह द्वन्द्व रहित हो जाता है। समाधि-काल में प्राप्त किये हुये ज्ञान के बल से वह व्यवहार-काल में भी कभी व्यथित नहीं होता; क्योंकि जहाँ अज्ञानी लोग भय देखते हैं वहाँ भी ज्ञानी ईश्वर को

देखता है। चराचर सम्पूर्ण जगत् का एकमात्र अधिष्ठान पर्मात्मा ही है। जैसे सर्प के अधिष्ठान रज्जु को जान लेने पर भय मिट जाता है, उसी प्रकार जगत् के अधिष्ठान परमात्मा को जान लेने पर भय के लिये कहीं स्थान ही नहीं रहता।

साधनहीनता के कारण जो परमात्मा का अपरोक्ष ज्ञान करने में असमर्थ हैं, वे भी यदि शास्त्र और ब्रह्मनिष्ठ सद्गुरुओं के शब्दों में श्रद्धा और विश्वास करना सीखें तो बहुत अंशों में उनका दुःख दूर हो जायेगा। जब तक अन्तःकरण में भ्रम बना हुआ है, तब तक लाख उपाय करने पर भी दुःख से सदैव के लिये छुटकारा नहीं मिल सकता। व्यथित मनुष्य को यदि मदिरा पिलाकर बेहोश कर दिया जाय तो अवश्य कुछ क्षणों के लिये, जब तक मदिरा का नशा रहेगा, वह अपनी व्यथा भूला रहेगा। परन्तु नशा उतरते ही वह पुनः उसी अवस्था को प्राप्त हो जायेगा। इसी प्रकार जगत् के विषयों में मन फँसा कर कोई दुःखों से छुटकारा पाना चाहे तो यह सम्भव नहीं।

आत्मा का ज्ञान होने पर सम्पूर्ण दुःख सदैव के लिये नष्ट हो जाते हैं। एक ही चैतन्य भिन्न-भिन्न नामों से पुकारा जाता है। पर्मात्मा ही सम्पूर्ण प्राणियों में आत्मारुप से व्याप्त है। आत्मा और परमात्मा में कोई भेद नहीं। जो आत्मा है वही चैतन्य जीव भी कहलाता है। भेद केवल उपाधि का है। उपाधि-युक्त चैतन्य ही जीव कहलाता है और सम्पूर्ण उपाधियों को त्याग देने पर वही चैतन्य आत्मा है। आत्मा और जीव का भेद ऐसा है जैसे धान और चावल का। जब तक एक भूसी बनी हुई है उसे धान कहा जाता है और जब उसकी भूसी हटा दी जाती है तब वही चावल कहलाता है। तत्वतः जो धान है वही चावल।

धान और चावल का व्यावहारिक भेद यह है कि धान में जल और मृत्तिका के योग से अंकुर उत्पन्न हो जाता है, परन्तु चावल चाहे जितने समय तक जल-मृत्तिका के संयोग में रहे उसमें अंकुर

नहीं हो सकता। इसी प्रकार जब तक शुभाशुभ कर्मों का बन्धन है, तब तक वही चैतन्य जीव है और कर्म-बन्धन क्षीण होने पर वह शुद्ध-बुद्ध आत्मा है। जीव का पुनर्जन्म ही उसका अम्कुरित होना है। शुभाशुभ कर्म जीव के के लिये भूसी के समान है। भूसी हटा देने से फिर अंकुर नहीं हो सकता। अर्थात्, शुभाशुभ कर्मों का परित्याग हो जाने पर फिर पुनर्जन्म नहीं होता।

जब तक भूसी लगी हुई है तब तक धान, धान ही है।

यद्यपि चावल भी उसी में है। परन्तु उसे उबालकर कोई खा नहीं सकता। यदि कोई धान उबाल कर किसी को खाने के लिये देवे तो उसे पागल ही समझा जायगा। ठीक इसी प्रकार जब तक कर्म-बन्धन नष्ट नहीं किया जाता, तब तक जीव परमानन्द की अनुभूति के वञ्चित रहता है।

अज्ञान से मोहित हुआ जीव कर्म के बन्धनों में पड़ता है। अज्ञान ही भ्रम कहलाता है। इनकी निवृत्ति यथार्थ ज्ञान से होता है। ज्ञान प्राप्त करने के लिये शास्त्र और सद्गुरु की सहायता अपेक्षित है। बिना गुरु के कोई जीवन भर माथा रगड़े, परन्तु आत्मज्ञान नहीं हो सकता। नदी पार करने वाले दस पुरुषों के दृष्टान्त में जब तक एक महात्मा ने आकर उनका भ्रम दूर नहीं कर दिया, तब तक वे अपने एक साथी के डूबने के भ्रम में विलाप करते रहे। जब महात्मा ने गणना करवा कर बतलाया कि 'दशमस्त्वमसि' दसवें तुम हो, तब उनका शोक नष्ट हुआ। इसी प्रकार गुरु के द्वारा ही 'तत्वमसिङ' का यथार्थ बोध होता है।

भगवान् के अस्तित्व और उसकी दयालुता में अपना विश्वास दृढ़ करो। धैर्यपूर्वक प्रारब्ध भोग करते हुये अपने-अपने वर्ण और आश्रम के धर्म का ठीक रूप से पालन करते जाओ। स्वधर्म का पालन करते रहने से अन्तःकरण पवित्र होगा और तभी आत्म-ज्ञान

प्राप्त करने की योग्यता प्राप्त होगी। ज्ञान-प्राप्ति के लिये व्यवहार से दूर भागने का आवश्यकता नहीं। संसार का व्यवहार तो चलाते रहो, परन्तु मन को उसमें न फँसाओ। संसार में जो राग हो गया है वही बन्धन का हेतु है, संसार बन्धन का हेतु नहीं है। अतः राग का त्याग करके अक्षय सुख का अनुभव करो। हम किताबी बातें नहीं कहते, यह सब हमारी अनुभूत बातें हैं। यदि आप निष्ठा-पूर्वक इनका पालन करें तो अवश्यमेव सुखी हो सकते हैं।

93

Suffering exists only in appearance, it is not real.

Nowadays, in all the four directions people appear to disturbed and unhappy. The real cause of this is lack of knowledge. By reasoning together with discernment it becomes clear that outer surroundings cannot influence us, if we make the effort to strengthen our natural tendency to be unaffected. When the mind allows external environments to give happiness or to give trouble, then they make us happy and sad, if we are continuously experiencing the existence of our *sthula* (gross), *sukshma* (subtle) and *karana* (causal) bodies. We are beyond these three bodies. You are the soul, you are *sachchidanandamaya*, pure Truth, Consciousness and Bliss, then in whatever the surroundings you are, you cannot be experiencing suffering.

Enduring fate cannot be avoided. Even the *gyaani* (realised) is to undergo it and the *agyaani* (unrealised) too. The difference is only this, that the *gyaani* then endures every kind of destiny - good and bad - with happiness but the *agyaani* (unrealised) weeps as he endures. When this is settled, that destiny will certainly be endured, then why not experience it with happiness? In truth there really is no *duhkha* (pain, suffering). The reason is that it only has the appearance of existing then. It is like having been in any room, seeing in the dark a rope, and trembling with fear presuming it to be a snake. But seeing that rope in the brightness of the sun he is not terrified and is not perplexed, although he is amongst people that are being frightened at the notion, that the rope is a snake. In this way a *gyaani* can remain in your midst but *duhkha* (pain, suffering) cannot make him unsteady.

You people see the reasoning, that the rope was the same for all? But he who has seen the real shape of that in the light, seeing that in the dark he is not frightened. He who does not understand the real shape, they become frightened and sorrowful - taking it to be a snake. If by any method these people's delusion is taken away then the fear will have no reality. It is certain that the cause of *duhkha* (pain, suffering) is delusion. Delusion can be removed, therefore *duhkha* also can be removed. If the origin of *duhkha* is not delusion and is of universal good then it's disappearance is impossible even for Vidhataa (the creator of the universe); since if something is good it can never cease to be.

There are two methods to destroy delusions. To understand this you ought to take the illustration of the rope and the serpent. With a lamp, on seeing the real shape of the rope, the delusion of the snake was able to be erased. With the rope no fear exists, then the cause of the alarm and trembling was really only at the notion of the snake. Therefore, with knowledge resting only on perception, it is not really a reality. The second method of destroying delusion is - to trust on the words of someone who knows. He who understands that in the daylight it is just a rope, trusting on his word, fear can also be erased.

Having performed reasoning, asceticism, the six *sampattis* (attainments) and *mumukshuta* (wishing salvation) etc., by *samadhi* the *gyaani* (realised) can acquire direct knowledge of the world and the true nature of Brahma. He understands that Paramatma pervades all forms whether *atma* (a soul) or *anatma* (soulless). Therefore, whilst remaining in the world he becomes without duality. With the strength of knowledge obtained in the period of *samadhi* he is not troubled in the time of everyday business; because wherever ignorant people see fear, the *gyaani* (realised) sees Ishwar (God). The sole support of the whole of the world of the living and lifeless is Paramatma. In the manner in which, when we know that the condition of the serpent is really the rope the fear is destroyed, by that very method, on understanding that Paramatma supports the world there is nowhere for the fear to remain.

On account of backwardness in *sadhana* (spiritual practice) they are unable to obtain direct knowledge of Paramatma. If they have faith in the *Shastra* and have faith in the words of the *sadgurus,* that are possessing knowledge of the immortal self, and trusting then they learn, a large part of the *duhkha* will become distant. Whilst there is delusion created in the inner self, then even with a thousand plans, the suffering can never be got rid of. If a man is troubled and he drinks some alcohol then certainly, for some moments, he will be senseless - whilst he is intoxicated with alcohol he will forget his suffering. But coming down from intoxication he regains that very condition. This is the way that the mind is ensnared in affairs of the world, wanting to get rid of the troubles, then it is not possible.

On knowing *atma* (the soul) then *duhkha* becomes destroyed forever. The one *chaitanya* (consciousness) is evoked by several names. Really Paramatma pervades all living beings in the form of *atma* (soul). There is no differentiation between *atma* (soul) and Paramatma (Supreme soul). That *atma* is the same as is also called *"chaitanya jiva"*. The difference is only that of condition. The proper condition of *"chaitanya"* (consciousness) is called *"jiva"* and on abandoning all the conditions, this consciousness is *"atma"*.

Separating *atma* and *jiva* is like that of paddy and rice. Whilst it has been with a husk it is said to be *"dhana"* (paddy) but when the husk is got out of the way then the same is called *"chawal"* (rice). Essentially, that *dhana* is the same as *chawal*. The usual distinction made between paddy and rice is that if paddy is in water and is planted in earth then it sprouts, but however much you would like it, planting rice in a mixture of earth and water, it cannot sprout. In this manner whilst bound to pleasant and unpleasant *karma* then there is the same *chaitanya jiva* (conscious life) and when the bondage to *karma* weakens, that *atma* (soul) is pure and awake. Transmigration (rebirth) of the *jiva* is really the sprouting. The pleasant and unpleasant *karma* is like the chaff for the *jiva*. If you do away with the husk then there can be no sprouting. That is to say, on completely surrendering the pleasant and unpleasant *karmas* then there is no transmigration.

Whilst the husk is attached then it is *dhana* (paddy), it is really *dhana*. Although it is also *chawal*. But if it is boiled you cannot eat it - if anybody boils any *dhana* for the purpose of eating then he will be understood to be *pagala* (mad, crazy). In just the same way, if the bondage to *karma* is not destroyed then the *jiva* (soul) is cheated of *paramananda* (highest bliss).

Deceived by *agyaan* (ignorance) the *jiva* falls into bondage of *karma*. Ignorance is really called delusion. The disappearance of these comes from correct true knowledge. For acquiring *gyaan* (knowledge) the help is needed of *Shastra* and *sadguru* (a good tutor). Without any *guru* and the whole life scouring the head, but you cannot get knowledge of the *atma*. As in the instance of when there were ten people crossing to the other side of the river, when one *mahatma* (great sage) appeared and took away their delusion. Up until then they were wailing, mistakenly thinking their associate had drowned. When the *mahatma* counted them he informed them; *"dashamastvamasi"* - 'You are the tenth' - then their distress became destoyed. This is the method, the way of the *guru* really, become aware of the reality of *"tatvamasi"* ('I am That I am').

Be resolute in your trust in the existence of Bhagwan and his graciousness. Together with courage endure the fate, cherish in good shape the *dharma* your *varna* (caste) and *ashrama* (stage of life). By cherishing one's own religion the inner self will be pure, and on this account you will have the capacity of gaining *atma-gyaan* (self-realisation). For gaining knowledge, you do not need to run far away from your daily business. Move to doing the business of the worldly existence but do not get the mind ensnared in that. If you become attached to *samsara* (worldly existence) **that** is the reason for bondage, *samsara* is not the cause of bondage. Therefore, renounce attachment, and experience eternal pleasure. We am not talking book speech, all this speech is all our experience. If you cherish these with faith then necessarily you can be happy.

९४

संसार शोक-सागर ही है
आत्म-ज्ञानी ही इसे पार कर सकता है

*

विचार-दृष्टि से देखा जाय तो संसार में सुख का लेश-मात्र भी नहीं है। यहाँ सुख की भावना करना ऐसा ही है, जैसे ससुराल की गाली सुनकर प्रसन्न होना। गाली तो गाली ही, है, उसमें प्रसन्नता कैसी? परन्तु नहीं, अनिष्ट में भी इष्ट बुद्धि रखने वाले लोग हैं। जैसे नाली में पड़ा हुआ मद्यप नाली में पड़े रहने में ही सुख मानता है; कोई उसे हाथ पकड़ करं बाहर निकालना चाहे तो भी प्रयत्न करके वह वहीं पड़ा रहना चाहता है। इसी प्रकार संसार में सुख की भावना करने वालों का हाल है। संसारी पदार्थों में सुख का लेश-मात्र नहीं, संसार तो शोक-सागर ही है। लिखा है कि - 'तरति शोकमात्मवित्' शोकोपलक्षित जो अज्ञान् है उसको आत्मवित् ही करता है। श्रुति कहती है -

'आचार्यवान् पुरुषो वेद'

अर्थात्, आचार्यवान् को ही ज्ञान होता है।

'धन्वान् पुरुषो वेद' 'पुत्रवान् पुरुषो वेद' 'स्त्रीवान् पुरुषो वेद' आदि यह नहीं कहा। 'आचार्यवान् पुरुषो वेद' यही श्रुति ने कहा है।

इसलिये शोक-सागर, संसार-सागर पार होने के लिए आत्म-ज्ञान प्राप्त करना आवश्यक है।

94

The drunk happily accepts falling in the gutter and remains there.

Having looked with discernment, there is not even a small portion of happiness in *samsara*. Here the feeling of happiness is like that in which you become delighted at the abuse in the father-in-law's house.

Abuse then is abuse, so what kind of happiness is in you?

But no, there are people who set their desires on the undesirable. Like falling in the gutter, the drunk happily accepts falling in the gutter and remains there. If anybody gives him a hand to get out then even for that effort he wishes to remain at the very place he has fallen. This is the kind of condition that people are feeling of happiness in *samsara* (worldly existence). In earthly things there is not even an iota, a small portion, of happiness. *Samsara* then is really an ocean of suffering.

It is written:-

"तरति शोकमात्मवित्"

"tarati shokamatmavit"
[*Chandogya Upanishad* 7:1:3]

'The knower of the Self goes beyond sorrow.'

Shruti (Scripture) says that:-

"आचार्यवान् पुरुषो वेद"

"acharyavan purusho veda"
[*Chandogya Upanishad* 6:14:2]

That is to say;

'Only the possessor of an *acharya* (teacher) gets knowledge.'

It does not say; 'The one with wealth gets knowledge', 'The one with a son gets knowledge', 'The one with a wife gets knowledge' etc.

"आचार्यवान् पुरुषो वेद"

"acharyavan purusho veda"

'The *acharyavan* (the one with a teacher) gets the *Veda* (knowledge) of *purusho* (man)'

This is what the *shruti* did say therefore, the ocean of distress - for crossing the ocean of *samsara* (worldly existence) it is necessary to gain the knowledge of the Self.

९५

भवसागर से पार होने का प्रयत्न करो

*

नौकारूढ़ होकर भी यदि डूब गये
तो इससे बड़ा दुर्भाग्य और क्या होगा

*

प्रत्येक मनुष्य यह चाहता है कि लोक में वह सुखी रहे और परलोक भी न बिगड़े। जो परलोक को नहीं जानता वह नास्तिक है। नास्तिक भी यह चाहता है कि वह सुखी और शान्त रहे। आस्तिक लोग दोनों लोक बनाना चाहते हैं। परन्तु सुख-शान्ति केवल इच्छा मात्र से तो हो नहीं सकती। इच्छा तो केवल प्रयत्न कराने वाली होती है, सुख-शान्ति प्रयत्न करने से ही मिल सकती है। इसलिए सुख-शान्ति के लिए प्रयत्न करो और ऐसा प्रयत्न करो जो वैध हो। वैध प्रयत्न वही है जैसा शास्त्र कहता है। किसी कवि ने कहा है:-

न पीतं जाह्नवी तोयं
न गीतं भगवद् यशः
न जाने जानकी जाने जाने
यमाह्वाने किमुत्तरम्।

गंगा-जल का पान नहीं किया। अब देखना यह है कि गंगाजल पान करने से होता क्या है? गंगाजल पान करने से पाप नष्ट होते हैं, पाप नष्ट होने से बुद्धि शुद्ध होती है और बुद्धि शुद्ध हो जाने पर भगवान् की ओर प्रेम बढ़ता है। ऐसा गंगा-जल यहाँ उपलब्ध है। सरल से सरल यह साधन यहाँ प्राप्त ही है।

भगवान् की भक्त-वत्सलता का चिन्तन और गान ही भगवान् का

गुणानुवाद है। हिरण्यकश्यपु के वध के लिये भगवान् का जड़ से उत्पन्न होना उसी प्रकार है, जिस प्रकार पिपीलिका मारने के लिए तोप लगाना। भगवान् के लिए यह साधारण सी बात रही। भगवान तो उसकी मति ही बदल सकते थे। फिर प्रह्लाद कार्य तो तभी हो गया जब-जब जिस-जिस तत्त्व से प्राह्लाद को कष्ट दिया गया तब-तब प्रह्लाद वही-वही तत्त्व हो गये। जब वे अग्नि में डाले गये तो अग्नि ही हो गये। अग्नि, अग्नि को क्या जलायेगा? जब प्रह्लाद जल में डुबोग्ये गये तो वे जल तत्त्व ही हो गये। परन्तु भगवान् ने ऐसा इसीलिए किया कि आगे के भक्तों को विश्वास हो, आश्वासन रहे। अपने यश के विस्तार के लिए वे प्रह्लाद के सामने प्रत्यक्ष प्रकट हुए। सांसारिक लोग कह सकते हैं कि भगवान् को अपने यश-विस्तार के लिए क्या पड़ी है। परन्तु यह भगवान् की भक्त-वत्सलता ही थी कि जिसके आगे के भक्त लोग गुणानुवाद करके, उनका यश-गान करके, भवसागर को पार करें। इसी लिये इस प्रकार भगवान् प्रह्लाद के लिए नृसिंह रूप में पैदा हुए।

द्रौपदी के कष्ट में भगवान् चीर ही हो गये। इस प्रकार भगवान् का स्मरण, चिन्तन और गान करने से बुद्धि शुद्ध होती है और भगवान् में विश्वास होता है। भगवान् को जानने का साधन वेद-शास्त्र पर विश्वास करना भी है। यदि वेद-शास्त्र पर विश्वास न करोगे, तो भगवान् की सत्ता पर भी विश्वास न होगा। भगवान् की सत्ता पर विश्वास न करने से संशय बना रहेगा। संशयवान् पुरुष का न लोक ही बनता है और न परलोक ही।

भगवान् को जानोगे नहीं, विश्वास नहीं करोगे, तो ढूँढोगे कहाँ? जैसे हमको रामनगर जाना है तो हम नक्षे में देख कर पता लगावेंगे कि रामनगर कहाँ है। तब आत्म-भवन में रुकेंगे। नक्षा है वेद-शात्र। वेद-शास्त्र द्वारा भगवान् को जानो। परन्तु भगवान् को जान लेने-मात्र से तो काम चलेगा नहीं, कुछ अनुभव भी करो। अनुभव

बहुत बड़ी चीज है।

एकान्तवास भगवान् के ढूँढ़ने का अच्छा साधन है। अतः एकान्त में रह कर अनुभवी महात्मा बनो। इस प्रकार साधू-सन्यासी ही नहीं, संसारी भी कर सकते हैं, क्योंकि संसारियों से ही तो महात्मा होते हैं। इनकी कोई खदान नहीं, इन्हीं माताओं के पेट से महात्मा भी हुए हैं। आज जो दुराचार-पापाचार-रत हैं कल वे ही उच्च कोटि के महात्मा हो सकते हैं।

एक समय की बात है, हम उपनिषद् का पाठ कर रहे थे। एक परमहंस आए और कहा कि क्या आप भी पूजा-पाठ करते हैं? हमको तो बड़ा आश्चर्य हुआ। हमने कहा, आप से अधिक आश्चर्य तो हमको हुआ कि रिटायर्ड होकर आप फिर दफ्तरों में धक्का खाते-फिरते हो। हम तो आश्रमी हैं, संन्यासी हैं। आप तो अपने को पर्ममहंस कहते हो, परमहंस तो आश्रमातीत होता है। कौन संसार में व्यभिचार कर रहा है, कौन पूजा-पाठ कर रहा है - यह देखते-फिरना तो आप का काम नहीं है। आप की वृत्ति तो निरन्तर स्वरूपाकार रहनी चाहिये। हम तो प्रिन्सिपल हैं; स्वयं पाठ-पूजा करेंगे क्योंकि दूसरों को सिखाना है। प्रयोजन यह है कि मन इतना बेईमान है कि वेदान्त के सहारे उपासना छोड़ देने पर न जाने कब फिसल जाय। अच्छे-बुरे कर्म तो प्रारब्धानुसार होते ही रहते हैं। उपासना तो अवश्य ही होती रहनी चाहिये।

जब तक प्रारब्ध हैं, कुछ न कुछ करना ही पड़ेगा। इसलिए भगवान् का चिन्तन करते हुए विहिताविहित का विचार करके कर्म करो। विहताविहित का निर्णय करने वाला शास्त्र ही हैं; इसका निर्णय कोई कमेटी नहीं कर सकती। हमारे संचालक तो वेद-शास्त्र ही हैं। व्यवहार चलाते रहो। मन भगवान् में लगाओ। अन्त समय में भगवान् का चिन्तन करते हुए जाओ। ऐसा न कर पाये तो कुछ भी नहीं कर पाये-नौकारूढ़ होकर भी नदी में डूब गये।

95

The *nastika* (atheist) also has this wish that he is being happy and serene.

Each human being wants to be happy in this world and also not spoil the other world. He who does not believe in the other world, he is a *nastika* (unbeliever, atheist). The *nastika* (atheist) also has this wish that he is being happy and serene. The *astika* (believer, theist) wishes to make both worlds [happy]. But from a mere desire you cannot be happy and peaceful.

If you desire, then simply become someone who makes an effort, happiness and peace can be got by effort. Therefore, make an effort for happiness and peace but make an effort that is *"vaidha"*. The effort that is *"vaidha"* is really that which is said to be according the *Shastra* (Scripture). A poet did say:-

"न पीतं जाह्नवी तोयं
न गीतं भगवद् यशः
न जाने जानकी जाने जाने
यमाह्वाने किमुत्तरम् ।"

*"na pitam jahnavi toyam
na gitam bhagavad yashah
na jane janaki jane jane
yamahvane kimuttaram."*

'If I did not drink the water of Jahnavi (Ganga),
If I did not sing of the fame of Bhagavad (the Lord),
If I do not know who is Janaki (Sita),
What reply is there to Yama (Death) when he calls?'

na pitam, I did not drink, *jahnavi-toyam,* the water of the Ganga. *na gitam,* I did not sing, *bhagavad-yashah,* the glory of the Lord. *na jane,* I do not know, *janaki-jane,* about the birth of Sita. *Yamahvane,* When Yama calls me, *kimuttaram,* what will happen to me?

By drinking Gangajal, sins are destoyed. By destroying sin the mind becomes pure and on the mind becoming pure, love grows towards Bhagwan. After this manner Gangajal is known here. Only by sincerity is this *sadhana* (devotion) gained.

To think of Bhagwan's tenderness of devotee and singing of Bhagwan's glorious virtues. Bhagwan's emerged from the immovable [pillar] for the execution of Hiranyakashyapu. In this way, that is like taking a cannon for killing an ant. For Bhagwan this is a commonplace thing. Bhagwan could have really changed his (Hiranyakshyapu's) thinking, but then Prahlad's role had become that, from whatever element Prahlad was being given hardship then Prahlad became that very same element. When they cast him in the fire then he became the fire. How will fire burn fire? When Prahlad was immersed in the water then he became the element of water. However, Bhagwan therefore came like this to be hope for the devotees, reassuring. For the spread of his own reputation he became apparent to Prahlad. Worldly people can say, 'Why did Bhagwan drop down? For his own fame?' But this was actually the tenderness of Bhagwan, for devotees in future to glorify the virtues, sing his fame, then they will cross to the other side of the ocean of existence. Therefore, in this manner he had been born in the form of Narsingh (the Man-Lion).

In Draupadi's suffering Bhagwan actually became the cloth. This is the remembering of Bhagwan, by thinking and singing the mind becomes pure and has faith in Bhagwan. The means to know Bhagwan is to also to have faith on the *Veda Shastra*. If you do not act with faith on the *Veda Shastra* then you will also not have faith in the existence of Bhagwan. By not having trust in the existence of Bhagwan you will create uncertainty. The suspicious man is really neither prepared for this world nor the other world.

If you do not know Bhagwan, you will not have faith. Then where will you search? In the manner we go to "Ram Nagar"* ('City of Ram' or 'City of God'), then we will apply ourselves with looking for the whereabouts on a map, 'Where is Ramnagar?' Then you will stop at "Atma Bhavan"* ('Building of the Self'). The map is *Veda Shastra*. Understand that the *Veda Shastra* is the way to Bhagwan. However, by merely knowing about Bhagwan then you will not fulfil your desire, also get some experience! Experience is a very great thing.

[* On 25th April 1952, at the request of Pandit ShriDatta Shastri, secretary of Baba Kalikamli Mission, Guru Dev stayed at Atma Vigyan Bhawan, Ram Nagar, Rishikesh (the ashram is known as Shankaracharya Niwas).]

In a secluded place, to seek Bhagwan is good *sadhana*. Therefore, living alone become an experienced *mahatma* (great soul). This is not only for the *sadhu* and *sanyasi*. *Samsari* (worldly people) can also do it, because a *mahatma* comes from worldly people. They are not from a hole in the ground, to their mother's womb the *mahatma* also they have been. Today, he who is occupied in wicked sinful living can tomorrow become a highly eminent *mahatma*.

One time we were reading the *Upanishad*. One *paramahamsa* came and said; 'What? You still worship and study?'

To us this came as a great surprise. We said, 'We are more surprised then by you, that you are *"retired"* but you are again returning to undergo the jostle in offices. We are in the *ashrama* (stage) of *"sannyasi"* (ascetic). You then call yourself *"paramahamsa"* (ascetic of the highest order). The *paramahamsa* then becomes *"ashramatita"* (beyond *ashram*).

Who in the world is fornicating?

Who is worshipping and studying?

This you are going about to see, then this is not your business. Your existence should be continuously remaining in the *swaroop* (form of the Self).

We then are the *"principal"*; I will personally study, and worship, to teach others.'

The purpose is this, that the mind is so dishonest that with the support of *Vedanta* (theology), leaving off *upasana* (prayer), one doesn't even know he has slipped. Good and bad *karma* then remain, existing according to destiny. You should continue to pray, this is really certain.

Whilst there is *prarabdha* (commenced actions, destiny), something or another is really to be done. Therefore, thinking of Bhagwan, do action which is duly considered. The *Shastra* really settles the arrangement, some *"committee"* cannot settle this. Our management then are really the *Veda Shastras*. Begin the day-to-day business. Attach the mind on Bhagwan. In the end time [of dying], as you go be thinking of Bhagwan. If you do not do like this then you will not get across, even though you have a boat, you will sink in the water.

९६

सिवाय परमात्मा के कोई सहायक नहीं

*

इस संसार में रहना किसी को नहीं। यहाँ तो धर्मशाले का निवास है। आ गये हो, दुर्लभ मानव शरीर मिल गया है, भव-सागर से पार हो सकते हो। इसी शरीर से ज्ञान-भक्ति पैदा कर सकते हो। अब न किया, अब न बनाया, तो कब बनाओगे? परमात्मा व्यापक है, सर्वत्र है; किन्तु हम एकदेशीय हैं। इसलिए हम व्यापक परमात्मा को भक्ति-द्वारा एक-देश में प्रकट करें, तभी हमारा काम बनेगा। साकार-निराकार है क्या? काष्ठ में अग्नि सर्वत्र परिपूर्ण है, परन्तु आप उससे जलते नहीं। चूल्हे में चैला लगा कर चाहो कि रोटी बन जाय तो क्या रसोई बन जायगी? उसी काष्ठ को घर्षण करके अग्नि प्रकट कर लो तो सब काम सिद्ध हो जायगा।

परमात्मा अखण्ड है, प्रत्येक देश-काल-वस्तु में है। कहीं भी कोई ऐसी वस्तु नहीं, जहाँ परमात्मा न हो। सर्वशक्तिमान् झोते हुए भी परमात्मा में एक शक्ति नहीं है। वह यह कि यदि वह चाहे भी तो हम से अलग नहीं हो सकता। अब आप ही बतावें, इतना हमारा और परमात्मा का अभेद होते हुए भी हम दुखी हैं, तो किसकी ओर से गलती है?

द्रौपदी का उदाहरण देखिये। पाँचो पति एक से एक वीर,

कृपाचार्य, द्रोणाचार्य एक से एक महारथी बैठे थे। एक कुलाङ्गना की बेइज्जती की जा रही थी। संसारियों का इस्तीफा देखो। इससे बड़ा ज्वलन्त उदाहरण और क्या मिल सकता है? आप चाहें कि पिता, पुत्र, भाई, बहिन, पति से कुछ सहायता मिल सकती है, तो सर्वथा असम्भव। परमात्मा न करे कोई आपत्ति का समय आये, नहीं तो सब सम्बन्धी इस्तीफा दे देंगे। सिवाय परमात्मा के कोई सहायक नहीं होगा। ऐसी भावना ही अनर्गल है कि अमुक हमारी रक्षा करेगा। जब द्रौपदी की रक्षा के लिये बड़े-बड़े महारथियों ने इस्तीफा दे दिया तो तुम्हारे सहायकों को क्या गिनती है! संसारियों से केवल शिष्टाचार चलाये जाओ, ये रागास्पद नहीं हैं। द्रौपदी को जब संसारियों से निराशा हो गई, तब भगवान् आये। प्रह्लाद के लिए जड़ से प्रकट हुए। यह भगवान् की व्यापकता है। परन्तु व्यापक परमात्मा से हमारा लाभ नहीं। व्यापक अग्नि से आपका काम नहीं हो सकता। काम के लिये काष्ठ का घर्षण करके अग्नि को एक-देश में लाना ही पड़ेगा। इसी प्रकार परमात्मा को भी उपासना द्वारा एक-देश में लाने से ही कल्याण है। भगवान् को देश में आने में कोई आपत्ति भी नहीं है, क्योंकि वे स्वयं कहते हैं कि -

यदा यदा हि धर्मस्य, ग्लानिर्भअवति भारत्।
अभ्युत्थानमधर्मस्य, तदात्मानं सृजाम्यहम्॥
परित्राणाय साधूनां, विनाशाय च दुष्कृताम्।
धर्मसंअस्थापनार्थाय, संभवामि युगे युगे॥

इतना ही नहीं, भगवान् यह भी कहते हैं कि:-

ये यथा मां प्रपद्यन्ते तांस्तथैव भजाम्यहम्।

अर्थात्, जो जिस प्रकार से मेरा स्मरण करता है, मैं उसी प्रकार से उसका स्मरण करता हूँ। कितना बड़ा आश्वासन भगवान् दे रहे हैं। अब भी हम न चेते तो हमारा दुर्भाग्य!

96

With worldly people only maintain good manners, they are not a basis for attachment.

Nobody is to stay in this *samsara* (worldly existence). Here then is a *dharmashala* (dwelling house for pilgrims). You become born and have obtained a scarce human body. You can cross to the other side of the *bhava sagara* (the ocean of existence). Only with this body can you gain *gyaan-bhakti* (knowledge and devotion). If now it is not done, if now you have not made, then when will you make? Paramatma is pervasive, is everywhere; but we are just of one place. Therefore, by way of devotion to Paramatma he will manifest in one place. On this account our desire will be achieved. What is *sakara* (that with form) and *nirakara* (the formless)? In wood, fire is completely everywhere, but from that you cannot burn. Putting pieces of wood in the oven, you want to make *roti* (flat bread), but how will you cook it? Only if that wood is rubbed will fire become manifest, then all work will be accomplished.

Paramatma is *akhanda* (indivisible) in each and every place, time and thing. There isn't anywhere that Paramatma does not exist. Having been All-Powerful there is however one strength that is not in Paramatma. Even if he wishes then we cannot be separate. Now, only you will tell. Even as much as we are one with Paramatma, we are sorrowful, then in which direction is the mistake?

You should look at the example of Draupadi. Five husbands, each one a hero, Kripacharya and Dronacharya, One by one the great warriors were sitting whilst a beautiful woman of their tribe was being dishonoured. Look at the resignation of the worldly people. How can you get a more brilliant example than this? You may want some help from father, brother, sister and husband, then this is altogether impossible. If Paramatma does not act in the time of a predicament, then all the relatives will be resigned. Without Paramatma there will be no supporter. So it is really a useless sentiment that so and so will be our protector. For Draupadi's protection, when very great warriors gave up resignedly, then why count on your helpers?

With worldly people only maintain good manners, they are not a basis for attachment. When Draupadi became despondent with worldly people, then Bhagwan came. For Prahlad he manifested from the immovable [pillar]. This is the extensiveness of Bhagwan. But our advantage is not from the pervasive Paramatma. Your work cannot be done by pervasive *agni* (fire). For work the wood is rubbed for *agni* to actually be produced in one place. Also *upasana* (worship) is the way to bring Paramatma to one place, this is really the welfare. For Bhagwan to come to a place is not even difficult, because he said himself that:-

"यदा यदा हि धर्मंस्य ग्लानिर्भंअवति भारत ।
अभ्युत्थानमधर्मस्य तदात्मानं सृजाम्यहम् ॥"

*"yada yada hi dharmamsya glanirbhamavati bharata.
abhyutthanamadharmasya tadatmanam sriijamyaham."*
[*Bhagavad Gita* 4:7]

'Whenever righteousness is in decline Arjuna,
and there is a rise of unrighteousness, then I manifest myself'

"परित्राणाय साधूनां विनाशाय च दुष्कृताम् ।
धर्मसंअस्थापनार्थाय संभवामि युगे युगे ॥"

*" paritranaya sadhunam vinashaya cha dushkritam.
dharmasamasthapanarthaya sambhavami yuge yuge.."*
[*Bhagavad Gita* 4:8]

'For the welfare of the good, for the destruction of the wicked I am manifest,
and for the establishment of *dharma* I am born from age to age.'

Not only this much. Bhagwan even said this:-

"ये यथा मां प्रपद्यन्ते तांस्तथैव भजाम्यहम् ।"

"ye yatha mam prapadyante tamstathaiva bhajamyaham."
[*Bhagavad Gita* 4:11]

That is to say,

'In whatever manner I am remembered, I am remembering him.'

How great a comfort Bhagwan is giving? If we are not acquainted then it is our calamity.

९७

जाति-पांति कल्याण-कारक नहीं

*

भगवान के भजन और स्वधर्म पालन
से काल्याण होगा

*

जन्म तो कर्म के आधीन है, परन्तु भगवान् की दयालुता कर्म के आधीन नहीं है, वह भाव के आधीन है। कोई भी-चाहे वह ब्राह्मण हो, क्षत्रिय हो, वैश्य हो, शूद्र हो - भगवान् में भाव बना कर भगवान् को प्राप्त कर सकता है। भगवान् का गुणानुवाद मनुष्यमात्र कर सकता है; ऐसा नहीं कि केवल ब्राह्मण ही भगवान् का गुणानुवाद कर सके। भक्त तो चारों वर्णों के लोग हो सकते हैं, परन्तु आचार्य चारों वर्ण के लोग नहीं हो सकते। इसके लिये तो आदि-शङ्कराचार्य का डंका है कि -

"यावत् वित्तोपार्जन सक्तः तावन्निज-परिवारोक्तः,
पश्चात् धावति जर्जर देहे वातां कोऽपि न पृच्छै गेहे।"

इसलिये -

"भज गोविन्दं, भज गोविन्दं। भज गोविन्दं मूढ़मते।"

कोई भी हो, किसी जाति का हो वृद्धावस्था आने के पहले ही

सचेत होकर भगवान् का भजन-पूजन पर्याप्त कर ले, इसी में कल्याण है। कल्याण किसी जाति में पैदा होने से नहीं होगा। कल्याण तो होगा भगवान् के भजन से और भगवान् के भजन का मनुष्य मात्र को अधिकार है। ब्राह्मण होने से ही मुक्त हो जायगा, ऐसी बात नहीं है। यदि भगवान् की भक्ति है तब तो ठीक है, नहीं तो ब्राह्मण भी नरक का अधिकारी हो सकता है और भक्तिमान् शूद्र भगवान् को प्राप्त कर सकता है। जहाँ कल्याण होता है, वहाँ न कोई ब्राह्मण है, न क्षत्रिय है, न वैश्य है, न शूद्र है। परमार्थ में कोई भेद ही नहीं है, भेद तो व्यवहार में है।

97

Happiness will not be being born in any caste.

Birth then is dependent on *karma*, but Bhagwan's kindness is not dependent on *karma*, that is dependent on *bhava* (emotion, feeling). Anybody who desires, be he *brahmana*, be he *kshatriya*, be he *vaishya*, be he *shudra* - [whoever] has a feeling for Bhagwan can gain Bhagwan. They can glorify Bhagwan, so really Bhagwan's glorifying cannot only be done by *brahmanas*. Four castes of people can do *bhakta* (service) then. But an *acharya* (preceptor) cannot be people of the four castes.

For this purpose then is the drum (proclamation) of Adi Shankaracharya:-

"यावत् वित्तोपार्जन सक्तः तावन्निज-परिवारोक्तः,
पश्चात् धावति जर्जर देहे वातां कोऽपि न पृच्छै गेहे ।"

*"yavat vittoparjana saktah tavannija - parivaroktah.
pashchat dhavati jarjara dehe vatam ko.api na priichchai gehe."*
[*Bhaja Govindam* v6]

'When one is alive, his family members enquire kindly about his welfare.
Later, when the body is old and decrepid, nobody in the house asks for word of him'

Therefore;

"भज गोविन्दं, भज गोविन्दं । भज गोविन्दं मूढ़मते ।"

"bhaja govindam, bhaja govindam. bhaja govindam murhamate."
[*Bhaja Govindam* v1]

'Worship Govinda, worship Govinda, worship Govinda O, foolish mind!'

Actually, before senility, anybody of any caste should be mindful to do sufficient *bhajan* and *puja* of Bhagwan, for in this is happiness. Happiness will not be being born in any caste.

Happiness will then be from *bhajan* of Bhagwan and to do *bhajan* to Bhagwan is just man's right.

There is no talk that one must be a *brahmana* in order to get *mukta* (liberation). If *bhakti* (service) of Bhagwan is done then [all] is well, [but if] not then *brahmanas* also come to the ruler of hell, and the devout *shudra* can gain Bhagwan. Wherever happiness is to be, there nobody is *brahmana*, is not *kshatriya*, is not *vaishya*, is not *shudra*. In Paramatma there is no difference in anyone, the difference then is in everyday affairs.

९८

दुर्जन के लिये दुर्जन बनना निन्दक के लिये स्वयं निन्दक बन जाना उचित नहीं

*

"क्षमा खड्गः करे यस्य, दुर्जनः किं करिष्यति"

अर्थात् क्षमा रूपी खड्ग जिसके हाथ में है उसका दुर्जन कुछ नहीं बिगाड़ सकता।

"अतृणे पतिते त्रहिः स्वयमेवोपशाम्यति"

जहाँ तृण न हो वहाँ अग्नि का अङ्गार गिरे भी तो क्या करेगा? स्वयं ही शान्त हो जायगा। इसी प्रकार जो क्षमावन्त हैं, उनके प्रति किए गए दुर्जनों के दुर्व्यवहार स्वयं ही समाप्त हो जाते हैं। इसी लिये सदैव ही उपेक्षावर्ती का सहारा लेना चाहिए।

इसी प्रकार मैत्री, करुणा, मुदिता और उपेक्षा इन्हीं चार वृत्तियों में रहते हुए व्यवहार चलाना चाहिये। और किसी पाँचवीं वृत्ति का सहारा नहीं लेना चाहिये। ऐसा करोगे तो कभी अशान्त होने का

अवसर नहीं आयेगा।

धन के दुरुपयोग के सम्बन्ध में यह बात है कि नम्बर एक का दुरुपयोग यह है कि पापाचार-दुराचार में धन खर्च किया जाय। नम्बर दो का दुरुपयोग यह है कि पूर्व की कमाई खाकर आगे के लिए कुछ संचय न किया जाय। धन को बुरे कामों में न भी लगाओ तब भी यदि उसको सत्कार्य में न लगाया गया तो उसका दुरुपयोग ही है। दुष्कर्म में धन का उपयोग न करते हुये यदि सत्कर्म में नहीं लगाया जा रहा है तो यही नम्बर दो का दुरुपयोग है।

धन का उचित उपयोग यही है कि उसकी 'प्रथम् गति हो अर्थात् सत्पात्र में उसका व्यय हो।

जीवन के सदुपयोग के लिये सचेष्ट रहना चाहिये। आज-कल लोग जाति-पाँति के फेर में पड़ कर ही व्यर्थ के वर्गवाद् में जीवन का अमूल्य समय नष्ट करते हैं। किसी जाति में जन्म हो गया, बस भगवान् को छोड़कर जातियों के संगठन के फेर में पड़ जाते हैं। जहाँ कहीं जिस जाति में जन्म हो गया हो, उसी से किसी तरह जन्म-मरण रूपी कारागार से निकलने का प्रयत्न करना चाहिये, न कि एक जाति रूपी कारागार का समर्थन करते रहो। अपनी जाति-पाँति से इतना ही लाभ उठाना चाहिये कि उसमें जो वेद-शास्त्रानुसार अच्छी बातें हों उन्हें तो अपनाओ और जो वेद शास्त्र के विरुद्ध प्रथायें हों उनसे कोई सम्बन्ध न रक्खो, उनका त्याग कर दो। इसी में जात्याभिमान की सार्थकता है। यह निश्चय रखना चाहिये कि अच्छी बात वही है जो वेद-शास्त्र के अनुकूल है। केवल हमारे विचार से कोई बात अच्छी-बुरी नहीं हो सकती। अच्छी बात वही है, जिसे वेद-शास्त्र अच्छा कहता है और बुरी बात वही है जिसे वेद-शास्त्र बुरा कहता है।

धन की इच्छा हो तो ऐसे धन का संग्रह करो जो साथ जाय।

जिसको यहीं छूट जाना है ऐसे 'टेम्परी' धन का संग्रह करने से क्या लाभ?

यह बात जरूर है कि अविवेक कारण -

"धनाहा जीविताशा च जीर्यत्ऽपिनजीर्यते।"

धन संग्रह करने की और जीते रहने की इच्छा जीर्ण-शीर्ण हो जाने पर भी नहीं मिटती। इस पर एक दृष्टान्त है कि:-

एक बहुत बृद्धा स्त्री थी। किसी तरह से लकड़ी बीन-बीन कर बेचकर अपनी आजीविका चलाती थी। उसका जीवन कष्टमय था। एक दिन जंगल में लकड़ी बीनते-बीनते लोभ के कारण उसने बहुत बड़ा गट्ठर बाँध लिया जो उससे उठाया नहीं उठता था। गट्ठर उटाने का उसने कई बार प्रयत्न किया, परन्तु उठा न सकी। अन्त में निराश होकर बड़े दुःख के साथ उसने कहा कि यदि किसी तरह मृत्यु आ जाती तो मैं इस जंजाल से छूट जाती। उसने इतना कहा ही था कि मृत्यु सामने आकर खड़ी हो गई। मृत्यु ने कहा कि कहिये माताजी किसलिए बुलाया है? वृद्धा ने पूँछा कि तुम कौन हो? मृत्यु ने कहा कि मैं मृत्यु हूँ; आपने अभी मुझको बुलाया, इस लिए मैं आई हूँ। बृद्धा ने कहा कि अच्छा हुआ, तुम आ गये। इसी गट्ठे को उठाने के लिए बुलाया था।

तात्पर्य यह है कि प्राणी चाहे जिस स्थिति में हो, वह मरना नहीं चाहता। परन्तु यदि केवल खाते-पीते हुये ही जीते रहना है तो ऐसे जीने से कोई लाभ नहीं। जीना वही सार्थक है कि जों कुछ आगे के लिए बनाया जाय। यदि केवल विषय-भोग के लिए जीना है तो इस प्रकार पाप सम्ग्रह करते हुए जीने से तो मर जाना ही अच्छा है।

व्यवहार में यह अवश्य स्मरण रखना चाहिये कि अपने से यदि किसी की भलाई न हो सके, तो किसी की बुराई भी न करना। साथ

ही साथ भगवान का भजन-पूजन कुछ न कुछ अवश्य करते रहना। मन तो चंचल है, मन लगे या न लगे, भजन-पूजन में समय खर्च करना चाहिये। यदि अभी नहीं लगता है तो थोड़े दिनों में लगने लगेगा, परन्तु करते जाना चाहिये। जिस गिलास में पीनी पीते हो, उसी गिलास से थोड़े दिनों में प्रेम हो जाता है, क्योंकि जब दूसरा गिलास आता है तो ऐसा लगता है कि वह पुराना गिलास कहाँ गया। इसी प्रकार जिस छड़ी को रोज हाथ में लेते हो, कुछ दिनों में उससे प्रेम हो जाता है। वैसे ही भगवान् के नाम को जपते-जपते, उस नाम में भी छड़ी-गिलास के समान प्रेम हो जाएगा। इसलिए बिना मन के भी भगवान् का नाम लेते रहना चाहिये, मन कहीं तो जाने दो।

98

It is not proper to be wicked to the wicked, to go and be abusive to those who are abusive.

"क्षमा खड्गः करे यस्य दुर्जनः किं करिष्यति"

"kshama khadgah kare yasya durjanah kim karishyati"
[a *subhashit* - wise verse]

That is to say;

'Whoever has the sword of forgiveness in his hand, nothing can destroy.'

"अतृणे पतिते त्रहिः स्वयमेवोपशाम्यति"

"atrine patite trahih svayamevopashamyati"
[continuation of above *subhashit* - wise verse]

'Wherever there is no grass then what will even falling embers of fire do? Yourself be peaceful, it will go out.'

This is really the method of a forgiving person, instead of bad treatment of the wicked persons, actually, automatically it becomes completed. Therefore you should always be giving the support of equanimity. This is really the method - *maitri* (friendship), *karuna* (compassion), *mudita* (cheerfulness) and *upeksha* (equanimity) - you should carry out your everyday business remaining in these four conditions and you should give no assistance to any of the five *vrittis* (*pramana, viparyaya, vikalpa, nidra & smriti*). If you act like this then you will certainly never be without peace.

In connection with the abuse of wealth, this is the instruction:- *"Number"* one abuse is; spending wealth on sinful conduct and wicked living. *"Number"* two abuse is; not saving anything of the former earnings to live on in the future.

Even if wealth is not applied to wicked acts but if it is not applied to good work then this is really abuse. If you do not employ the wealth in *dushkarma* (wicked action), if you do are not employing it in *satkarma* (virtuous action) then this is really *"number"* two abuse.

This is really the proper use of wealth, that the first condition, that is to say, you spend on *satpatra* (good object).

You should remain energetic in making proper use of life. Nowadays people ruin the precious time of their life in falling again to make exchange about line of *jati* (caste). Any caste you are born in is enough, but then you let go of Bhagwan to fall into argument about organisation of castes.

Wherever you have become born, in whatever *jati* (caste), you should make an effort to escape being possessed of life and death, which is a kind of prison, not supporting one prison in the form of *jati* (caste). You should benefit so much from the advantage of you own line of caste, this much, that you apply the good words according to the *Veda Shastra* and not engage in a relationship with anyone whose custom is to live contrary to the *Veda Shastra*, avoid them. Really in this is useful caste pride. You should certainly keep to good words, the very same that coincides with the *Veda Shastra*. From our view alone we cannot state what is good and bad. This is the really the good thing - that which the *Veda Shastra* say is right. And the bad thing? - That which *Veda Shastra* say is bad.

If you desire wealth then collect that wealth which goes with you. You are going to get freedom from this place, so what is the advantage of collecting *"temporary"* wealth?

This thing is certain - this is the cause of lack of discrimination:-

"धनाहा जीविताशा च जीर्यत्ऽपिनजीर्यते ।"

"dhanaha jivitasha cha jiryat.apinajiryate."
[*Brahma Purana* 12:45]

'The desire for collecting wealth and being successful does not become destroyed, even on becoming time-worn and broken.'

On this is an illustration:-

There was a very old lady. Somehow she was making a livelihood for herself out of selling firewood she had been picking up. Her life was *kashtamaya* (suffering illusion). One day picking up firewood in the *"jungle"*, because she was greedy the tied bundle so very large she was not able to lift it up. She made an effort to lift the bundle several times, but was not able to get it up. In the end she grew desperate and with the suffering she said. 'If by some means Mrityu (death) were to come, I would be free from this misfortune.'

She had just said just that and in front of her stood standing Mrityu (death)!

Mrityu remarked saying, 'Mata ji, why did you call?'

The old woman asked, 'Who are you?.'

Mrityu said, 'I am Death, just now you called to me, therefore I am come.'

The old woman said, 'It is good you have come. I have called for you to lift this bundle.'

The significance of this is, even if a person is in a position of want, they don't want to die. But if life is only successfully lived eating and drinking then there is no advantage living in this way. To live a life, the very same having a meaning, you should make something for the future. If you are to live for experiencing things then by this method you live to collect sin, then really it is good to go and die.

In your day-to-day business, this you should certainly remember, that if you are cannot do any goodness to anyone, then not to do any badness either. As well as this you should certainly do some chanting hymns and worship of Bhagwan. The mind is restless, mind applied or not applied, you should spend time in chanting hymns and worship. If it is not connected just now, then in a few days it will be connected, but you should just do. That *"glass"* you drink your water in, in a few day you come to love that very *"glass"*. Since when another *"glass"* comes, then you are so attached, "Where is that old *"glass"* gone?' This is also the way that you take your walking stick in your hand every day, in a few days a love comes for that. So it is really with *japa,* of the name of Bhagwan, in that name will come the love, similar to the walking stick and the *"glass"*. Therefore even without the mind you should take the name of Bhagwan, if the mind goes somewhere then let it.

९९

त्याग और ग्रहण से मुक्त होकर स्वरूपानन्द में निमग्न रहो।

त्यागोगे क्या?

संसार तो पहले से ही त्यक्त है। शब्द, रूप, रस, गन्ध आदि जितने पदार्थ हैं वे तो तुमसे अलग हैं ही, उनकी सत्ता ही तुमसे भिन्न है। जब संसार तुमसे अलग ही है तो उसको त्यागोगे क्या? तुम्हारे त्यागने के पहले ही वह तुम से त्यक्त है, अलग है। इसलिए किसी के त्याग की बात कहना या त्याग का भाव मन में बनाना मिथ्या दम्भ ही है। मरे को मारने से क्या गौरव? कोई मरे हुए शेर को गोली मार कर कहे कि मैंने शेर का शिकार किया है - वह इसी तरह की बात है, जिस प्रकार यदि कोई कहे कि मैंने अमुक वस्तु का

त्याग किया है। संसार में सब कुछ त्यक्त ही है, कोई ऐसी वस्तु नहीं है जो त्यागने योग्य हो। स्वभाव से तो सभी कुछ तुमसे त्यक्त ही है।

ग्रहण क्या करोगे?

संसार में ग्रहण करने योग्य कुछ भी नहीं है, क्या ग्रहण करोगे? यह जो कुछ देख रहे हो, सब मदारी के रुपये के समान मिथ्या है, इसमें कोई तथ्य नहीं है। ग्रहण करने योग्य तो वह वस्तु तो सकती है जो सुखास्पद हो या शान्ति-प्रद हो। संसार की सभी वस्तुइँ क्षण-भंगुर हैं, वियोगान्त हैं। इनके संयोग में जितना सुख नहीं मिलता उतना इनके वियोग में दुःख होता है और इनका संयोग भी परिणाम में दुःखद ही होता है। इसलिए कोई भी वस्तु यहाँ की संग्रहणीय नहीं है, संसार में तो कुछ भी ग्रहण करने योग्य नहीं है।

तत्व दृप्टि से देखो तो भी 'सर्व खल्विदं ब्रह्म' की भावना से देखो। यह संसार सब ब्रह्म ही है, यहाँ स्वरूप के अतिरिक्त और कुछ है ही नहीं। तो फिर जब सब कुछ अपना स्वरूप ही है, अपने से भिन्न कुछ दूसरी वस्तु ही नहीं है, तो ग्रहण किसका करोगे? इस प्रकार भी संसार में ग्रहण करने योग्य कुछ नहीं है। अतः किसी भी दृष्टि से संसार में ग्रहण करने योग्य कुछ है ही नहीं।

इसीलिए कहा जाता है कि यहाँ न कुछ ग्रहण करने की भावना बनाओ और न कुछ त्यागने की ही इच्छा करो। त्याग ग्रहण से सर्वम्था अलग रहो। जब न कुछ त्यागने की इच्छा करोगे और न कुछ ग्रहण करने की इच्छा तो वासना रहित होकर अपने स्वरूप में स्थिति हो जाओगे। इसीलिए विचार करते हुए यह बात अपने मन में दृढ़ कर लो कि यहाँ न कुछ त्यागने योग्य है और न कुछ ग्रहण करने योग्य। ऐसा विचार पुष्ट करके अपने स्वरूपानन्द में निमग्न रहो - यही मनुष्य-जन्म की सार्थकता है।

99

When *samsara* is separate from you, then what will you abandon?

What will you be unattached to? From the first, *samsara* (worldly existence) is really not attached. Sound, form, taste, smell etc., whatever thing, they are separate from you, their existence is really different from you. When *samsara* is separate from you, then what will you abandon? Before you abandon it, it is already abandoned by you, it is separate. Therefore this talk of *tyaaga* (abandoning) or making an emotion of *tyaaga* (abandoning) is really an arrogant falsehood. What is the glory in killing that which is dead? Will anyone shoot a dead tiger with a bullet and then say, 'I have hunted the tiger' - this is really the kind of talk. That is the way if anybody says, 'I gave up such and such thing.' In *samsara* everything is actually abandoned, there isn't any such thing that is suitable to be abandoned. By nature then everything is really abandoned by you.

What will you acquire?

In *samsara* there isn't even anything fit to be acquired, so what will you acquire? This, that something that you are looking at, all are false like the *rupees* of the trickster, in this there isn't any reality. The thing fit to be acquired is that which can give happiness or give peace. All things of *samsara* are destroyed in an instant, are having a sad end. The pleasure we get from getting connected with these is as much as the suffering at their loss and even the effect of the connection becomes trouble-giving. Therefore there is nothing here to acquire, in *samsara* then there is nothing fit to be acquired.

By seeing the nature then look also to;

"सर्वं खल्विदं ब्रह्म"

"sarva khalvidam brahma"
[*Chandogya Upanishad* 3:14]

'Indeed, all this manifested universe is Brahma'

- look with that feeling.

Brahma

[*'India and Its Inhabitants'*, Caleb Wright, Brainerd, 1856]

'This *samsara* (worldly existence) is really all Brahma.' Here there isn't really anything in addition to *swaroop* (the form of the Self). Then again, when everything is really oneself, then there is really nothing other than oneself, then what is to be acquired? By this way too, there is nothing fit to be acquired in *samsara* (worldly existence). Consequently, any way by which you look, there is nothing in *samsara* fit to be acquired.

Therefore it is said that there is nothing here to make an emotion of acquiring and nothing to wish to give up. Completely separate from giving up and acquiring. When you will have no wish to give up, and no wish to acquire something, then without *vasana* (imagination) you become in the position of your own true Self. Therefore, having considered this information, strictly hold in your own mind that there is nothing here fit to be given up and nothing fit to be acquired. After this strong consideration be engaged in *swaroopananda* (the bliss of real form of the Self) - this is really the meaning of man's birth.

१००

अविवेक से मनुष्य बहुत कष्ट उठाते हैं

*

सर्वदानन्दमय सर्वशक्तिमान् भगवान् सर्वान्तर्यामी हैं। सबके हृदय में अभेद रूप से स्थित हैम्; फिर भी लोग दुःखी और अशान्त देखे जाते हैं। संसार का सारा दुःख और सारी अशान्ति अविवेक के ही कारण है। सुख शान्ति के भण्डार-स्वरूप भगवान् का तो अन्दर ही निवास है, परन्तु अविवेक के कारण सुख-शान्ति की प्राप्ति के लिए लोग बाहर भटक रहे हैं। भौतिक सामग्री संचय में सुख-बुद्धि हो गई है, यही सारे दुःखों और कष्टों का कारण है।

औरों को क्या कहा जाय, द्रोपदी तक को भ्रम हो गया था। जब दुःशासन ने उठकर द्रोपदी की साड़ी खींचना प्रारम्भ किया तो एक बार द्रोपदी ने एक से एक महाबलशाली अपने पाँचो पतियों की ओर देखा, पितामह भीष्म की ओर भी देखा। जब सब असहाय से बैठे रह गये, तब द्रोपदी को पता चला कि आपत्ति-काल में कोई भी सहायक नहीं होता। बड़ी-से-बड़ी भौतिक सामग्री समय आने पर सब बेकार सिद्ध हो जाती है और हितैषी सब मुँह फेर लेते हैं। यह सोचकर निस्सहाय अवस्था में उसने भगवान् कृष्ण का समरण किया - उन्हें पुकारा - "हे नाथ! द्वारिका-वासिन्!"

अब यहीं विचार का विषय है। यदि द्रोपदी को विवेक होता तो वह भगवान् को द्वारिका-वासिन् कह कर न पुकारती। भगवान् तो अहर्निष अन्तर्यामी अन्तर्वासिन् हैं। भगवान् को अपने निकट अपने में न देखकर द्रोपदी ने उन्हें द्वारिका से बुलाया, यही अविवेक है। सर्वशक्तिमान् भगवान् को सदा सर्वदा सर्वव्यापक न मानना ही सबसे बड़ा अविवेक है। इसी के कारण लोग अनन्त दुःख भोगते हुए भी भगवान् की कृपा प्राप्त नहीं कर पाते।

जब द्रोपदी का चीर बढ़ने लगा तो द्रोपदी समझ गई कि भगवान् आ गये। तब उसने कहा – "भगवन्! आपको आने में कुछ विलम्ब हुआ।" भगवान् ने कहा – "द्रोपदी! मैं तो तेरे पास ही था, तूने मुझे द्वारका से बुलाया (द्वारका-वासिन् कह कर) तो मुझे वहाँ जाकर फिर आना पड़ा, इसी में विलम्ब हुआ।"

स्पष्ट ही है कि भगवान् सर्वत्र विराजमान हैं और भक्त पर सब प्रकार का अनुग्रह करने को तैयार हैं।

"जो मुझे जैसा भजता है, उसे मैं वैसा ही मानता हूँ," यह भगवान् की प्रतिज्ञा है:-

"ये यथा माँ प्रपद्यन्ते
तां स्तथैव भजाम्हम्।"

– "गीत"

इसलिए भगवान् को सर्वत्र विराजमान मानते हुए उनकी उपासना करके एक बार उनकी कृपा के पात्र बन जाओ, तो फिर सदा के लिए दुःख और अशान्ति से छुटकारा मिल जाएगा।

100

All the pain and all of the unrest of *samsara* (worldly existence) is really caused by *aviveka* (absence of discrimination).

The All-Blissful, Omnipotent Bhagwan is All-Pervasive. The semblance of his identity is situated in the hearts of all; yet even then people appear sorrowful and restless. All the pain and all of the unrest of *samsara* (worldly existence) is really caused by *aviveka* (absence of discrimination). The form of treasure of happiness and peace has it's dwelling inside, but because of *aviveka* (lack of discrimination) people are caused to miss the way of acquiring happiness and peace outside. [They believe] that in accumulating material goods they will have happy minds, this is really the cause of all pain and suffering.

Besides that what can be said? For [even] Draupadi became confused? When Dushasana rose up and was beginning to drag off Draupadi's saree. Then she looked in the direction of those possessing great strength, at her own five husbands, one by one. She also looked in the direction of *"pitamaha"* Bhishma.

[The warrior Bhishma was known as *"pitamaha"* 'the grandfather' out of respect as the family elder, even though he was a life-celibate.]

When all sat helpless, then Draupadi realized that there was to be nobody else to support her in this predicament. When the time comes, even the greatest of the greatest material goods are all proved useless, and all are giving lip service to well-wishing. In this helpless state she remembered Bhagwan Krishna - she called out to him:- *"He natha! Dwarika-vasin!"* ('Oh Lord who dwells in Dwarka').

Now consider this point here. If Draupadi had been reasoning then she would not have called out to Bhagwan *"Dwarika-vasin"*. Bhagwan then is dwelling inside day and night.

Not seeing Bhagwan near to herself, Draupadi called him from Dwaraka. This is lacking discrimination. It is a great absence of discrimination really of all to assume the Omnipotent Bhagwan is not constantly at all times pervading everywhere. This is the reason people eternally endure pain and also do not gain the grace of Bhagwan.

When Draupadi's cloth lengthened then Draupadi knew that Bhagwan had come, then she said, 'Bhagwan, you did delay a little in coming!.' Bhagwan said, 'Draupadi, then I was really with you, but you called to me to release myself from Dwaraka, so I had to go there and come back again, in this I have been delayed.'

It is really clear that Bhagwan is shining everywhere and is ready to help the devotee in all sorts of ways.

'According to the worship to me, so do I accept, like that,' - this is the vow of Bhagwan:-

"ये यथा माँ प्रपद्यन्ते तां स्तथैव भजाम्हम् ।"

"ye yatha man prapadyante tam stathaiva bhajamham."
[*Bhagavad Gita* 4:11]

Therefore accepting that Bhagwan is shining everywhere, pray to Him, become an object of His grace, then you will always get release from *dukha* (pain) and *ashanti* (unrest) too.

KRISHNA.

[*'Daily Life and Work in India'*, W J Wilkins, T Fisher Unwin, 1890]

१०१

स्वार्थ प्रबल है

*

संसार इतना स्वार्थी है कि मनुष्य का चमड़ा यदि किसी काम में आता होता तो चमड़ी खिंचवाकर चिता पर भेजता। इसमें लेश-मात्र भी सन्देह नहीं है। जब तक लोगों का स्वार्थ सिद्ध होता है तभी तक सब मान-सम्मान और अनुराग दिखाते हैं। भगवान् आदि-शंकराचार्य ने ठीक कहा है:-

यावत् वित्तोपार्जन सक्तः
तावन्निज परिवारो रक्तः।
पश्चाद्धावति जर्जर देहे
वार्ता कोऽपि न पृच्छति गेहे॥

अर्थात्, जब तक धन कमाने की सामर्थ्य है, सब तक अपने स्वजन कुटुम्बी लोग भी अनुराग करते हैं। फिर जब वृद्धावस्था आती है और शरीर जीर्ण-शीर्ण हो जाता है, तब घर में उससे कोई बात भी नहीं पूछता। इसलिए -

'भज गोविन्दं' 'भज गोविन्दं'। 'भज गोविन्दं मूढ़ मते॥

हे अज्ञानी! मतिमन्द जीव! भगवान् का भजन कर।

101

Self-interest is prevalent.

Self-interest is prevalent. In *samsara* (worldly existence) there is so much self-seeking that if there came to be any business of the hide of man then instruction would be sent to cause the skin* to be extracted. There is not an iota of doubt in this.

[* the word for skin used is *"chamari"*. One of Guru Dev's devotees, who it appears was responsible for the photos being taken of Guru Dev in Mussoorie, was a prominent businessman going by the name of *chamari* - Shri Ratan Lal Chamaria (see pp17/18, 'Beacon Light of the Himalayas' 1955)]

Whilst people's self-interest is accomplished, then they show dignity, respect and love. Bhagwan Aadi Shankaracharya accurately said:-

"यावत् वित्तोपार्जन सक्तः
तावन्निज परिवारो रक्तः।
पश्चाद्धावति जर्जर देहे
वार्ता कोऽपि न पृच्छति गेहे ॥"

" yaavat vittopaarjana saktah
taavannija parivaaro raktah.
pashchaaddhaavati jarjara dehe
vaarta ko.api na priichchati gehe.. "
[*Bhaja Govindam* v5]

That is to say; 'Whilst there is the ability to get wealth then all one's family and kinsmen are loving. But when senility comes and the body is old and broken, then nobody in the house even asks his news.'

Therefore,

"भज गोविन्दं। भज गोविन्दं। भज गोविन्दं मूढ़ मते ॥"

"bhaja govindam. bhaja govindam. bhaja govindam muudha mate."

[*Bhaja Govindam* v1]

'Oh, 'Ignoramus! Foolish soul! Worship Bhagwan!'

१०२

भौतिकवाद सुख-शान्ति देने में समर्थ नहीं

*

भौतिक उन्नति माया के प्रसार की ही उन्नति है। माया के सहारे सुख-शान्ति की इच्छा करना अन्धकार को अन्धकार से ढूढ़ने का प्रयत्न करना है। जिस प्रकार बिल के ऊपर लाठी पीटने से अन्दर का सर्प नहीं मारा जा सकता, उसी प्रकार शारीरिक भोग-विलास की सामग्री के बाहुल्य से सूक्ष्म शरीर (मन) में होने वाली अशान्ति को भी नहीं मिटाया जा सकता। सुख-दुःख मन में होता है। सोये हुए को गाली दो, तो उसे दुःख नहीं होगा; क्योंकि उसका मन उस समय अपने कारण अविद्या में लीन रहता है। तात्पर्य यह है कि मन ही सुखी-दुःखी होता है। इसलिये मन जब तक तृप्त नहीं होगा, तब तक अशान्ति जा नहीं सकती। मन तब तक भटकता रहेगा, जब तक वह पूर्णानन्दमय भगवान् न प्राप्त न कर सकेगा। जैसे छोटे-छोटे बच्चों को खिलौना देकर बहलाते हो, वैसे ही आप लोग धन, स्त्री, पुत्र, मान-प्रतिष्ठा आदि से मन को बहला सकते हो। पर ये वस्तुयें मन को सन्तुष्ट नहीं कर सकतीं। मन उसी को पाकर सन्तोष मानता है जो सब से बड़ी वस्तु है। संसार में परमात्मा ही ऐसी बड़ी वस्तु है जिसके जान लेने के बाद और कोई वस्तु जानने योग्य नहीं रह जाती।

102

Materialism is not capable of giving happiness and peace.

Materialism is not capable of giving happiness and peace. Material advancement is really the advancement of the expansion of *maya* (illusion). To desire happiness and peace with the help of *maya* is to attempt to search darkness with darkness. In the way that by beating above the opening you can't beat the serpent within, you cannot erase the unrest in the *sukshma sharira* (subtle body) by an abundance of material goods to give pleasure and enjoyment. Happiness and pain exist in the mind. If abuse is given to [someone] who is asleep then he will not suffer because at that time his mind remains immersed in ignorance. The meaning of this is, that it is the mind that becomes happy or sorrowful. Therefore, whilst the mind is not satisfied then the unrest cannot go. Whilst the mind will be caused to miss the way, then that enjoyment of perfect bliss - Bhagwan - cannot be acquired. In the manner that you give small children a plaything as a diversion, so really you people can be diverted by wealth, woman, son, dignity, respect etc. The mind cannot be satisfied on [getting] these things. The mind expects to get satisfaction from the biggest thing of all. In *samsara* only Paramatma is such a great thing, who after knowing, nothing else is fit to be known.

१०३

उदर पोषण के लिये
अपने भाग्य पर विश्वास रखो

*

किसी के दबाव में आकर अनुचित कार्य करके
पाप का संग्रह मत करो

*

"यदस्मदीयं न हि तत्परेशाम्" जो हमारे भाग्य में है वह अवश्य ही हमें मिलेगा, उसे कोई दूसरा नहीं पा सकता - यह कर्म-मीमांसा-शास्त्र का अकाट्य सिद्धान्त है। हमारा तो यह कई बार का सिद्ध अनुभूत प्रयोग भी है। ऐसे घनघोर वनों में जहाँ कोई मनुष्य की कल्पना भी नहीं कर सकता है। वहाँ अपना भाग्य अपने साथ रहता है! प्रारब्ध का भोग्य वहाँ भी प्राप्त होता है। जिस समय प्रारब्ध समाप्त हो जायगा, उसी समय शरीर छूट जायगा। यह निश्चय है - जब तक शरीर है, तब तक प्रारब्ध का भोग अवश्य है, इसमें सन्देह की बात नहीं। इसलिये अपने योग-क्षेम के लिये चिन्तन होना, अपने पूर्व संचित-कोष की विस्मृति का परिचायक है।

जो पहले की कमाई है वह तो मिलेगी ही, इसमें सन्देह नहीं। बैंक में जमा किया हुआ रुपया अपने को ही मिलेगा, इसमें सन्देह ही क्या? संसारी बैंक का रुपया तो कभी बैंक के फेल होने पर डूब भी जा सकता है; परन्तु अपने कर्मों के फल जिस बैंक में जाकर जमा होते हैं, वह बैंक कभी फेल होने वाला नहीं है। वह सर्वज्ञ सर्वशक्तिमान् का अक्षय कोष है, जिसमें कभी हिसाब में भी भूल नहीं हो सकती। अतः जिसने जो जैसा किया है, वह उसे रत्ती-रत्ती

भोगना पड़ेगा।

अपने समीप जो आता है वह अपना ही प्रारब्ध-भोग है। पर जो सामने आये उसे विचार-पूर्वक ही भोगना चाहिये। मनुष्य और पशु में केवल यही अंतर है कि पशु उचितानुचित का विचार नहीं कर सकता कि क्या उचित है और क्या अनुचित। आप मनुष्य हैं, इसलिये उचितानुचित का विचार करते हुए ही व्यवहार चलाओ।

कभी भी किसी के दबाव या संकोच में आकर कोई ऐसा कार्य मत कर बैठो जिसमें पाप का संग्रह हो। पाप से आगे का मार्ग बिगड़ता है। जैसा पहले कर आये हो उसका फल इस समय भोग रहे हो - इसी से शिक्षा लेकर ऐसे उत्तम कार्य करो जिससे आगे तरक्की में जाओ। कहीं ऐसा न हो कि जिसने भोजन-वस्त्र का प्रबन्ध कर दिया, उसके अच्छे-बुरे सभी कार्यों का समर्थन करने लगे। "जाकर खाई ताकर दुहाई" तो कुत्तों का काम है; मनुष्य को तो विचार-पूर्वक कार्य करना चाहिये। उचित का ही समर्थन करो और अनुचित का यदि खंडन नहीं कर सकते तो कम से कम उससे तटस्थ तो रहो।

103

‘If that is in our destiny, that is really certain that we will get it’

For supporting the stomach put your trust in fate.

Do not show any compulsion for collecting sin by improper action.

“यदस्मदीयं न हि तत्परेशाम्”

“ yadasmadiyam na hi tatparesham”

‘When it is ours then it is not that of others.’

That is, ‘If that is in our destiny, that is really certain that we will get it’, no one else can get it. - this is the firm standpoint of *Karma Mimamsa Shastra* (one of the six systems of Hindu philosophy).

Without effort, we successfully experienced this several times in this way in very dense woods, wherever there cannot be any person’s plan. There one stays along with one’s own *bhagya* (destiny)! The *prarabdha* (commenced action, fate, destiny) that is worthy of being experienced is also gained there. At that time the *prarabdha* becomes completed, that time the body will be go and be relinquished. This is certain that whilst there is a body then *prarabdha* (commenced action, destiny) is certain to be experienced, in this information there is no uncertainty. Therefore, to be thinking for one’s own *yoga-kshema* (connection and protection) is to be forgetting one’s own acquaintanceship with previously gathered treasure.

That which was earned before, that you will get exactly then. In this there is no uncertainty. You will get your own *rupees* that have been deposited in the *“bank”*. Really, what is the uncertainty in this? The worldly *“bank”* of *rupees* then, sometimes the operation of the *“bank”* can become sunk; but the fruits of your actions become accumulated in that *“bank”* - that *“bank”* never fails. That is the imperishable repository of the All-Knowing Omnipotent, wherein never can there be a slip in the account. Consequently, whatsoever you did, so you get, that he will endure, little by little.

That which comes near to you is your *prarabdha* (commenced action) which is really to be endured. You should really endure together with consideration that which comes in front of you.

The only difference between man and beast is really that the beast cannot consider what is right and wrong, what is proper and what is improper. You are man, therefore proceed with your daily business considering what is proper and what is improper. Don't be habituated to such action, out of pressure or shame, wherein sin is accumulated. By sin the road ahead is spoiled. According to that which came first, at this time you are enduring the fruits thereof. Take a lesson from this. In this way do the best action and from that go to improve the future. We are not saying this, that because arrangement is made for food and clothing that you support all action, good and bad;

"जाकर खाई ताकर दुहाई"

" jakara khaii takara duhaii "
'To go to eat, to jeer at justice.'

This then is the action of dogs; to man then you should act with consideration. Support only that which is proper and if you cannot revoke that which is improper then little by little be indifferent from that.

१०४

जितना हो सके शुभ कार्यों का सम्पादन करो

*

आत्म-सुख की प्राप्ति इन्द्रिय संयम से होगी, विषयोपभोग से नहीं

*

इन्द्रियों के द्वारा शब्द, स्पर्श, रूप, रस, गंध का ही अनुभव होता है। क्योंकि इन्द्रियाँ वहिर्मुखी होने के कारण केवल बाहर के ही विषयों का ज्ञान प्राप्त कर सकती हैं, अन्दर का ज्ञान इन्द्रियों से नहीं हो सकता। आत्मा अपने निकट से निकट है, नित्य प्राप्य है, कभी भी उसका अभाव नहीं होता - फिर भी हम उसे देख नहीं पाते, जान नहीं पाते। जो सब को देखने वाला है उसको किससे देखा जाय? आँखें सब को देखती हैं; परन्तु स्वयं अपने को नहीं देख पातीं, उन्हें देखने के लिये दर्पण चाहिये। आत्मा को देखने का दर्पण अन्तःकरण है - अतः माने 'भीतरी' कारण माने 'ज्ञान' का साधन। आन्तरिक ज्ञान का साधन होने के कारण इसे अन्तकरण कहते हैं। दर्पण यदि स्वच्छ होता है, तभी उसमें प्रतिबिम्ब पड़ता है। मलिन दर्पण में कभी भी प्रतिबिम्ब दिखाई नहीं देता। इसी प्रकार निर्मल अन्तःकरण में ही आत्मा का प्रतिबिम्ब दिखाई देता है; मलिन अन्तःकरण वाले उसे नहीं देख सकते। इसलिये अन्तःअकरण को स्वच्छ बनाने की आवश्यकता है।

जाति, कुल, रूप, यौवन, धन, मान इत्यादि का अभिमान करना अज्ञान है। जब तक इनके अभिमान का त्याग नहीं किया जाता, तब तक आत्मा का ज्ञान कैसे हो सकता है। अज्ञान के नाश होने पर ही आत्मा का ज्ञान होता है। अज्ञानी अपने को परमात्मा से

अलग मानता है और स्थूल शरीर को ही वह अपना स्वरूप समझता है। नाश होने वाले जगत् के पदार्थों में उसकी विशेष आसक्ति रहती है। इसी लिए किसी न किसी निमित्त को लेकर वह दुःखी होता रहता है।

शास्त्र और गुरु लोग जगत् को मिथ्या बताते हैं। मिथ्या वह है जो दिखे तो, परन्तु जिसकी सत्ता स्थिर न हो - जैसे मन्दान्धकार में पड़ी हुई रज्जु को देखकर किसी को उसमें सर्प का भ्रम हो जाय, पर वास्तविक सत्ता सर्प की नहीं है; परन्तु भ्रमकाल में तो उसकी प्रतीति सत्य ही है। जब तक ठीक-ठीक रज्जु का ज्ञान नहीं होता, तब तक सर्प-भ्रम की निवृत्ति नहीं हो सकती। अब इस भ्रम को दूर करने के लिए कोई लाखों रुपये व्यय करके अश्वमेध यज्ञ आदि करे तो इससे भी वह भ्रम दूर नहीं होगा। भ्रम मिटाने का उपाय यह है कि दीपक लेकर उसके प्रकाश में रज्जु कों ठीक ठीक देख लिया जाय। रज्जु का निश्चय बोध हो जाने पर ही वह व्यक्ति किसी के प्रयत्न करने पर भी रज्जु को सर्प नहीं मान सकता। इसी प्रकार जिसे जगत् के अधिष्ठान-रूप परमात्मा का बोध हो चुका हैं, वह कभी भी जगत् को सत्य नहीं मान सकता। अज्ञानी ही उसे सत्य मानते है। जगत् के मिथ्यात्व का बोध हो अज्ञान-निद्रा से जागने पर होता है। जागृत अवस्था लाने के लिए बन में जाने की आवश्यकता नहीं है। बन में रहने मात्र से किसी को ज्ञान नहीं प्राप्त हो सकता। न जाने कितने कोल-भिल्ल बनेचर वहाँ रहते हैं, पर महामूर्ख हैं। एकान्तवास तब लाभदायक हो सकता है। जब अज्ञान को मिटाने के साधन प्राप्त हों। अज्ञान को दूर करने के साधन सद्गुरु और शास्त्रों से प्राप्त होते हैं। परन्तु जो शास्त्रों पर ही श्रद्धा नहीं करता, महात्माओं के बचनों का विश्वास नहीं करता, उसके अज्ञान की निवृत्ति कैसे हो सकती है? इसीलिए लिए विश्वास सम्पादन करने की आवश्यकता है।

"असंशयवतां मुक्तिः
संशयाविष्ट चेतसाम्।
न मुक्तिर्जन्म जन्मान्ते
तस्माद् विश्वासमाप्नुयात्।"

सारांश में, मुक्ति का अर्थ है - संसार में लौट कर न आना। दूसरा अर्थ यह है कि दुखों का स्पर्श न हो।

जिसे स्त्री, पुत्र, धन, मान, प्रतिष्ठा आदि की वासना नहीं है, उसे अवश्य आत्मा का अनुभव हो सकता है। आत्मा को तत्वतः जानने वाला ही शोक-सागर से पार होता है।

अन्तःकरण वासनाओं से मलिन रहता है; इसलिए वासनाओं को नष्ट करने की आवश्यकता है। भोग के द्वारा कोई वासनाओं को तृप्त नहीं करना चाहे तो यह 'न भुतो न भविष्यति' - न हुआ है न और न हो सकता है। तृप्ति विचार से होती है, चाहे आज करो, चाहे दस वर्ष बाद। इन्द्रियाँ जब शान्त होंगी तब विचार के द्वारा हों। भोग से भोग की वासना और दृढ़ होती है। कहीं खुजलाने से आज तक किसी की खुजली अच्छी हुई हो तो हम यह भी आशा करें कि विषय-भोग से इन्द्रियाँ शान्त होंगी।

सब जानते हैं कि साथ में कुछ नहीं जाता, अपना शरीर भी चिता तक ही जाता है। पर वेद - शास्त्रों पर विश्वास करो तो साथ जाने वाली भी एक वस्तु है। परलोक - मार्ग में जीव के साथ उसके किये हुए शुभाऽशुभ कर्म जाते हैं। शुभ कर्म करने वाला उत्तम लोकों को प्राप्त होता है और अशुभ कर्म करने वाला नरक को। इसलिये जितना हो सके, शुभ कर्मों फा सम्पादक करो।

104

By self-restraint of the senses you will be happy in your self

By self-restraint of the senses you will be happy in your self, not by anything perceived by the senses. By means of the senses, sound, touch, form, taste and smell are perceived. Since the purpose of the senses is external, only knowledge of anything perceived by the senses outside can be known - knowledge of inside cannot be had from the senses. *Atma* (the soul) is the nearest of the nearest to oneself, is constantly available, there is never a deficiency even - on the other hand we cannot get to see it either, nor get to know it. That All-Seeing One, when has he been seen? The eyes see all; but you do not get a view of your own self, you need a mirror to see yourself.

The *antahkarana* (conscience, inner self) is the mirror of the *atma* (soul) - therefore, *"antah"* means *"bhitari"* (inner), *"karana"* (causing) means the cause of realisaton of *gyaan* (knowledge) - from this we say *"antahkarana"*. If the mirror is cleaned, then the reflection falls onto it. If it is dirty it will not show a reflection. This is the way, if the *antahkarana* (inner self) is clean it actually displays a reflection of the *atma*; the one who has a dirty *antahkarana* (inner self) cannot see it (the *atma*). Therefore it is necessary to make the *antahakarana* clean.

It is ignorance to be proud of caste, tribe, appearance, youth, wealth, weight etc. Until you have abandoned pride in these, then how can you have knowledge of *atma* (soul)? Knowledge of *atma* comes only when the ignorance fades away. The ignoramus assumes that he is separate from Paramatma and understands himself to only be the *sthula sharira* (gross body). He stays with a characteristic attachment to things of the world. Therefore, not for any other reason, he remains unhappy.

The *Shastra* and those people who are *gurus* tell; 'The world is *mithya* (untrue, false, delusory, illusion)' - *"mithya"*, that is that which is to be seen then, but of which the existence is not true. In the manner in which befalls one in dense darkness, to see a rope and become confused that is a serpent. In truth there is no serpent; but in the period of confusion that is actually the experience. Until whenever there comes the accurate knowledge of the rope, until then the confusion about the serpent cannot disappear. Now, to put distance to this confusion, any amount of expense then [can be made] making an *ashvamedha yagya* (sacrifice of a horse) etc., - but even by this the confusion will not be distanced. The means of destroying the confusion is this, that; taking a lamp, in the light the rope is accurately seen. Actually, on becoming aware that it is certainly a rope, even with effort that person cannot accept the rope as a snake. In this way, he that becomes adjusted to the form of Paramatma as ruler of the world, he can never accept the world as real. Only an ignoramus accepts that as the truth. Understanding of the falsehood of the world occurs on waking up from the sleep of ignorance. In order to produce the waking state it is not necessary to go to the forest. Merely by living in the forest you cannot obtain *gyaan* (knowledge). I don't know how many Kol and Bhil (wild tribals) there remain browsing about the forest, but they are very foolish. Living in a secluded place can be beneficial, when it is used as a *sadhana* (solution, devotion) to destroy ignorance. The *sadhana* to distance ignorance is acquired from the *sadguru* and the *Shastras*. But if you do not have faith in the *Shastras*, you do not trust the utterances of the *mahatmas*, then how can the ignorance disappear?

"असंशयवतां मुक्तिः
संशयाविष्ट चेतसाम्।
न मुक्तिर्जन्म जन्मान्ते
तस्माद् विश्वासमाप्नुयात्॥"

"asamshayavatam muktih samshayavishta chetasam.
na muktirjanma janmante tasmad vishvasamapnuyat.."

'Therefore it is a necessity to attain faith.'

In summary, the meaning of *"mukti"* is 'not returning to *samsara* (worldly existence).' Another meaning is this; 'not being touched by troubles.' Whoever does not long for wife, son, wealth, dignity, respect etc., he can certainly perceive the *atma*. Only the one who understands the reality of *atma* crosses to the other side of the ocean of distress.

From desires, the *antahkarana* remains dirty; therefore it is necessary to destroy desires. By means of experience you do not need to satisfy any desires, as then;

"न भुतो न भविष्यति"

"na bhuto na bhavishyati"
[*Mahabharata* 1:1:18]

'It did not exist and will not exist.'

Satisfaction comes from discernment, have the desire today, [still] desire ten years after. When the organs of the senses will be quiet then a way for discernment exists. By experience the longing for more experience becomes resolute. If by scratching somewhere today any itching sensation will be made good, then we will also fulfil this hope that by experiencing anything perceived by the senses we will quieten the senses!

All understand that really nothing goes with you [after you die], even your own body only goes as far as the funeral pyre. But have trust on the *Veda Shastras,* then one thing will be going with you too. Accompanying the soul on the road to the other world go the *shubha* (happy, auspicious) and *ashubha* (unfortunate, inauspicious) *karmas*. By doing *shubha karma* (auspicious action) then the best worlds are gained and by doing *ashubha karma* (bad work) you go to *naraka* (hell). Therefore, as much as you can, be someone who performs auspicious actions.

'A Brahmin reading the Shasters'
[*'India and Its Inhabitants'*, Caleb Wright, Brainerd, 1856]

१०५

सतर्क रह कर जीवन का सदुपयोग करो

*

संसार में तीन चीजें हैं - तन, मन और धन। यही संसार कहा जाता है। तन-मन-धन का उपयोग बन जाय तो कभी अशांति न आवे। इनका उपयोग नहीं बनता, इसी से अशान्ति भोगनी पड़ती है। इसका उपयोग सिखाने के लिये कोई स्कूल कालेज नहीं है। धन की तीन प्रकार की गति-होती है - जो न दान देते हैं और न उसका अपने लिये ही उपयोग करते हैं, उनका धन तृतीय गति को अर्थात् नाश को प्राप्त होता है। तुलसीदास ने भी लिखा है:-

"सो धन धन्य, प्रथम गति जाकी।"

अर्थात् वह धन धन्य है, सार्थक है, जिसकी प्रथम गति हो, जो दान में व्यय किया जाय। तुलसीदास ने तो केवल धन के ही लिये कहा है, पर हम कहते हैं कि -

"सो तन धन्य प्रथम गति जाकी।"
"सो मन धन्य प्रथम गति जाकी।"

अर्थात् वह तन और मन भी धन्य है, जिसकी प्रथम गति हो।

तन की प्रथम गति है कि शरीर भगवान् की अर्चना पूजा में लगा रहे - आंख भगवान् के रूप को देखे; कान भगवान् का यश सुने, वाणी भगवान् का यश गान करे। अर्थात् प्रत्येक इन्द्रिय भगवत्संबंध को अपना विषय बना कर भगवान् रस-पान करती रहे। प्राण भगवान् की आराधना में लगा रहे - यही तन की प्रथम गति है। मन की प्रथम गति है - भगवान् में ही मन लगा रहे। धन

की प्रथम गति कही गई है – सत्पात्र में दान, परन्तु दान के पहले उचितानुचित विचार पूर्वक ही उसका अर्जन होना चाहिये। ऐसा नहीं होना चाहिए कि जैसा मिला, वैसा ही अर्जन कर लिया। अनर्थ और पाप के द्वारा जो धन कमाया जायगा वह धन तो यहीं पड़ा रह जायगा, परन्तु पाप का फल अपने साथ जायगा, पाप पीछा नहीं छोड़ेगा। इसलिये धन-संग्रह में पाप न होने दो। पाप धन के साथ यहीं छूट जाय, ऐसा नहीं होगा। इससे धन-संग्रह में बहुत विचार करना चाहिये।

एक महात्मा ने ऐसी सिद्धि प्राप्त कर ली थी कि जो कोई उनके पास आता था, उसके अच्छे-बुरे कर्मों को वह कह देते थे। एक समय हमारा उनका समागम हो गया। कहीं से घूमते हुये हम उसी तरफ से निकल पड़े। हमने उनसे कहा कि जगत् पाप करता है और उसका चिंतन आप करते हो, यह तो बड़ा घाटा है। जिस मन को परमात्मा में लगा रहना है, वह मन जगत् के किये हुये अनाचार-पापाचार का चिन्तन करे – यही मन का दुरुपयोग है। साधु होकर फिर मन का इतना दुरुपयोग!!

तन-मन का और भी एक प्रकार से दुरुपयोग किया जाता है कि लोग जाति-पांति के समर्थन में ही लगे रहते हैं। मनुष्य का शरीर मिला है; किसी जाति में उत्पन्न हो गये-ब्राह्मण, क्षत्रिय, वैश्य, शूद्र – किसी भी वर्ण में जन्म हो गया तो भगवान् के स्मरण का सब को अधिकार है और भगवान् के निकट पहुँचने का भी सब को अधिकार है। बीच में, क्लास में अन्तर रहे, यह अन्तर कोई ऐसा विषय नहीं है जो बहुत अधिक विचार की चीज हो। जहाँ जन्म हो गया, तो हो गया। अब तो ऐसा प्रयत्न करना चाहिये कि फिर जन्म न हो; ऐसा नहीं कि जहाँ जिस जाति में जन्म हो, उसी के समर्थन में अपना जीवन का समय खो दिया। यह तो धर्मशाल है। यहाँ आकर अपना मुख्य काम बनाना चाहिये, न कि धर्मशाले का ही समर्थन

करते रहो। मनुष्य जीवन में जो मन भगवान में लगाने की चीज है, उससे अनाचार-पापाचार करना उचित नहीं।

105

Live carefully - make proper use of existence.

In *samsara* (worldly existence) there are three things - *tana* (body), *mana* (mind) and *dhana* (wealth). Right here *samsara* (worldly existence) is said to be. If proper use is made of the *tana* (body), *mana* (mind) and *dhana* (wealth) then *ashaanti* (anxiety) will never come. If you do not make use of these, you will undergo anxiety from only this. There isn't any *"school"* or *"college"* for teaching use of this.

The *dhana* (wealth) passes in three ways - that not given in charity, and not for your own use, and that wealth which is the third condition, that is to say it becomes lost. Tulsidas too wrote:-

"सो धन धन्य, प्रथम गति जाकी।"

"so dhana dhanya prathama gati jaki."
[*Shri Ramcharitmanas - Uttarakhand* - 7:126:4]

That is, 'That wealth is auspicious, is fruitful, which is the *"prathama gati"* (best condition), that is the expenditure in charity.'

Tulsidas was only really speaking of wealth, but we speak of:-

"सो तन धन्य प्रथम गति जाकी।"
"सो मन धन्य प्रथम गति जाकी।"

"so tana dhanya prathama gati jaki."
"so mana dhanya prathama gati jaki."

That is to say, '*tana* (body) and *mana* (mind) are also *dhanya* (auspicious, blessed), which are for the *"prathama gati"* (best condition).' Of the body, the best progress of the body is to apply it in worship and homage of Bhagwan. The eyes to see the form of Bhagwan, the ears to hear the fame of Bhagwan, the voice to sing the fame of Bhagwan. That is to say, to make one's own enjoyment of each and every organ of one's perception relating it to Bhagwan, drinking the Bhagwan flavour. The *prana* (breath) applied to the worship of Bhagwan. This is the *"prathama gati"* (best condition) of *dhana* (body). The *"prathama gati"* of the *mana* (mind) - the mind is only applied in Bhagwan. The *"prathama gati"* of *dhana* (wealth) has been spoken of - charity to a worthy person - but before the act of giving alms, very proper consideration should really be taken regarding the acquisition thereof. It should not be that you earn in just any way. If you will earn wealth that come by means of misfortune and sin that, that wealth will stay here [when you die] but the effects of the sin will go with you, sin pursuing will not let go. Therefore do not get sin in collecting wealth.

Is the sin that comes together with the wealth left right here?

It will **not** be so!

By this [understand] you should be very considerate in collecting wealth.

One *mahatma* obtained such a *siddhi* that he was able to tell of the good and bad *karmas* of any whom came to him. One time we became associated. Having wandered from somewhere we appeared by his side. We said that, 'The world does sin and you are thinking thereof, that then is big loss. That mind which is to remain applied to Paramatma, that mind is thinking of the improper conduct and sinful living of the world - that is really a misapplication of the mind. To become a *sadhu,* then so much misapplication of the mind!!'

Another way of misapplication of the body and mind is that people stay attached in supporting caste and the height of the lineage. You have gotten the body of a human being; any caste you have become born in - *brahmana, kshatriya, vaishya, shudra* - whatever caste you have become born in then all have the right to remember Bhagwan and all have the right to reach near to Bhagwan. In between, difference of *"class"* stays, this difference, any such matter is not a thing for much consideration. Wherever you have been born, then you have been. Now then you should make such effort that you are not born again; not so that whatever caste you are born in, your life is lost in support of it.

This then is a *dharmashala* (halting house for pilgrims). Having come here you should perform the principal work, not work in justifying the *dharmashala*. In the life of a human being that mind is a thing to be applied in Bhagwan, from that [understand] it is improper to do improper conduct and/or sinful living.

१०६

विचार पूर्वक प्रवृत्ति बनाने से ही मन सुमार्ग की ओर जाता है

अखंड ब्रह्माँड-नायक आनन्द-कंद सच्चिदानन्द भगवान् वेद वेद्य हैं। वेद-मार्ग द्वारा ही उनको जाना जा सकता है। वेद अपौरुषेय है, दिव्य दृष्टि के दाता हैं। भगवान् के दिव्य स्वरूप को देखने के लिये दिव्य दृष्टि ही अपेक्षित है। चर्म-चक्षुओं से भगवान के उस स्वरूप के दर्शन नहीं हो सकते हैं। भगवान ने गीता में अर्जुन को उपदेश देते हुये कहा है:-

न तु मां शक्यसे द्रष्टुमनेनैव स्वचक्षुषा।
दिव्यं ददामि ते चक्षुः पश्य मे योगमैश्वरम्॥

वह दिव्य दृष्टि प्राप्त करने की चेष्टा करना ही पुरुषार्थ है। इसी में मनुष्य जन्म की सफलता है।

भौतिक पदार्थ ही चर्म-चक्षुओं से देखे जा सकते हैं। फिर भी भिन्न-भिन्न पदार्थों के लिये भी भिन्न-भिन्न दृष्टि होती है। सभी भौतिक पदार्थ एक दृष्टि से नहीं देखे जा सकते। उदाहरण के लिये सोचि-माता-पिता, भाई-बहिन, स्त्री इत्यादि सभी भौतिक शरीरधारी हैं। क्या इन सब को एक दृष्टि से देखा जाता है? माता को और दृष्टि से देखते हैं, बहिन को और तथा स्त्री को और ही दृष्टि से देखा जाता

है। पुनः भिन्न-भिन्न दर्शक के अधिकारानुसार एक ही वस्तु भिन्न दृष्टि से देखी जाती है।

इसी भाँति उपासना भी अधिकार-भेद से पृथक-पृथक है, वेद का मूल प्रँणव है। परन्तु सब को प्रँणव के उच्चारण का अधिकार नहीं है। प्रँणव तो शुद्ध ब्रह्म है। केवल एक सन्यासी जो सभी भौतिक पदार्थों के रागों को त्यागकर ही सम्यकन्यासी होता है, उसके साथ कोई राग-द्वेष सांसारिक बंधन नहीं रह जाता। वह तो केवल निताँत एक ही रह जाता है। अतः उसे ही शुद्ध प्रँणव के उच्चारण का अधिकार है। गृहस्थ जिसका राग घर-गृहस्थी, स्त्री-पुत्रादि में बना हुआ है, उसे प्रँणव के जपने का अधिकार नहीं। क्योंकि प्रँणव के जपने का फल भी तो वही होना चाहिये जो वह है यानी माया रहित विशुद्ध ब्रह्म केवल एक सच्चिदानन्द स्वरूप। गृहस्थ के लिये प्रँणव का जप सुफलप्रद नहीं होता, नाश अमंगल-कारक होता है। अतः गृहस्थों के लिये यही विधान है कि वे केवल प्रँणव का उच्चारण (जप) न करके किसी न किसी मंत्र के साथ जोड़ कर उच्चारण करें। प्रँणव को मंत्र के आदि में जोड़ कर मंत्र का जप करें - ऐसा न करना अनधिकार चेष्टा है। अनधि-कार चेष्टा का प्रभाव हृदय पर भी नहीं पड़ता, सब परिश्रम विफल हो जाता है। प्रायः लोग यही कहते हैं कि मन की चण्चलता नहीं मिटती, मन स्थिर नहीं होता। पर मन की चंचलता तो विधि-विधान द्वारा नित्य नैमित्तिक कर्मों द्वारा ही दूर हो सकती है। उसे तो करते नहीं, एकदम ध्यानस्थ हो जाने की कल्पना करते हैं, सो कैसे सफल हो।

शब्द, स्पर्श, रूप, रस, गंध में ही तो मन जाता है। मन तो इनके पीछे दौड़ते-दौड़ते मलिन हो रहा है, शुद्धता की ओर जा कैसे सकता है। मन को वृत्ति तो श्वान-वृत्ति बन रही है। सुख की चाह में इधर-उधर भटकता हुआ कभी रूप के पीछे, कभी गंध के पीछे, कभी स्पर्श के पीछे, कभी शब्द के पीछे, श्वानवत् मन दौड़ा करता है,

परन्तु स्थिर नहीं हो पाता। वह तो निरंतर विषयाराम बना हुआ है, आत्माराम कैसे बने। विषयों से हट कर यदि आत्मा की ओर झुकाव हो जावे तो आत्माराम बने, विषयाराम न बने। जिसका मन भगवत् दर्शन् की ओर लग गया है, वह सिनेमा देखने नहीं दौड़ेगा। जो भगवान के रूप का प्रेमी बन गया है, वह किसी सांसारिक रूप की ओर आँख नहीं उठायेगा। जो भगवत्-चरण के स्पर्श का अक्षय सुख अनुभव करने लगता है, वह भौतिक स्पर्श की इच्छा नहीं करता।

इसी प्रकार रूप-रस-गंध-स्पर्श-शब्द के पीछे श्वानवत् दौड़ने वाले मन को भगवान् के किसी विग्रह के रूप की ओर लगाओ। उन्की सेवा से स्पर्श-सुख अनुभव करने का स्वभाव डालो। भगवान् के प्रति सुगंधित द्रव्य अर्पण कर प्रसाद रूप से उन्हें ग्रहण करना सीखो।

106

Celestial vision is needed in order to see the heavenly form of Bhagwan.

The *akhanda* (perfect), *brahmanda-nayaka* (assistant of the Universe), *ananda-kanda* (the root of bliss), *satchitananda* (Truth, Consciousness, Bliss) is the object of knowledge of the *Vedas*.

By way of the path of the *Vedas* you can actually go and understand Him. The *Veda* is *apaurusheya* (divine, not of human beings), is the benefactor of celestial vision. To see the heavenly form of Bhagwan, celestial vision is needed. With ordinary sight you cannot have *darshan* (sight) of the *swaroop* (true form) of Bhagwan. When Bhagwan gave *upadesha* (instruction) to Arjuna he said, in *Gita*:-

"न तु मां शक्यसे द्रष्टुमनेनैव स्वचक्षुषा।
दिव्यं ददामि ते चक्षुः पश्य मे योगमैश्वरम्॥"

*"na tu mam shakyase drashtumanenaiva svachakshusha.
divyam dadami te chakshuh pashya me yogamaishvaram.."*
[*Bhagavad Gita* 11:8]

'But you can't see me even with your own eyes,
I give thee the divine eye, behold my Lordly Yoga.'

To acquire celestial sight is really the activity of *purushartha* (the object of man's creation, willpower). In this is the success of a human being's life.

Only material stuff can be seen by the ordinary sight, yet again there are different 'sights' for different things. Not all material stuff can be seen by one sight. Consider for example, mother and father, brother and sister, wife etc. - all have the support of a material body. Are all these seen with the same 'sight'? Mother is seen with a sight, to sister another, and to wife with yet another sight is seen. Again, according to the entitlement of different spectators, one thing is to be seen from several perspectives.

This is really the manner that there are several separate different entitlements, the root of the *Veda* (divine knowledge) is the *prannava.* [*Pranava* is a Sanskrit word meaning a humming-mystical or sacred syllable - it is also defined as 'OM'.]

But, not all have the right to the utterance of the *prannava* - *prannava* then is pure Brahma. Only a *sannyasi* that has abandoned all material stuff is really a *sannyasi*, there is not any attachment and animosity, or bondage to worldliness. He then is alone, living really alone. Consequently, only to him is the right to the utterance of pure *prannava*.

The *grihastha* who has attachment to the house and to the duties of a householder, wife, children etc., has no right to do the *japa* (repetition) of the *prannava*.

Because the results of *japa* of the *prannava* should also be the same then, and this is, that is to say, be devoid of *maya* (illusion), only pure Brahma, alone the Self form of *sachchidananda* (Truth, Consciousness, Bliss). But for the *grihastha* the *japa* of the *prannava* does not give good effects, it will be responsible for decline and misfortune. Consequently, for *grihasthon* (householders) this is the arrangement; that they do not do the utterance of *prannava.* But affixed with other *mantra* they will do utterance. You will do *japa* of the *mantra* having affixed it to the *prannava*. Not to do it after this manner is not a right exercise. Also the [beneficial] influence of this unauthorised exercise on the heart does not occur, all endeavours become unsuccessful.

Generally, this is what people say, that the activity of the mind is not erased, mind does not become calm. But the restlessness of the mind can only be made to recede by way of doing the commanded, arranged, fortuitous activities. He does not do this, [but] is continuously musing and speculating, therefore, how does this become fruitful?

Actually the mind goes to sound, touch, form, taste and smell. Mind is becoming dirty as it runs after these then. How can it go in the direction of purity? The condition of the mind is becoming the condition of the dog. In wanting pleasure it becomes misled here and there, sometimes after a form, sometimes after a smell, sometimes after a touch, sometimes after a sound. Like a dog the mind runs, but cannot get calm.

He has been continuously making things to be enjoyed by the senses. How can *"atmarama"* (enjoyment of the Self) be achieved? To get sensory things out of the way, if you come to lean towards *atma* (the soul) then *atmarama* (enjoyment of the Self) is achieved - not enjoyment of sensory things. He whose mind is applied to the *darshan* (sight) of Bhagavat (God), he will not run to see the *"cinema"*. He who becomes a lover of the form of Bhagwan, his eyes will not become attentive in the direction of any worldly form. He who is applied to perceiving the permanent pleasure of touching the feet of Bhagavad (God), he does not desire the material touch.

So in this way, like a dog, to run after form, taste, smell, touch and sound, apply the mind in the direction of any form of Bhagwan. Throw [yourself] into the habit of experiencing the pleasure of contact by *seva* (service). Learn to make offering of "*sugandhita dravya*" ('aromatic substance' - incense) towards Bhagwan, the *prasad* (blessing, gift) from the appearance of Their acceptance.

१०७

जो अपना लक्ष्य भूल गया, वह पथ-भ्रष्ट हो ही जायगा

अनन्तान्दमय, सर्वशक्तिमान, ज्ञानस्वरूप परमात्मा की प्राप्ति ही मनुष्य-जीवन का सर्वश्रेष्ठ लक्ष्य है। अपने इस उत्तमोत्तम लक्ष्य का जिसे सदा स्मरण रहता है और जो इस लक्ष्य की प्राप्ति करने के लिये वेद-शास्त्र के बताये हुए मार्ग का अनुसरण करता है अर्थात् जो अपने शरीर, इन्द्रिय, मन, बुद्धि आदि की हलचल शास्त्रानुसार रखते हुये अपना जीवन धर्मानुकूल व्यतीत करता है, वही वास्तव में पुरुषार्थ-शील एवं भाग्यशाली है। ऐसे सत्पुरुषार्थवान् पुरुष की सब मनोकामनायें पूरी होते हुये उसे लक्ष्य की प्राप्ति अवश्य होती है, इसमें सन्देह नहीं।

जो अपने जीवन का चरम-लक्ष्य बनाया जाय उसके लिये उसी विषय के किसी अच्छे विशेषज्ञ को श्रद्धा-पूर्वक अपना मार्ग-प्रदर्शक बनाना चाहिये, जिससे कि उस विषय में उसके अनुभवों का तुम्हें लाभ हो सके। दूसरी बात यह है कि तुम्हारे जीवन की प्रवृत्ति ऐसी रहनी चाहिये कि जो तुम्हारे लक्ष्य की प्राप्ति के मार्ग में बाधक न होकर साधक हो।

हर समय सतर्क रहो कि कहीं ऐसा न हो कि अपने लक्ष्य-प्राप्ति

के मार्ग से इधर-उधर भटक जाओ। मत भूलो कि व्यवहार ही परमार्थ का मार्ग है। व्यवहार यदि अपने अधिकारानुसार शास्त्रोक्त है, तो वही तुम्हें लक्ष्य-प्राप्ति में आगे बढ़ायेगा। यदि मन विषयों के वशीभूत होकर व्यवहार में यथेच्छा-चरण में आया और शास्त्र-मर्यादाओं का उल्लंघन हुआ, तो व्यवहार ही लक्ष्य-पथ से तुम्हें हटाकर पारमार्थिक-लक्ष्य के विपरीत अनर्थ सम्पादन की ओर आगे बढ़ायेगा।

इसलिये सदा अपने परम लक्ष्य का स्मरण करते रहकर उसकी प्राप्ति के लिये अनुभवी गुरु का पथ-प्रदर्शन और सतर्क होकर गुरुपदिष्ट मार्ग का अनुसरण करना आवश्यक है।

107

Don't forget that everyday business is really the way of *paramarth* (salvation).

The paramount objective of a human being's life is to gain the *Anantanandamaya* (limitless bliss), Sarvashaktimana (Omnipotent), *gyaanswaroop* (the real form of knowledge) of Paramatma (the Supreme Self). One who is constantly remembering the highest goal and who for gaining this goal has been informed of the *Veda Shastra*. To follow the way, that is that of the perplexity of one's own body, senses, mind, intellect etc. is kept according to the *Shastra*, one's own life passes favourably to *dharma* (duty, religion). In truth that is the quality *purushartha* (willpower) and he is fortunate. In this way a good man is a man whose every desire is fulfilled, he will certainly gain the goal, in this there is no uncertainty.

He who makes this the ultimate goal of his own life should have faith in a good knowledgeable person of this subject who has demonstrated these qualities in their own path - from his experiences of that subject you can be advantaged. Another thing is this, that the flow of your life should remain so that acquiring your goal isn't a *badhaka* (hindrance) to your path, be a *sadhaka* (devoted to spiritual accomplishment).

All the time be alert so it is not that somewhere you are caused to miss the way and go here and there from the way of gaining your own goal. Don't forget that everyday business is really the way of *paramarth* (salvation). If business is done according to the authority as ordained by the *Shastras*, then it will be an advantage in gaining your goal. If the mind becomes overpowered by things of the senses, in business the order becomes according to one's own wishes with the boundaries set by the *Shastras* being violated, then really business will move you away from the path [leading] to the goal. You will produce *anartha* (misfortune), the reverse of the goal of the *paramarthika* (highest good, *summum bonum*, salvation) will be accomplished. Therefore, be constantly remembering the utmost goal. For gaining this, [find] an experienced *guru* who can demostrate the way, and be alert, having received the *guru's* instruction it is requisite to follow the way.

१०८

जो भगवान् की और झुका उसे किसी वस्तु की कमी नहीं

सत्सङ्ग करने से उचितानुचित, पाप-पुन्य, अधर्म और कर्त्तव्य का बोध होता है, विवेक उत्पन्न होता है। इसलिये सत्संग करने वाला अधर्म से बचता है और धर्म में प्रवृत्त होता है। पाप से बचकर वह पुन्य-कर्म करता है। सिद्धाँत है कि 'धर्मेण पापमपनुदति' धर्म करने से पाप नष्ट होता है। इस प्रकार सत्संग से पाप का नाश होता है।

सत्संग में बैठने से, भगवत्सम्बन्धी वार्ता श्रवण करने से, स्वाभाविक ही आन्तरिक दुख-उद्वेग आदि मनुष्य के हृदय को दहने वाला ताप शान्त होता है। सत्संग करने वाले के अन्तः- करण में स्वाभाविक ही शान्ति रहती है।

सत्संग के द्वारा मनुष्य सर्वशक्तिमान सर्व समर्थ भगवान् की ओर झुकता है। जो भगवान् की ओर झुका है उसके लिये कभी भी किसी वस्तु की कमी नहीं रह जाती, उसकी सारी दीनता-दरिद्रता नष्ट हो जाती है। इस प्रकार सन्त-समागम से पाप, ताप और दैन्य सभी का निवारण होता है।

108

‘By performing *dharma*, sin becomes destroyed.’

By doing *satsang* you get a feeling for what is proper and what is improper, sin and virtue, *adharma* (unrighteousness) and *karttavya* (obligation) - it produces *viveka* (discrimination). Therefore by being someone who does *satsang* you escape from *adharma* and become inclined to *dharma* (virtue, duty, righteousness). Refraining from sin he does virtuous action. The established doctrine is:-

“धर्मेण पापमपनुदति”

“dharmena paapamapanudati”
[*Mahanarayana Upanishad - Ekonashititamo Anuvakah* v7]

‘By performing *dharma*, sin becomes destroyed.’

In this way, sin becomes destroyed by *satsang*.

By sitting in *satsang*, by hearing tidings related to Bhagavat (God), the innate internal pain and anxiety etc. of the human being that burns the heart, that heat becomes smoothed. Indeed the *antah-karana* (inner conscience) of one who does *satsang* stays naturally peaceful.

By means of *satsang* man bows in the direction of Omnipotent, All-Capable Bhagwan. For him who bows in the direction of Bhagwan there is never any shortage of anything, his entire poverty becomes destroyed. In this way then, by association with saints, *paapa* (sin), *tapa* (mental agony) and *dainya* (poverty), all become prevented.

Glossary

aachaarya, acharya teacher
aadhyaatma, spiritual contemplation
aananda, joy, bliss
aastika, religious
aatmaa, soul
abhyaasa, practice
adharma, vice, sin
agni, fire
agyaana, ignorance
ahamkaara, egotism, arrogance, conceit, empty pride, vanity
ahimsaa, non-violence, inoffensiveness, benevolence
akshara, permanent
amrita, nectar
anishta, mishchief, evil
antahkarana, conscience, inner self
artha, wealth
arya, noble
ashaanti, unrest
ashram, hermitage
ashrama, stage of life
ashubha, unfortunate, inauspicious
asura, demon
atma, atman, Soul
avataar, incarnation
aviveka, absence of discrimination
bhaagya, destiny
Bhaarata, India
Bhagwan, Bhagwan, *bhagavaana*, Supreme Being, God
Bhagavat, God
bhagavattatva, essence of the divine
bhajan, hymn
bhakti, devotion

Bharat, *bhaarata* India
bhavaroga, birth-sickness
bhavasaagara, sea of experience
bhavateet, transcendental
bhoga, the experience of pleasure or a pain
bhuta-preta, ghosts
biij, seed
brahmana, brahmin, Hindu caste
Brahma, Absolute Divine Truth, Hindu god of creation
brahmachari, celibate student
brahmacharya, celibacy
Brahmanand, *brahmananda* Absolute bliss
brahma-nirguna brahma, without qualities),
brahmavidyaa, theology taught in the Upanishads
brahmin, learned or priestly caste
brhmanishtham, possessing knowledge of immortal self
chaitanya, consciousness
charan, ray of sun or moon
chela, disciple
chimtaa, the funeral pyre
chit, consciousness
chitaa, worry
chitta, faculty of reasoning
daana, charitable gift
daitya, demons
darshan, darshana Holy look, vision
deepak, light, lamp
Devaloka, the world of the gods, paradise
devataa, god
devataaon, gods/goddesses
dhaarmik, (virtuous, devout, religious, godly, upright, etc.)
dharma, righteous duty
dharmashaala, a dwelling house for pilgrims
dhoop, sticky incense, fragrant lamp
dhoti, sheet
dhyaana, dhyan, meditation
diksha, initiation
duhkha, pain, suffering

dushkarma, wicked action
Gangajal, the sacred waters of the River Ganga
Ganapati, Ganesha Hindu god with elephant trunk
Gandharvas, celestial musicians
Gandharva-Ved, Indian classical music
ganja, marijuana
gita, song
grihastha, householder
grhasthon, householders
guna, quality
gupha, cave
guru, teacher, master
gurudwara, Sikh temple
gyaanii, learned
gyan, gyaan, gnan, jyaan knowledge
hansa, swan
hare, lord
hawaii, pertaining to the air
Ishwar, Isvara, God
ishta, deity
jaati, caste
jagadguru, world teacher, universal teacher
jai, jay, jaya, jaaya hail, glory
japa, repetition of *mantra*
ji, term of respect
jiiva, the individual soul
jiivanmukti, liberated soul
jyotir, light
jyotishi, Indian astrology
kalpa, period of time
kalyaana, happiness, welfare, benediction, prosperity
kama, love
kamandalu, wooden pot
karma, law of action and reaction
karunaa, compassion
Kashi, Benares, Varanasi
kaupeen, loincloth
kiirtana, singing praise of God

kripa, grace
Krishna, dark, name of principal character of *Mahabharata* poem
kriyamaana, work now being done
kshatriya, caste of warriors, administrators
kshema, prosperity
kusang, kusanga, the company of evil men
ladduu, Sweetmeat made of *ghii* (ghee)
lingam, phallus
maayaa, maya, delusion of
maharaja, king
maharishi, maharshi, Great sage
maharishon, sages
mahatma, mahaatma, great soul
Mahesh, name of Hindu god Shiva
maitrii, friendship
mala, maalaa, rosary, necklace, garland
mala-mutra, excrement & urine
mandir, temple
manoraajyam, the realm of the mind
mantra, word or words of spiritual power
Manu Smriti or *Manu Samhita*, law book
maryaadaa, principled code of conduct
math, monastery
mauna, maun, silent
moksha, final liberation, beatitude, redemption, absolution, salvation, freedom
muditaa, cheerfulness, delight
mukti, liberation
naastika, nastika, unbeliever
nagar, town
niraakaara, without form
nirguna, without qualities
nitya, eternal
nityaananda, always happy
paapa, sinful
pandit, learned man
parabrahma, the Supreme Soul
Paramatma, *paramaatmaa,* Supreme Spirit, Supersoul, God

parmartha, the ultimate good, salvation
pishaachinii, she-devil
praana, breath
praanon, the five vital airs
praarabdha, already commenced *karma*
prana, breath
pranaama, salutation
pranava, name of OM *mantra*
prasad, blessing
pravritti, tendency, inclination or perseverance of mind
puuja, puja, pooja, ceremony, ritual
puujana worship
punya, meritous *karma*
purnima, poornima, full-moon night
purusha, male
purushartha, "human wealth", willpower, work for fulfilment
puurna, poorna, perfect
raaga, attachment
raaj, *raja,* royal, king
rajasic, energetic, passionate
rajogunii, pleasure seeking, passion of love and pleasure
Rama, Raama, Raam, name of hero of *Ramayana* poem
raurava, a hell
rish,i sage, wise man
roga, disease
Rudra, name of Hindu god Shiva
saadhaka, one engaged in spiritual discipline
saadhana, spiritual practice or discipline
sachchidananda, Truth, Consciousness, Bliss
sadguru, genuine *guru*
sadagati, salvation, good conduct
sadhu, wandering holy man
sanchita, collected *karma*
samaadhi, stillness of the mind
sampradaaya, sect
samsaara, samsara, worldly existence, mortal world, transmigration
samsaarii, worldly

samskaara, mental impressions
sannyas, vow of renunciation
sanyaasi, renunciate
Saraswati, name of Hindu goddess of learning, name of river
Sarvashaktimaan, Omnipotent, Almighty
satogunii, purity
satsanga, to take the company of the good or pious
sattvic, satvik, pure
satya, truth
shaanti, *shaanti* peace
Shastras, shaastra, Hindu Scriptures
Shankar, name of Hindu god Shiva
shikshaa, instruction
shishya, pupil
Shiva, name of Hindu god of destruction, lord of the *yogis*
Shivalinga, symbol of creative forces
Shivaratri, night(s) dedicated to worship of Hindu deities Shiva and his consort Shakti
shloka, verse
shraddha, faith, veneration, reverence
shravana, devotion
shri, blessed
shrotiyan, well-versed in *Vedas*
shruti, information heard from the *Veda*
shubha, happy, auspicious
shuudra, one of the four castes, labourer
siddha, perfected being
siddhi, one who has acquired supernatural powers
smarana, remembrance
smriti, remembered, from the *Shastra.*
sthuula shariira, gross body
stotra, hymns of praise
suukshma shariira, subtle body
svarg, svarga, swarg, heaven
swami, renunciate
swaroop, svarupa, swarupa, divine form, real self, true self
tamasik, impure
tamogunii, impure, ignorant

tapasya, tapas, austerity
tilaka, tilak, mark of sandalwood paste applied to forehead, emblem of a sect
tri, three
tyaagi, unattached renunciates
upaasanaa, sitting near, devout meditation, worship, prayer
upadesha, upadesh, lecture, advice instruction, discourse, sermon
Upanishad, texts on *yoga*, to sit near
upekshaa, equanimity, indifference
vaanaprastha, forest dweller
vaidya, physician
vairagya, freedom from worldly desires
vaishya, trader
vanaprasthas, forest dwellers
varna, caste
Veda, ancient religious texts, *Rig Veda*, *Sama Veda*, *Yajur Veda*, *Atharva Veda*
veshyaa, whore
vigyaana, knowledge, wisdom, science, learning, philosophy, the soul
Vishnu, Hindu god of preservation
vishvambhara, (universal support)
viyoga, separation, disunion, detachment etc
vritti, flow of mental activity
vrittiyon, mental conditions, of friendship, compassion, delight & indifference
yaatra, yatra, journey, tour, pilgrimage
yagya, yajna, ritual, religious sacrifice
yakshini, demi-gods,
karna-pishachi, demons
yogadarshanam, Patanjali's Yoga Sutras
yogamaayaa, inner power
yoga-shaastra, yogadarshanam, of Patanjali, Yoga Sutras
yuga, period of time

Lightning Source UK Ltd.
Milton Keynes UK
UKHW02f2155220818
327654UK00002B/225/P

9 780956 222800